INTERNET activities

ADVENTURES ON THE SUPERHIGHWAY

GARY L. ASHTON
Product Line Manager—API/SDKs
Novell GroupWare Product Marketing
Provo, Utah

KARL BARKSDALE
Computer Technologies Teacher
Dixon Middle School
Provo, Utah

MICHAEL RUTTER
Christa McAuliffe Fellow
Brigham Young University
Provo High School
Provo, Utah

EARL JAY STEPHENS
Foundation Project Manager
Utah Information Technologies Association
Salt Lake City, Utah

SOUTH-WESTERN EDUCATIONAL PUBLISHING

ISBN: 0-538-65147-4

4 5 6 7 8 9 10 BN 00 99 98 97

Printed in the United States of America

Vice-President/Editor-in-Chief: Robert E. First
Managing Editor: Janie F. Schwark
Developmental Editor: Anne Noschang
Production Editor: Becky E. Peveler
Marketing Manager: Kent Christensen
Production Artist: Sophia Renieris
Production Coordinator: Jane Congdon
Consulting Editor: Bob Sandman
Production Services: Electro-Publishing
Cover/Internal Design: Lou Ann Thesing

I(T)P®
International Thomson Publishing

South-Western Educational Publishing is a division of International Thomson Publishing, Inc. The ITP logo is a registered trademark used herein under license by South-Western Educational Publishing.

Library of Congress Cataloging-in-Publication Data

Internet activities : adventures on the superhighway / Gary L. Ashton
... [et al.].
p. cm.
Includes index.
Summary: Provides an explanation of the various parts and functions of the Internet plus cross-curricular, hands-on activities.
ISBN 0-538-65147-4
1. Information superhighway — Juvenile literature. 2. Internet (Computer network) — Juvenile literature. [1. Information superhighway. 2. Internet (Computer network)] I. Ashton, Gary L.
HE7570.I57 1995
004.6'7--dc20 95-24625
CIP

ACKNOWLEDGMENTS

The authors would like to thank the following people whose contributions made this book possible:

Shelly Adams
Hilary Barksdale
Eugene Paulsen
Jay Biddulph
Matt Urban
Todd Allen
Tom Rasmussen
Bob Sandman
Bob First
Anne Noschang
Becky Peveler
Sophie Renieris
Janie Schwark
Ann Small
Brad Van Alfen
Charlie Wicks
And their families and friends

The Authors would also like to thank the following individuals who contributed to the review process for this edition:

Dr. Ken Brumbaugh
Mounds View Public Shools
St. Paul Minnesota

Patrick Douglas Crispen
University of Alabama
Tuscaloosa, Alabama

John Steffee
Robert E. Lee High School
Tyler, Texas

Gary Ashton
Karl Barksdale
Michael Rutter
Earl Jay Stephens

USING THIS BOOK

Welcome to the Internet —
the largest computer network in the world.

The Internet is used by students on every continent and in nearly every country. The chances are that, sometime in the near future, you will be asked to complete a research project using the Internet. It is very likely, furthermore, that you will be able to use the Internet once you enter the job market. In order to be successful in class or on the job, you will need to know how to get the most out of using the Internet.

That is where *Internet Activities* comes in. This book will give you the skills you need to navigate the Internet. As you do, new electronic worlds will open up: the World Wide Web, Gopherspace, and USENET, to name a few.

Internet Activities is divided into three sectors, or sections. If you are new to the Internet, complete Sectors 1 and 2 before moving to the Sector 3. After you complete the first two sectors, you will have the skills you need to get the most from the interdisciplinary activities in Sector 3.

SECTOR 1:
Welcome to the Net . . . Cyber Views of Cyberspace

The first sector, *Welcome to the Net*, gives you a quick overview of the Internet and other on-line resources. Sector 1 is divided into three Cyber Views, or short chapters. As you read through the Cyber Views, you will find many new terms. Terms in **bold** are explained in the Glossary at the end of the book. At the end of each Cyber View, there is a Cyber Quiz. The questions in the quizzes will help you double-check your understanding of what you have read.

SECTOR 2:
Going On-Line . . . Applying the Tools of the Internet

The second sector, *Going On-Line*, takes each major Internet tool and uses it. Mosaic, Netscape, Gopher, Archie, Veronica, and FTP open up the Internet. In Sector 2, you will experience firsthand what being on-line is all about. Each Cyber View in Sector 2 ends with a Cyber Quiz.

Starting with Cyber View 4, you will be out on the Internet applying what you have learned. Activity is what the Internet is all about. And the activities are what this book is all about. Complete the activities and the on-line world of tomorrow will become second nature to you. Each activity in Sector 2 is divided into several parts.

Introduction and Objectives Explain briefly what you are about to do.
Resource Tables Provide advice and information to help you past sticky problems on the Internet.
Inter Steps Give a step-by-step way of accomplishing the activity on-line.
Screen Shots and Graphics Screen shots and pictures are included to help you visualize what you are doing.
Cyber Logs While you are on-line, you will collect lots of resources: a piece of data, a file, a graphic, an idea. The Cyber Logs allow you to record important information about your travels.
Cyber Quests The Cyber Quests allow you to explore the Internet on your own, applying the tools or knowledge you have just obtained.

SECTOR 3:
On-Line Activities . . . Instructional Adventures in Cyberspace
http://www.thomson.com/swpco/internet/wq50ab1.html

The third sector, *On-Line Activities*, will give you practical examples of how you can apply your on-line skills at school, at work, and at home in your leisure time. But enough chatter. It is time to Cyber View.

README file

You will find README files everywhere. There are four different types of README files:

Net Notes: Provides additional information and points of interest on the Internet.
Netiquette: Gives important tips concerning Network Etiquette, that is, tips for how to behave on the Net.
Soft Notes: Supplies hints on how to get the most out of your software tools, and explains differences in the various platforms you will encounter on-line.
FAQ's: Answers Frequently Asked Questions about the Internet.

README boxes contain important information. Don't miss any of them!

CONTENTS

PREFACE

SECTOR 1

SECTOR 2

Art Acknowledgments

For permission to reproduce the screen captures on the pages indicated, acknowledgment is made to the following:

21	Jet Propulsion Laboratory
27,28, 30,31,32, 38,39,40, 46,47,48, 49,71,72, 80,85,101	NCSA Mosaic™ from the Software Development Group at the National Center for Supercomputing Applications. NCSA Mosaic™ is copyrighted by and is property of the Board of Trustees of the University of Illinois.
27,53,174	World Wide Web Consortium
28	Whale Watching Web
29,159	Space Telescope Science Institute
29,32,38 39,47,49	Netscape grants permission to use Netscape Navigator home page screens and descriptions.
55	Enterprise Integration Technologies
65	WSGopher Development
67,90,113, 116	Minuet *Minnesota Internet User's Essential Tool* Version 1.0 Beta 14.1 Copyright 1994 University of Minnesota Developed by: S.E. Collins; G.R. Gonzalez; P.H. Kachelmyer; K.S. Person; and E.A. Scheske
165,232	Yahoo
168	Bernard Hodes Avertising, Inc.
182	Syracuse University
184	Carnegie Mellon University
187	NASA EOS IDS Investigation Volcanology Team
194	SURAnet
197	The Electronic Newsstand
199	Purdue University On-Line Writing Lab

202	Copyright Institute of Latin American Studies, University of Texas at Austin. This page cannot be reproduced without written permission from the Institute of Latin American Studies, University of Texas at Austin.
206	The Legal Information Institute
208	PC Catalog
212	American Mathematical Society
216	National Center For Atmospheric Research (managed by the University Corporation for Atmospheric Research under the sponsorship of the National Science Foundation)
222	University of California, Irvine
236	The State University of New York at Buffalo

WELCOME TO THE NET...

...Cyber Views of Cyberspace

The Internet is the world's fastest-growing computer network with millions of computer users on every continent. There are thousands of new Internet users every day.

Just ten years ago, the Internet was reserved for selected educational researchers and military planners. Not anymore. Anyone with the right equipment can connect from home, work, or school.

As you begin your tour of the Internet, you will be joining some of the most important people in the world: presidents and leaders of nations, heads of business, research scientists, and students in nearly every country. When you are on the Internet, everyone is on equal footing.

The Internet has been compared to an electronic wilderness. You never know what you might encounter. Before you go out into uncharted territory, you should learn a few survival skills. The Cyber Views in this Sector will give you a basic understanding of the Internet.

1

Networks, Hosts, Clients, and Names

In this first Cyber View, you will learn the basics of the Internet. The Internet starts with your computer, extends to your local area network, and expands across the world to tens of thousands of other networks and millions of computers around the world.

In this Cyber View, you will explore the following topics:

- Networks
- The Net or Internet
- Hosts
- Clients and servers
- Names and addresses

The Internet Starts with Local Networks

A **network** is created anytime two or more computers are linked together to share information. A network can be created by connecting a few computers, or by linking thousands of computers.

Bringing Networks Together

The **Internet** is often described as a "network of networks." The Internet is not a single network, but a super network of more than 50,000 smaller subnetworks (as in Figure 1-1).

Net is short for network. The Internet is called the Net because it is the largest computer network ever created.

ReadMe file 1

FAQ's: What is Cyberspace?

The Internet is adding new words to our vocabulary. Words like **superhighway** and **Cyberspace**.

The Internet started out as a small computer network for a few researchers and military planners. It is growing into a super-sized electronic highway that everyone can use.

When you are on the electronic superhighway, you are considered to be in Cyberspace. When you are chatting with someone electronically, you are conducting a *Cyberchat*. The new Internet vocabulary is called *Cyberspeak* or *Cyberese*.

The word *Cyberspace* refers to the field of cybernetics. **Cybernetics** is the science that compares the functions of the brain with the functions of a computer. Cybernetics may someday lead to more sophisticated computers.

Hosts

Any computer attached directly to the Net and providing services to Internet users is called a **host**. The term **server** is also used to describe these important computers.

Strictly speaking, a computer is only a host if computer users can log in from a personal computer and use its resources. For example:

- A host in Texas may allow you to **download,** or copy, a file rating the top ten software programs.
- A host in Florida may allow you to research a paper for an English class.
- A host in Ottawa may allow you to join a discussion group about your favorite hobby or sports team.

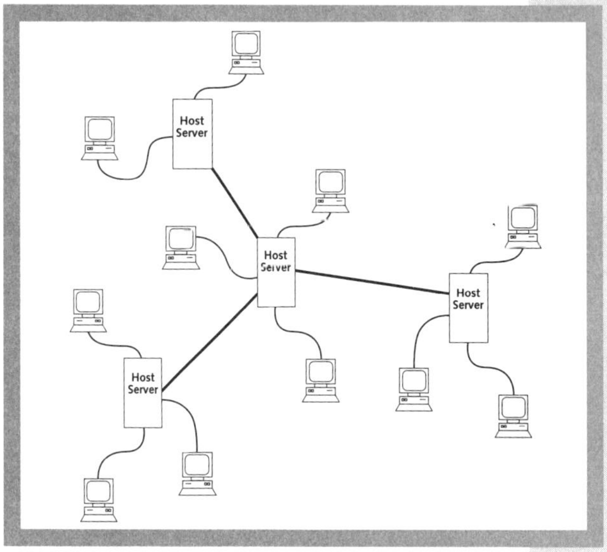

f 1-1 The Internet is a network of networks.

Client and Server Software

In order for you to talk to the Net, you must run special software on your computer called **client software**. When you log in to an Internet host, your computer becomes an Internet **client**. In short, a client is any computer that runs client software.

Internet hosts must have the same software to speak back to you. The Net is a little like an expensive French restaurant. The French-speaking waiter is the host, or server. When ordering, you as the client must speak French to be understood by the server. If you order in German or English, you will not be able to communicate your request.

One problem on the Internet is the variety of server and client software available to users. When the software from a particular server or host does not support your client software, there is an **incompatibility**. Gradually, incompatibilities are being eliminated as the Net becomes more user-friendly.

READ ME **file 2**

FAQ's: What is the language of the Internet?

Internet hosts and servers speak a language called **TCP/IP**, short for Transmission Control Protocol/Internet Protocol.

TCP/IP is really two things:

IP, or the Internet Protocol, is like an address label on a package you send through the mail. Packages on the Net are called **packets**. This address makes sure the packet arrives at the right place.

TCP, or Transmission Control Protocol, keeps track of every item in the package or packet. If an item in the packet does not arrive or is broken, TCP asks the host to send the packet over again. *

READ ME file 3

NET NOTE: Internet domain names

You can tell a lot about someone by looking at their Internet names. The Internet is divided into areas or sections called **domains**. For example, many Internet names end in a domain extension like the following:

.mil = military domain
.edu = educational domain
.com = commercial domain
.org = organizational domain
.gov = governmental domain
.net = network provider domain

What can you guess from these Internet names?

http://ericir.syr.edu/

spacelink@msfc.nasa.gov

maxwell@spies.com *

Hosts can reject clients for a number of other reasons. Some hosts are **password-**protected and only let people who know the special word or phrase log in. Other hosts may have old or unreliable hardware and software. Some hosts may have quit providing certain services. Many times a host server may have more client requests than it can support, so it rejects additional requests to log in.

Internet Names and Addresses

Before a host can recognize you and let you log in you must have an Internet **address**. An address is a number, like 158.91.6.2. People have a lot of problems remembering numbers, so the **Domain Name System**, or **DNS**, was created. DNS allows those using the Internet to substitute **names** that are easier to remember.

Internet names are funny-looking things. For example:

president@whitehouse.gov

alt.fan.disney.afternoon

askeric@syr.edu

http://www.jpl.nasa.gov

Computers communicate in numbers. Net names are converted to numbers by DNS computers. These numbers become addresses that other computers understand.

Names are assigned by computer technicians that manage local networks. These local **Network Administrators** *must* assign you an Internet name. And with good reason. Every name on the Net must be different, or **unique**, so that data like **E-mail**, or electronic mail, will know where to go. If everyone created their own Internet names, odds are there would be thousands of duplicate names. Duplicate names make it impossible for E-mail to arrive at the correct location.

In a sense, the Internet is like a huge electronic postal service, and every Internet computer is like a home or an apartment. All the houses and apartments must have different addresses so the postal person will know where to deliver the mail. Your Network Administrator is like the postal supervisor, making sure the mail arrives (as in Figure 1-2).

Your teacher may have your Internet address already. In some schools, each individual computer has a unique Internet address. At other schools, each student has a unique name or address.

Saying and Writing Internet Names

If someone were to call you on the phone and ask for your Internet name, how would you say it? Following are a few tricks in saying and writing Internet names:

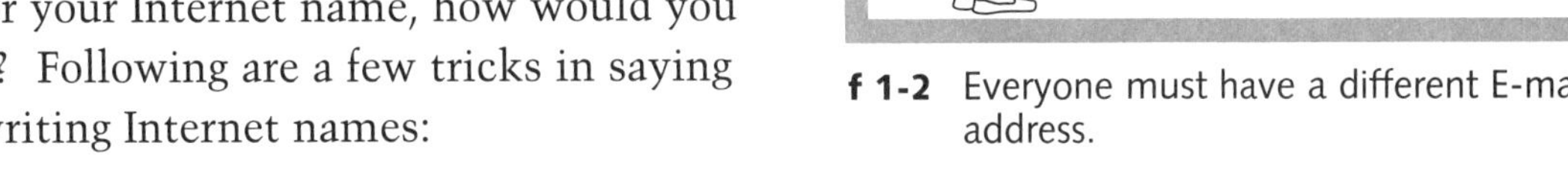

f 1-2 Everyone must have a different E-mail address.

- The @ sign is pronounced "AT."
- A period (.) is a "DOT."
- Spell out each letter unless the name is obvious.
- There are no spaces in an Internet name.
- All letters in an Internet address should be in lowercase.

To say **askeric@ericir.syr.edu**, you might say "askeric, AT, e, r, i, c, i, r, DOT, s, y, r, DOT, edu." You may say "askeric" and most people will understand what you mean. You will have to spell the rest of the name, letter by letter, until you get to "edu." Since "edu" (pronounced "ed u") is a common Internet term, experienced Internet users will know it immediately.

The Internet name of the vice-president of the United States is **vice-president@whitehouse.gov**. You could say "vice, HYPHEN, president, AT, whitehouse, DOT, gov." In this example, you may not have to spell out any of the words since most people will know what you are talking about. Remember, White House is one word **(whitehouse)**.

For **spacelink@msfc.nasa.gov**, you would say "spacelink, AT, m, s, f, c, DOT, nasa, DOT, gov."

file 4

NET NOTE: Names and newcomers

Most people are very new to the Internet and are confused by new Internet names. As you share an Internet name or address, speak slowly and clearly. *When in doubt, spell the whole name out, letter by letter.* Even a name as common as "edu" may need to be spelled out "e, d, u" for the Internet rookie.

How would you say the following Internet addresses?

help@cerf.net

farrell@rice.edu

admin@surfnet.nl *

CyberQuiz 1

On a separate piece of paper or on a handout provided by your teacher, answer the following questions.

Circle Yes if the statement is true or No if the statement is false.

1. **Yes or No** When you are on the Internet, you are considered to be in Cyberspace.
2. **Yes or No** The Net refers to the Internet.
3. **Yes or No** The Internet domain `.mil` stands for millions of users.
4. **Yes or No** TCP is like an address label on an Internet packet or package.
5. **Yes or No** Client and server software must match to avoid incompatibilities.

For questions 6 through 8, circle the letter that corresponds to the best answer.

6. **Who generally assigns Internet names:**
   - a. the government
   - b. the postal service
   - c. a Network Administrator
   - d. your personal computer
   - e. your best friend

7. **Cybernetics is**
   a. the science of studying the human brain and the functions of a computer
   b. the study of Cyberspace and Internet technology
   c. the science of Internet File Transfer Protocols
   d. a new video game

8. **In Cyberspeak, a period (.) is called a**
   a. dot
   b. point
   c. period
   d. click

For questions 9 through 10, write the correct answer in the space provided.

9. **What do the following domain extensions mean?**
   .mil ________________
   .edu ________________
   .com ________________
   .org ________________
   .gov ________________
   .net ________________

10. **In your own words, describe the Internet.**
    Write your full Internet name here: ____________________________.
    How do you say your Internet name?

    ____

    ____

2 On-Line Resources, Tools, and Connections

Everything you find on the Net is called a resource. This Cyber View introduces the resources and the tools you need in order to use the Net effectively.

In this Cyber View, you will read about:

- **Internet resources**
- **The electronic city**
- **Internet tools**
- **Network connections**

ReadMe file 5

NET NOTE: The Internet in Antarctica
The Internet is truly on every continent, including Antarctica. An Internet host at the South Pole passes scientific data and weather information to researchers around the globe. *

Net Resources

The Internet reaches schools in more than 140 countries around the world. On the Internet you can also reach government agencies, chambers of commerce, libraries, colleges, universities, travel agencies, banks, military bases, research labs, and friends you meet in Cyberspace.

All of the people, places, hosts, and data you can find on the Internet are called **resources** (see Figure 2-1).

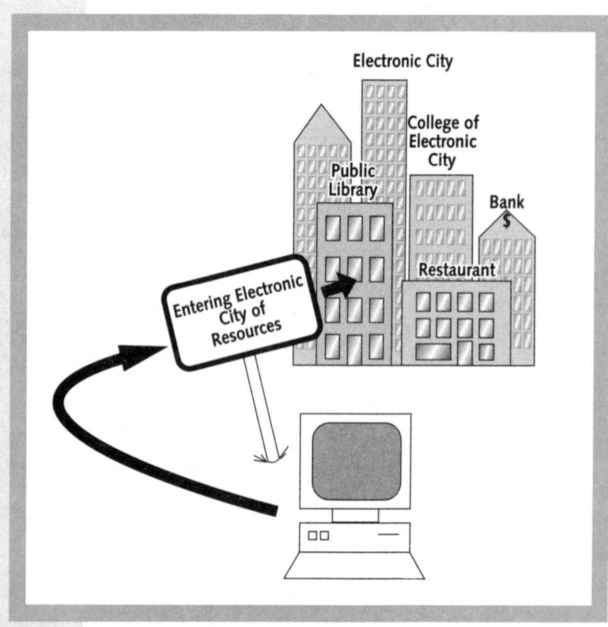

f 2-1
Internet resources are like an electronic city.

An Electronic City of Resources

Before the creation of the Internet, in order to visit a library, attend school, transfer funds from your checking account to your savings account, mail letters, and shop, you had to travel from location to location. You can now do these same things **on-line** by using your personal computer's connections to the networks.

When you use on-line resources, you become part of a new electronic city. In the electronic city of the future, you will not be limited to the books in your local library, the classes offered at your nearby school, or the goods sold in your local stores. Instead, you will be able to:

- browse a thousand different libraries in a hundred countries
- shop in electronic stores around the world
- pay your bills on-line without writing a check
- take classes from professors and teachers a thousand miles away
- book a trip, secure your own airline ticket, become your own travel agency
- search banks around the world for the best interest rates
- send mail without a stamp
- download the video titles or electronic games of your choice
- and much, much more

In the electronic city, you will not be limited by your physical location. If you have the necessary equipment, no matter where you live, you can have the same access to the Net as anyone else. You can be in the center of things from Topeka, Moab, Escondido, Tyler, Chicago, Miami, Champaign, Wheeling, Birmingham, Lethbridge, Buffalo, Little Rock, or Slick Rock.

Where you live is of little consequence. Quite literally, the world becomes your electronic city or town.

README **file 6**

NETIQUETTE: Netiquette

With so many people crowding onto the Internet, it is important that everyone knows how to act and relate to each other in this new on-line world.

Rules of conduct and behavior are called **etiquette**. **Netiquette** is Cyberspeak for Internet etiquette. Read the README: NETIQUETTE boxes throughout the book for hints on Internet etiquette. *

README file 7

FAQ's: Who is on the Internet?

People are the most important resource in the electronic city. The Net is used by nearly every kind of person, in every walk of life:

accountants, administrative assistants, airline pilots, artists, astronauts, authors, butchers, bakers, candlestick makers, CEOs, computer programmers, computer technicians, congressmen and congresswomen, dentists, doctors, engineers, executives, financial consultants, generals, governors, historians, inventory clerks, investment brokers, lab technicians, lawyers, librarians, marine biologists, marketing consultants, mechanics, newspersons, politicians, presidents of the United States, professors, psychologists, receptionists, salespersons, Santa Claus, sports fanatics, systems administrators, tax consultants, teachers, travel agents, weatherpersons, zoologists, and . . .

. . . millions of students like you. ✱

On-Line Internet Resources

The Internet electronic city opens up millions of new on-line resources. While not everything described in the previous section is available to you today, it soon will be. If you have an Internet connection, you can share and publish your ideas, stay up to date on key issues, research nearly any topic, exchange jokes, chat, download software, or simply play games ... starting today.

In Sector 3, you will use the Internet to:

- explore your favorite sports
- view space from the view of the Hubble Space Telescope
- write your congressperson or the president and vice-president of the United States
- visit Germany, France, Chile, and Bolivia
- see the inside of a volcano
- track storm clouds
- read on-line newspapers
- dissect a frog
- explore the law
- download articles, books, and graphics

To access these and hundreds of other Internet resources, you need to first master the tools of the Net.

The Tools of the Internet

To find and use Internet resources, you need several Internet tools. These software tools are improving every day by becoming more **user-friendly**. The basic Internet tools are explained in more detail in Sector 2, Cyber Views 4 through 9. Following is a list of these tools:

- **Browsers:** Browsers enable users to search the World Wide Web, the most significant new resource on the Net. WWW, or W3, is a network of computers bound together by a linking system that allows you to jump from one document to another by clicking on keywords. To read a WWW document, you need a W3 Browser. Mosaic® and Netscape® are excellent W3 Browsers. (Cyber View 4)

- **Gopher:** Named for the Golden Gophers of thc University of Minnesota, the Gopher is a tool that allows you to burrow and tunnel through lists of computer menus, directories, and files until you find what you want. (Cyber View 5)
- **FTP:** FTP is short for File Transfer Protocol. FTP transfers files from distant computers to your computer. Find something interesting on the Net? A way to get your own copy is to use FTP. (Cyber View 6)
- **Telnet:** Telnet gives you the ability to log in to a distant computer host in another state or country and use that computer as if you were there. (Cyber View 6)
- **E-mail:** The most widely used application on the Internet is electronic mail, or E-mail. E-mail allows you to receive and send memos, notes, and letters to anyone in the world with an Internet address. There are many E-mail software packages that can send and receive mail from the Internet. (Cyber View 7)
- **USENET Newsgroup Readers:** A USENET Newsgroup can be found for almost every topic you can imagine. Newsgroups can be very informative, but full of controversy. USENET has more than 6,000 discussion and news groups, but to read them you need a Newsgroup reader. (Cyber View 8)
- **Commercial Tools:** Chat software allows you to have interactive conversations with other people on-line. Internet Relay Chats (IRCs) are becoming increasingly popular, especially on commercial subnetworks like America Online℠, Prodigy®, and MCI®. Other Net tools can download graphics and sound files. Shopping and other commercial activities are available on the Net with the help of other specialized commercial software tools. (Cyber View 9)

Types of Connections

Before you can use your Internet tools, you have to be connected to the Internet in some way. When you are on-line, you will be operating several computers at a time; for example:

- Your desktop computer
- The host computer that connects you to the Internet (also called a *connection server*)
- The remote host or server that has the information you are after

The links between these computers are called **connections**. The connection between you and your local host will determine what kind of Internet tools you can use and what kind of network resources are available to you. There are three major types of connections:

- Direct
- SLIP-PPP
- Dial-in

Direct Connections

With a direct connection, communications hardware physically connects you to the Internet. This is the most efficient connection for Internet travel. With a direct connection, information you select will be transferred directly from the remote host to your computer at the highest possible speeds and with the highest degree of reliability.

SLIP-PPP Connections

If you can't have a direct connection to the Internet, the next best thing is SLIP or PPP. **SLIP** is short for Serial Line Internet Protocol. **PPP** is short for Point to Point Protocol.

With SLIP and PPP connections, some of the communications hardware is replaced with a telephone modem. A **modem** is a simple communications tool that converts computer signals into signals that can travel over telephone lines.

SLIP and PPP allow you to act like you have a direct connection over your phone line. Your computer and your host computer work together to process and store Internet data. However, with SLIP and PPP, the **transfer rate** at which data is exchanged is slower between you and your Internet host, and the connections are not considered to be as reliable as a direct connection.

READ ME file 8

NET NOTE: Modem Speed

Speed is a major issue with modems. Modem speed is measured in **bits per second,** or **bps**. For most Internet uses, it is best to use a modem with 9,600bps or faster speeds. Slower modems will get the job done, but you will spend a great deal of time waiting, and waiting, and waiting.... *

Dial-in Connections

With a dial-in connection, you link to the Internet with a modem. Millions of people use dial-in connections to get on-line from their homes. Many small businesses and a large number of schools use dial-in connections because they are generally less expensive and easier to install than direct connections.

When you dial-in, your host computer must do most of the work. Your desktop computer will simply display what the host computer has processed. With most dial-in connections, the tools are located on the host. You will be able to use only the tools that the host provides.

Every kind of connection has its advantages and disadvantages. Even with the limitations of a dial-in connection, there is a lot you can accomplish on the Net. The main thing is to find a reliable connection that will run your Internet tools effectively (as in Figure 2-2).

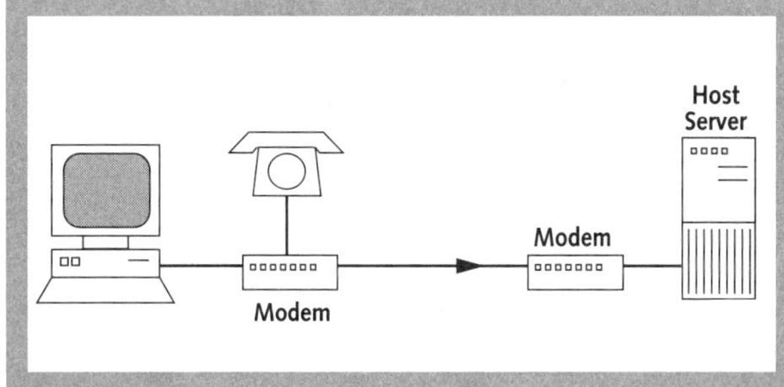

f 2-2
Typical SLIP, PPP, or dial-in connection

CyberQuiz 2

On a separate piece of paper or on a handout provided by your teacher, answer the following questions.

Circle Yes if the statement is true or No if the statement is false.

1. **Yes or No** The people and places you find on the Internet are called resources.
2. **Yes or No** Modem speed is measured in miles per hour, or MPH.
3. **Yes or No** Netiquette is Cyberspeak for Internet etiquette.
4. **Yes or No** When you are on-line, you may be operating several computers at a time.
5. **Yes or No** On-line resources allow you to send mail without a stamp.

For questions 6 through 8, circle the letter that corresponds to the best answer.

6. **The links between computers are called**
   a. connections
   b. contacts
   c. extensions
   d. cybernetics

7. **Gopher**
   a. moves the mouse pointer arrow on your computer screen
   b. describes the rules for using the Internet
   c. allows you to pay your bills without writing a check
   d. is named for the Golden Gophers of the University of Minnesota

8. **When you dial-in to the Internet with a modem, you**
   a. use a phone line
   b. have a direct connection to the Internet
   c. must have a VCR
   d. have to be on Channel 3

For questions 9 through 10, write the correct answer in the space provided.

9. **What do the following terms mean?**
   WWW ________________
   W3 ________________
   FTP ________________
   SLIP ________________
   PPP ________________
   E-mail ________________

10. **What kind of connection do you have to the Internet?** Direct, SLIP, PPP, or Dial-in?

    ____

    ____

    ____

CYBER VIEW

3 THE NET: PAST, PRESENT, AND FUTURE

There has never been, in the history of the world, anything quite like the Net. The number one rule you need to know about the Net is that it will change—and change quickly! Whatever you see today in Cyberspace is about to become ancient history.

In this Cyber View, you will trace the history of the Net and examine its future with such topics as:

- Past networks
- Present networks
- Future networks

READ ME file 9

NET NOTE: Morse Code
Morse Code is simply a system that uses short and long clicks to represent letters of the alphabet. Widely used even today, here is Morse Code:

.-	a	.---	j	...	s
-...	b	-.-	k	-	t
-.-.	c	.-..	l	..-	u
-..	d	--	m	...-	v
.	e	-.	n	.--	w
..-.	f	---	o	-..-	x
--.	g	.--.	p	-.--	y
....	h	--.-	q	--..	z
..	i	.-.	r		

Use the code above to decipher the following message:

... ..- .-. ..-. - .... -.
- . .-. -. . - *

Networks Past

Several networks from the past led up to the Internet of today.

The Telegraph

The first electronic network was the telegraph. Perfected by Samuel Morse in 1837, the telegraph used electromagnets to send and receive clicks from one telegraph operator to another. The length of time between the clicks was important in understanding Morse Code, a system of short and long clicks used to transmit letters of the alphabet.

The Telephone

Alexander Graham Bell was the inventor of the telephone. On March 10, 1876, Bell had the first telephone conversation with his assistant Mr. Watson, by uttering the now famous words, "Mr. Watson, come here, I want you."

The telephone network covers almost all of the globe. The worldwide telephone network, like the Internet, is a network of networks working together. For example, a person can call from a California Pacific Bell pay telephone, call long distance over MCI, use AT&T lines for part of the transmission, and talk with a friend in London, England, over the British Telecom phone network. In this example, four different telephone networks work together to allow one conversation.

The worldwide telephone system is the communications backbone of the Internet. The fact that the Internet can use the existing phone system to communicate means the Internet has extensive global coverage and tremendous growth potential.

The ARPANET

The earliest ancestor of the modern Internet was called the ARPANET, short for the Advanced Research Projects Agency Network. The ARPANET was born out of both scientific and military needs. Scientists and military experts in the 1960s needed to share information and research data even if nuclear war or a natural disaster, like an earthquake, destroyed large sections of their communications system.

In theory, if any computer or part of the ARPANET ever went down (say from an enemy attack), the ARPANET had the ability to reroute computer data and information down different network paths, ensuring that at least part of the computer network would remain alive.

Iraq set up a computer network similar to the ARPANET, which survived aerial bombing attacks by American and Coalition forces in the Desert Storm conflict in 1991-92. This event helped prove the value of the ARPANET system. The Internet inherited many of the technologies developed for ARPANET.

READ ME **file 10**

FAQ's: Who is in charge of the Internet?
Quite literally, *no one is in charge of the Net.* Because of its ARPANET heritage, the Internet is a **distributed network**. This means that there is no central authority guiding its growth, use, and development.

The Net is managed by the cooperative effort of Network Administrators and millions of users like you. Because of this independence, those who use the Net need to work with others to solve problems in Cyberspace.

Read the README: NETIQUETTE boxes for hints and helps on network courtesy. *

The Present Internet Network

In the mid 1980s, the National Science Foundation (NSF) funded six supercomputers for scientific research. The computers were located in Princeton, New Jersey; San Diego, California; Champaign, Illinois; Pittsburgh, Pennsylvania; Ithaca, New York; and Boulder, Colorado.

In 1986, the NSF expanded its network by funding the NSFNET. Since there were only a few supercomputers, it was

README file 11

NETIQUETTE: SPAM—Inappropriate use of the public Internet

If you use the public Internet for personal business reasons you will be accused of Spamming. Unwanted Internet garbage, particularly advertising, is called **Spam**. Many people think the term comes from the *Monty Python* skit. Whatever the origin of Spam, one thing is for certain—if you *Spam the Net* you will get *flamed.*

Flames are rebukes sent by agitated Internet users. Avoiding flames is important, unless, of course, you want to spend hours deleting unwanted irate messages from a thousand unhappy people.

decided that scientists living in other parts of the country should be allowed to log in to the supercomputer centers remotely. To accomplish this **remote access**, a communications backbone was created.

The **backbone** is simply a system of high-speed phone lines carrying computer data. The backbone first connected the supercomputer sites to each other. Later, the ARPANET was connected to and absorbed by the new system.

The NSFNET established a backbone to which everyone with the necessary equipment and software could connect. Soon, colleges and universities from all over the country hooked to the backbone. The National Aeronautics and Space Administration (NASA), the Department of Energy (DOE), and other government agencies soon hooked up as well. Later, elementary and secondary schools were encouraged to join the new system, and the modern Internet was born.

Many students first experienced the Net while in college in the late 1980s and early 1990s. After leaving school, they missed the convenience of the Internet and demanded access. Many new companies were started to meet this new demand. They began to provide access to the Internet for a fee.

New Cyber companies were born, like Prodigy, America Online, CompuServe®, NETCOM®, and Delphi®. Established companies like MCI and AT&T® began to provide Internet connections to businesses and homes. Apple®, IBM®, and Microsoft® have also joined in. By the end of 1992, there were more business hosts on the Internet than educationally sponsored hosts.

The Growing Internet

Counting the number of hosts is a good way to see the rapid growth of the Internet in the last few years (see Figure 3-1).

Growth can be difficult to manage. When the Net was small, the communications links were like the roads in a small town. With just a few people traveling around the town, the small, narrow streets could easily handle the traffic. Rapid growth

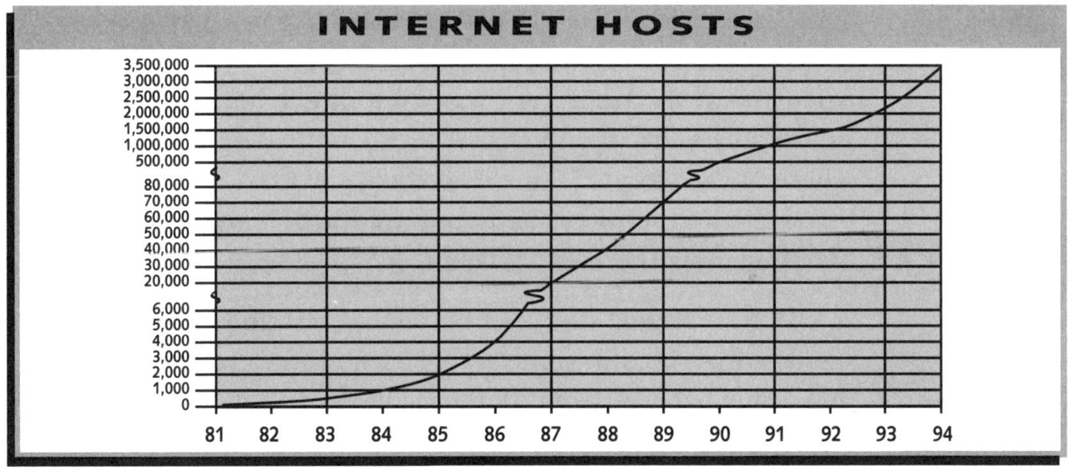

f 3-1 There were less than 300 hosts on the Internet in 1982. Now there are millions of hosts, and the growth is just beginning.

soon made the narrow roads obsolete. New communications highways and toll roads had to be built to handle the electronic traffic. Congress began to fund construction of an *electronic superhighway* to help keep up with the demand for on-line access. Businesses have also jumped in to help people reach the Net and use its resources. However, even with this help, sometimes the traffic on the Net is "bumper to bumper." Electronic traffic jams can prevent you from reaching your favorite on-line destinations.

READ ME file 12

NETIQUETTE: Reduce traffic ahead

Help reduce traffic on the Net by car pooling; that is, team up to search a site. Work in teams. This way there are less hits on your remote host, and a greater likelihood of other people getting through. Also, log off your remote host as soon as you have found what you're looking for.

The Changing Internet

The Internet of the recent past was, for the most part, text-based. **Text-based** Internet simply means the main thing you could get from the Net was a page full of words, or text.

In the early 1990s, a new way of looking at information generated a whole new set of resources on the Net called the World Wide Web. The World Wide Web changed the way people use the Net and increased its popularity among average people.

The World Wide Web is also called the Web, WWW, or W3. Anything with four names has to be good! The basic technology was not widely available until 1993. However, in just a few short years, W3 has become one of the most popular and powerful Internet resources.

The World Wide Web was born at CERN, near Geneva, Switzerland, at the European Laboratory for Particle Physics. Scientists at the laboratory wanted to find a better way of linking the work of one researcher to another scientist anywhere in the world. Using **hypertext**, scientists are able to link ideas and results found on one computer with results found on any other W3 server.

A WWW hypertext document contains certain keywords. The words are marked in some way. Sometimes the words are underlined, appear in a different [color], or show up as [reversed text] When you select hypertext keywords, or **links**, you jump automatically to another selection of text. The new text may be located in:

- the document you are currently in
- another document on your WWW host
- another document on a WWW host in Alaska, Switzerland, Kenya, or anywhere else in the world

Hypertext documents also allow you to do hyper jumps from pictures or graphics. As shown in Figure 3-2, click on a picture from a Home Page in California ...

... and you will jump to a colorful page from a picture database at NASA (see Figure 3-3).

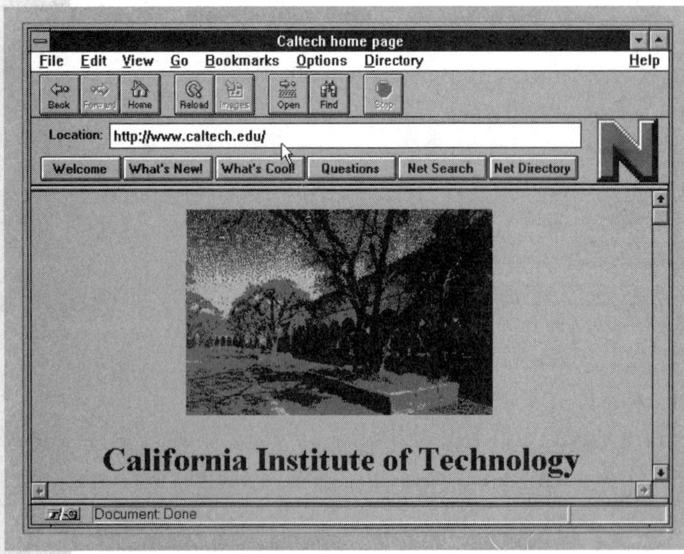

f 3-2 California Institute of Technology Home Page

A Browser, like Mosaic® or Netscape®, is required to explore the Web. A Browser allows you to read hypertext documents. You will learn how to use a hypertext Browser in Cyber View 4.

The Future Superhighway

The WWW and its hypertext technologies are only the beginning of a new wave of changes coming to the Net. The Internet will continue to grow into the information superhighway of the future. It will undergo many, many changes. In ten years, we will probably look back and think of the Internet the way we now think of the old and limited ARPANET.

Businesses

The future of the Net will largely be governed by business, which as of 1992 accounted for more than half of the subnetworks available on the Internet.

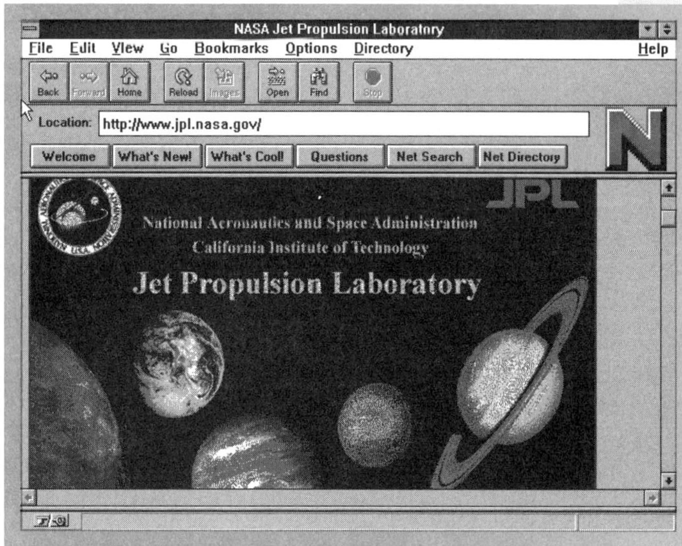

f 3-3 NASA's Jet Propulsion Laboratory

The early Internet was a not-for-profit system. Today, many are calling the Internet the gold rush of the 1990s as companies plot how to make mega-dollars over the Net. Many companies realize that if they don't participate in the Internet revolution, they may not be in business in the year 2010.

While most users of the early Internet did not have to pay directly for use of the Net, the superhighway network of the future may cost you a monthly connection and subscription fee. Fortunately, there are many new companies offering on-line access. Competition between these companies should keep the price of an on-line subscription low.

NREN

While still a senator, Vice-President Al Gore laid the groundwork for the next phase of the Internet when he introduced and Congress passed The High-Performance Computing Act. Al Gore desired to link universities, schools, government agencies, and everyone else for that matter to a much faster network than currently exists. This network he envisioned is called the National Research and Education Network, or NREN. NREN will help ensure that students have even greater access than they do today on the growing and changing Net.

READ ME file 13

FAQ's: How fast will NREN be?

At current speeds, it can take a few seconds to transfer this entire book electronically from one computer to another.

The new National Research and Education Network will be able to transfer this book in a fraction of a second.

The bottleneck of data transfer is often the phone connection between you and your access provider, and the modem in your computer. With a 9,600bps modem, it will take several minutes to transfer the book. With a slower modem, you'll have plenty of time to review for tomorrow's test, eat dinner, and watch your favorite movie while you wait and wait ....

The Electronic Superhighway

The future electronic superhighway will be faster and easier to use than the Internet of today. It will also have increasingly more graphics and visual information than ever before.

The old ARPANET and early Internet systems were primarily text-based; that is, all you could get were files containing words. People are demanding that pictures, graphics, video, and sound files be transmitted along with text.

In the future, you may not send an E-mail, but talk to people directly with video and voice mail. You will literally be able to conduct a two-way video call on the Net. If your party is out, you will be able to record your message for video/sound/computer playback at a later time.

The networks of the future will become increasingly wireless, with computers acting like cellular phones. Additionally, more satellites will be dedicated to sharing computer data, increasing speed and distribution.

Future *super-networks* will combine your telephone, computer, and television into one interactive system. This new system will expand what we mean by "on-line." You will be able to "talk back" to your new flat-screen TV stuck to your wall. No more trips to the video store: You can order any movie you want instantly. You will be able to play interactive computer/TV games with partners anywhere on the planet, with light-speed interactive response times. And your picture, graphics, and sound quality will be much better than anything currently available.

These new interactive systems will redefine our lives. You will have much more control and freedom of choice as you participate in the electronic city of tomorrow.

Get started on the future today. It is time for you to go on-line.

CyberQuiz 3

On a separate piece of paper or on a handout provided by your teacher, answer the following questions.

Circle Yes if the statement is true or No if the statement is false.

1. **Yes or No** British Telecom is the communications backbone of the Internet.

2. **Yes or No** NREN should provide greater access to the Internet for students.

3. **Yes or No** The Internet jumped from a few hundred hosts to millions of hosts in less than ten years.

4. **Yes or No** In 1993, education accounted for most of the subnet-works on the Internet.

5. **Yes or No** In the future, the television, the telephone, and the computer may become one single technology.

For questions 6 through 8, circle the letter that corresponds to the best answer.

6. **Who is in charge of the Internet?**
   - a. the United States government
   - b. the school districts
   - c. your local university
   - d. the Cybermaster
   - e. no one

7. **Unwanted Internet garbage, particularly advertising, is called**
   - a. cybergarbage
   - b. spam
   - c. flames
   - d. tuna

8. **The High-Performance Computing Act was introduced by**
   a. Al Gore
   b. Samuel Morse
   c. Alexander Graham Bell
   d. the National Science Foundation

For questions 9 through 10, write the correct answer in the space provided.

9. **What do the following terms mean?**

   NREN ________________
   ARPANET ________________
   NSF ________________
   NSFNET ________________
   The Web ________________
   Flame ________________

10. **What was the most important event in the development of the Internet? There are many correct answers. Defend your answer in a short essay.**

   ____

   ____

   ____

   ____

Going On-Line...

... Applying the Tools of the Internet

2

The purpose of the Internet is to bring the resources of the world to your personal computer. Resources can take many forms. When you are on-line, you can search a host computer and download news, personal mail, articles, graphics, library references, books, and other useful data. If you have the proper tools, you can even download and play video and sound clips.

On the Internet, you can chat with a friend electronically, join a discussion group, shop, pay your bills, and subscribe to hundreds of new services being added to the Net each month. These new services are dramatically increasing the popularity of the Internet.

Soon, on-line access will be as important to people as their phones, radios, newspapers, magazines, and televisions are today. For many people, being on-line is already a necessity.

Students, more than any other group, need access to the Net and *must* be able to use the tools of the Internet effectively. The following Cyber Views will teach you the tools you need to know to become an Internet expert.

BROWSER ACTIVITIES

In this Cyber View, you will learn about Internet Browsers. Browsers, like Mosaic and Netscape, have revolutionized the Internet. Browsers have made the Net easier to surf, more fun to use, and more interesting.

Browse the following topics in this Cyber View:

- Hypertext
- GUI icons
- GUI Browsers
- Uniform Resource Locators

Following this Cyber View, there are four activities:

Activity 4-1: Manipulating Your GUI Browser
Activity 4-2: Building and Using a Bookmark or Hotlist
Activity 4-3: CERN-*tainly*
Activity 4-4: Learn about Cyberspace in Cyberspace

README file 14

NET NOTE: Where and what is NCSA?

The supercomputer center at Urbana-Champaign was established in 1985 with a National Science Foundation (NSF) grant. Since then, many businesses, the state of Illinois, the university, and other federal agencies have also supplied money to support NCSA projects.

The center provides High-Performance Computing and Communications (HPCC) resources to a growing community of users. The NCSA has made significant contributions in the world of computing and communications, while creating tools like Mosaic. The National Center for Supercomputing Applications will continue to be an essential contributor in the development of NREN (README file 13) and the superhighway proposed by the Clinton/Gore presidential administration. *

Cheers to the University of Illinois at Urbana-Champaign

Mosaic deserves much of the credit for starting the Browser revolution. Mosaic was developed at the National Center for Supercomputing Applications, or NCSA®. NCSA is located deep in the heart of Illinois, at the University of Illinois in Urbana-Champaign. There, a group of dedicated professors and students designed and programmed the Mosaic Browser client. Later, many of the programmers that worked on the original Mosaic went on to develop commercial Browsers like Netscape.

Browsers have changed the way people relate to being on-line. There are many versions of hypertext Browsers available. If you learn one Browser, any other Browser you encounter will be easy to learn.

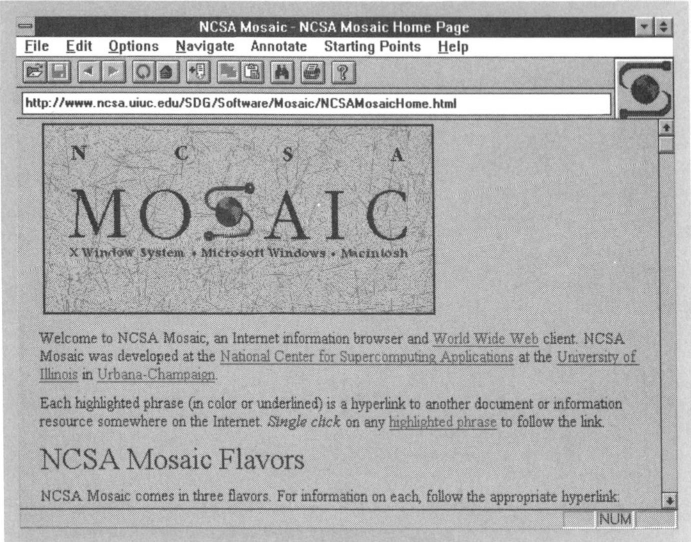

f 4-1 NSCA Mosaic, Champaign, Illinois

Hypertext

Browsers allow you to use hypertext links. Hypertext allows you to select a word with your mouse, then jump to another document that contains more information on the topic you are reading. For example, if you click on the text *WWW* in a document located on a host in Illinois (see Figure 4-1), you will be taken to another document that talks about the World Wide Web, located on another host server in Switzerland (see Figure 4-2).

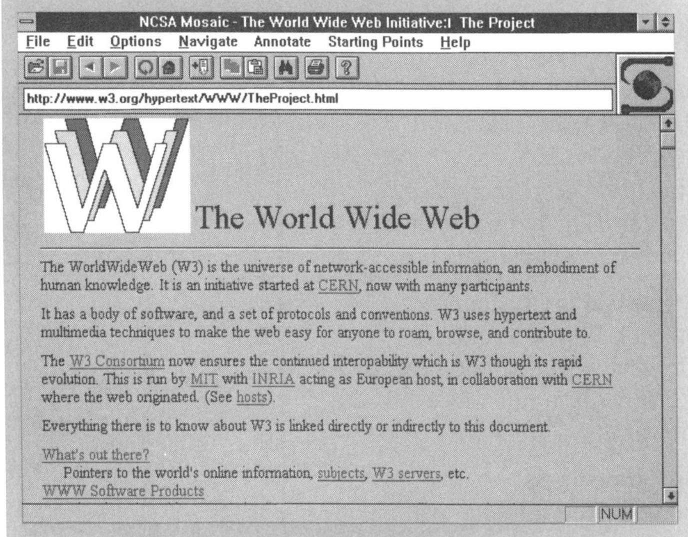

f 4-2 The World Wide Web at CERN in Switzerland

Hypertext words are usually underlined, show up as [reversed text], or appear [shaded in a different color], as shown in figures 4-1 and 4-2. If you see a hypertext word you like, simply click on the keyword and jump to the document that has the information you desire.

Hypertext links can also be used with pictures or graphics. Click on any of the little graphic boxes on this hypertext page from Finland, and you will be able to view some wonderful pictures of whales from the World Wide Whale Watch (see Figure 4-3 on page 28).

GUI Icons

Mosaic and Netscape have **iconic** or **GUI** interfaces. An **icon** is a picture or graphic. GUI, pronounced *gooey*, is short for Graphical User Interface. GUI icons allow you to send your computer commands by selecting graphical icons with a mouse.

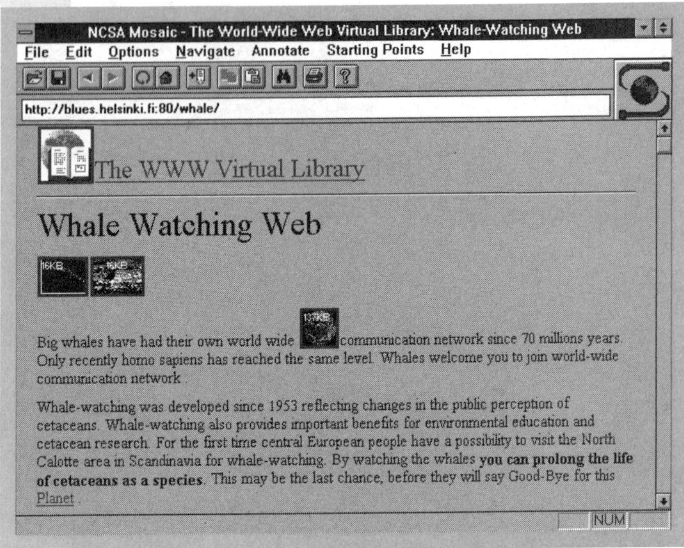

f 4-3 The Whale Watching Web, Helsinki, Finland

Click on an icon with your mouse, and the computer will execute the command. For example, click on the home icon (see Figure 4-4) to return "home" to your starting point.

f 4-4 Home Icon

Study Your Browser

Study the different parts of your GUI Browser. The following are two examples. The first shows Mosaic running on a Windows computer (see Figure 4-5). The second shows a different version of Netscape running on a Macintosh computer (see Figure 4-6). Compare your Browser's features to the figures below.

READ ME file 15

NET NOTE: Hypertext, hypermedia, and multimedia

It is often easy to confuse the terms hypertext, multimedia, and hypermedia.

Hypertext is a system connecting keywords in one document to text in other documents in other locations.

Hypermedia documents contain links to more than one kind of media. Media is simply another way to say, video, sound, pictures or graphics, graphs, or animation.

Multimedia is widely used to explain systems that use more than one media; i.e., a multimedia computer is one that can run software that uses sound, video, graphics mixed with text, or sound mixed with pictures.

The Microsoft® Internet Explorer Browser

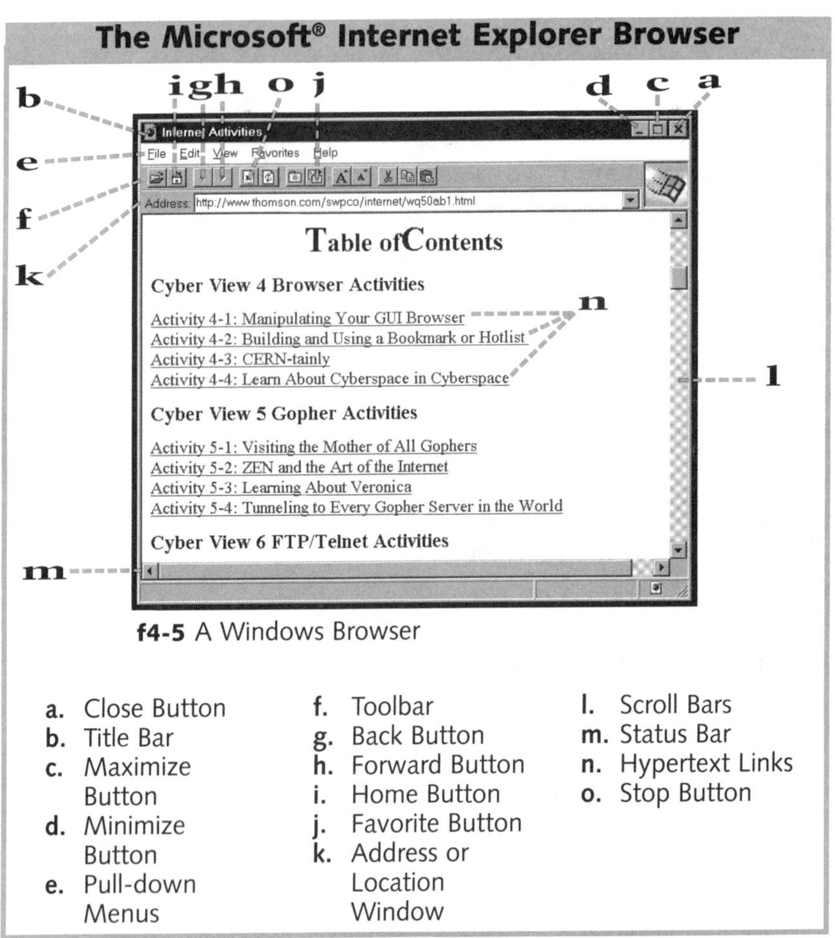

f4-5 A Windows Browser

a. Close Button
b. Title Bar
c. Maximize Button
d. Minimize Button
e. Pull-down Menus
f. Toolbar
g. Back Button
h. Forward Button
i. Home Button
j. Favorite Button
k. Address or Location Window
l. Scroll Bars
m. Status Bar
n. Hypertext Links
o. Stop Button

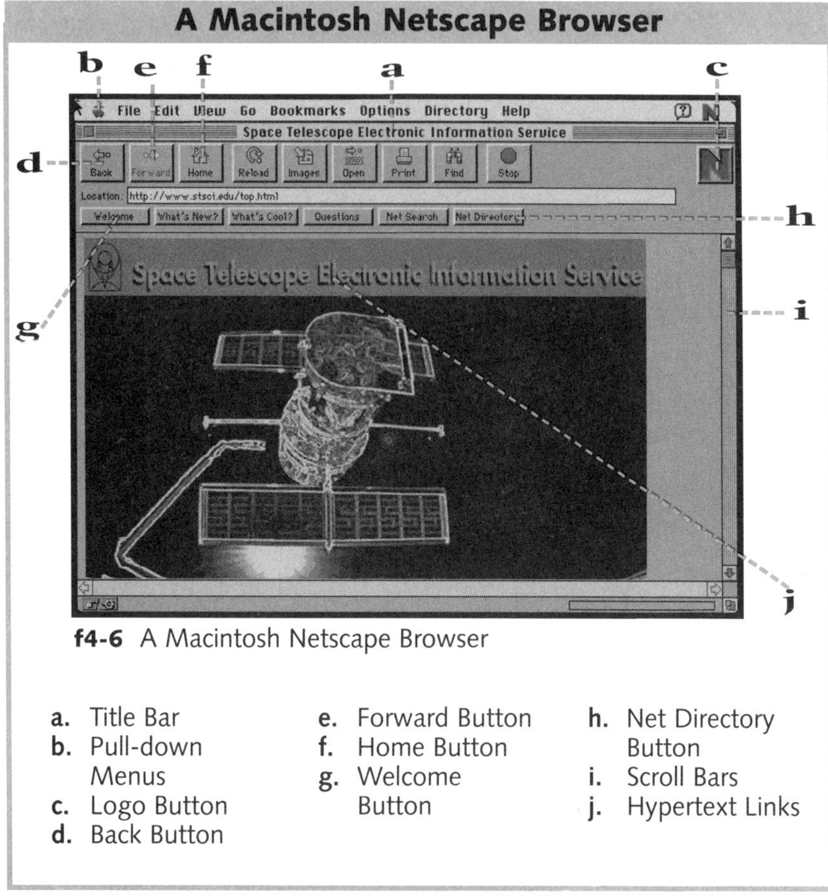

f4-6 A Macintosh Netscape Browser

a. Title Bar
b. Pull-down Menus
c. Logo Button
d. Back Button
e. Forward Button
f. Home Button
g. Welcome Button
h. Net Directory Button
i. Scroll Bars
j. Hypertext Links

If you are using a GUI Browser other than Mosaic or Netscape, your buttons and windows will look slightly different. However, the main functions will be the same. For example, most GUI Browsers will have a URL or Location address box, a Back Button, and a Home Button.

Using Your GUI Browser

Mosaic and other GUI Browsers are very easy to learn and use. If you have your own Browser client, you have probably figured it out already. Here are some basics to make your GUI Browser work for you.

Home Pages

When you start your GUI Browser, you will automatically come to a Home Page. **Home Pages** are like indexes that list specific topics on a single subject. The first Home Page that appears is *your* starting point Home Page. GUI Browsers allow you to find other Home Pages.

ReadMe file 16

NET NOTE: Home Pages and Welcome Pages

Many people confuse a Home Page with a Welcome Page. This is easy to do since the two pages look similar and both use hypertext.

A Welcome Page simply introduces you to a WWW host site. A Home Page relates to one topic, like art or travel. *

READ ME file 17

FAQ's: What is an HTML?

One of the big problems on the Internet is that documents are not consistent. One set of documents may be formatted in an old version of WordPerfect, and another may be in Microsoft Word. Some documents are DOS or ASCII formats, while others are Macintosh documents.

To solve this problem, **HTML** was developed. HTML stands for HyperText Markup Language. HTML consists of a set of commands that describe a file to the GUI Browser. HTML descriptions allow each Browser to display the document clearly. You will see **.html** at the end of URLs.

Your Starting Home Page

Many Mosaic clients use the NCSA Home Page as their starting point Home Page (see Figure 4-1). Netscape also has a Home Page for Netscape users. However, your starting Home Page may be different. Your local Internet Administrator has the option to change your Home Page. Don't worry. With your GUI Browser, you will be able to link to any other Home Page.

Uniform Resource Locators (URLs)

Behind each hypertext link is a **Uniform Resource Locator,** or **URL**. A URL is an address or reference code, like the library code used to locate a library book. URLs make it possible for Mosaic and other GUI Browsers to find specific hypertext documents on any host server in the world.

URL addresses are funnier looking than normal Internet addresses. These long names are seen everywhere in this new hypertext world, sometimes called hyperspace. Following are some examples:

- **http://www.dcc.uchile.cl/**
- **http://info.er.usgs.gov**
- **http://info.cern.ch/hypertext/WWW/TheProject.html**

The first URL address belongs to The University of Chile. The second is a URL addressing the United States Geological Survey. The third example is the URL address for the World Wide Web project of CERN in Switzerland.

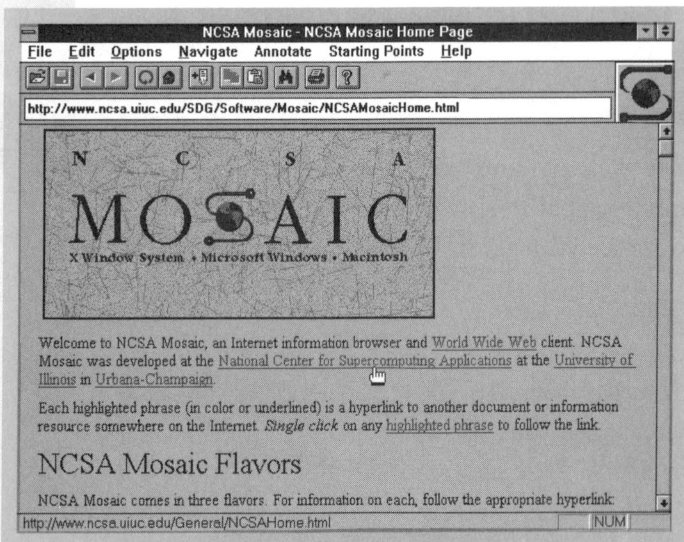

f 4-7 Hypertext link shows in URL display

If you rest your mouse pointer on any hypertext word, you will be able to see the URL for that hypertext link in the URL display (as shown at the bottom of Figure 4-7).

Hotlists and Bookmarks

Keeping track of important URLs can be a problem. Fortunately, Browsers allow you to create catalogs or lists of your favorite URLs.

In Activity 4-2, you will catalog interesting Home Pages in a list. In Mosaic, your catalog is called a **Hotlist**. In Netscape, your catalog is called a **Bookmark** list.

Play with Your GUI Browser

Browsers are very similar in most ways. Minor name changes and buttons in slightly different places should not bother you. If you play with your GUI Browser options for a few minutes, you will quickly find the commands and features you need.

Keeping Track of Where You Are

It is easy to get carried away with hypertext and jump from place to place. In a matter of seconds, you can be from your starting point to a Home Page halfway around the world. At some point, *you will get lost* and find a topic or Home Page you are not interested in.

GUI Browsers keep track of the path you follow so you can return to where you started. You can back up one page at a time with the Back Button (see Figure 4-5). Or you can return to your original starting point by selecting the Home Button (see Figure 4-5).

file 18

FAQ's: What is HTTP?
At the start of URLs, you will see the letters `http://`. **HTTP** is short for HyperText Transfer Protocol. Protocols are instructions computers understand that tell them how to handle and send hypertext documents from

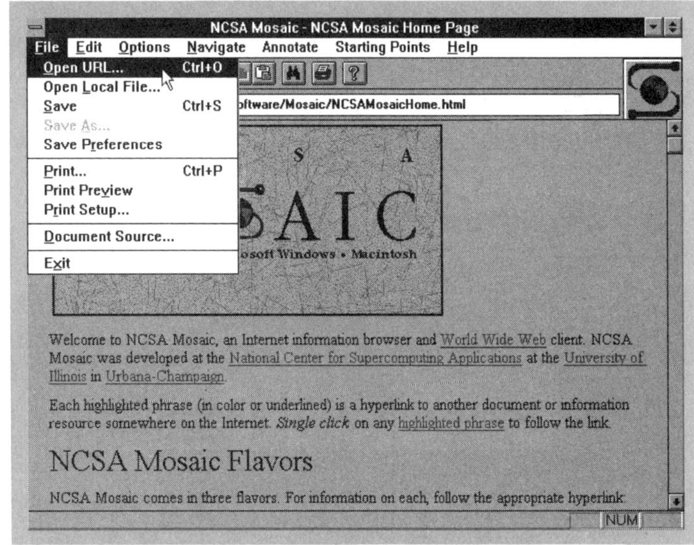

f 4-8 Open URL pull-down menu

Entering a URL

URLs are critical to completing activities with your GUI Browser. You can enter a URL in Mosaic by clicking the *Open URL* command located in the File pull-down menu (as shown in this Windows example in Figure 4-8).

In Netscape, this same option is also found under the File pull-down menu. However, the command is *Open Location* (as seen in this Windows example in Figure 4-9).

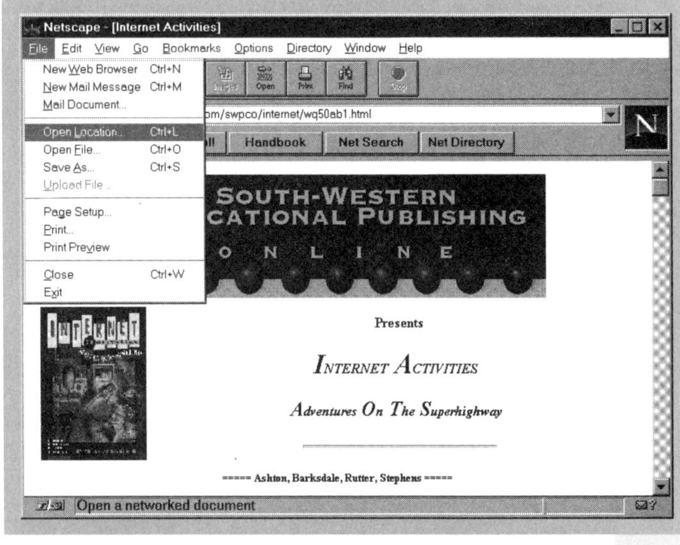

f 4-9 Open Location pull down menu

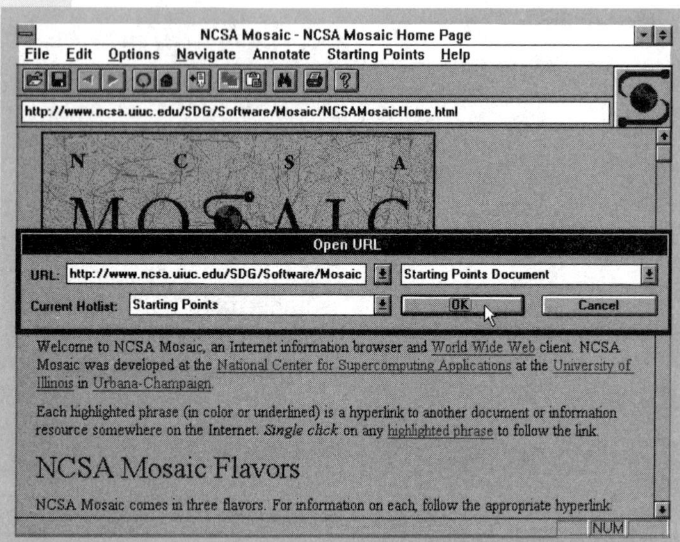

f 4-10 Windows Mosaic URL entry box

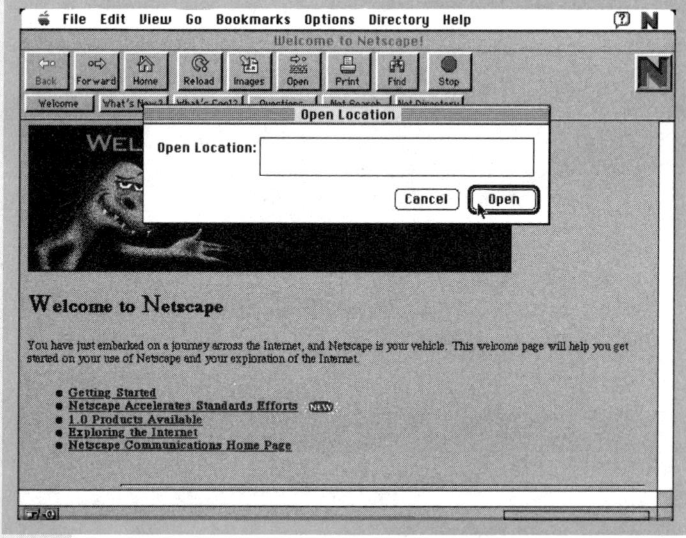

f 4-11 Macintosh Netscape URL entry box

When the URL entry box appears, click in the URL entry box and key a URL address (see figures 4-10 and 4-11).

After you key the URL, select OK or OPEN to load your new hypertext document.

A Few Warnings

URLs must be keyed exactly as they are written. URLs are case-sensitive. This means that every capital letter or lowercase letter must be keyed correctly; for example, *www* and *WWW* are different from each other. Also, every (.) and (/) must be keyed properly; for example, a (\) is not a (/).

CyberQuiz 4

On a separate piece of paper or on a handout provided by your teacher, answer the following questions.

Circle Yes if the statement is true or No if the statement is false.

1. **Yes or No** An icon is a picture or graphic.
2. **Yes or No** Browsers use hypertext keywords to jump to other text.
3. **Yes or No** A URL allows you to find Home Pages by clicking on hypertext links.
4. **Yes or No** Netscape is a GUI hypertext Browser.
5. **Yes or No** Protocols are instructions computers understand that tell them when you are violating Netiquette.

For questions 6 through 8, circle the letter that corresponds to the best answer.

6. **GUI Browsers will NOT have**
   a. a URL address box
   b. a Back Button
   c. a Home Button
   d. a Belly Button

7. **When you start your GUI Browser, you will automatically come to**
   a. Gopherspace
   b. a Home Page
   c. hypertext links
   d. a Hotlist

8. **This URL, http://www.ncsa.uiuc.edu/general/ncsahome.html, is from (HINT: Look at the URL.)**
   a. the Stanford Medical Center
   b. the University of Minnesota
   c. the United States Geological Survey
   d. the National Center for Supercomputing Applications

For questions 9 through 10, write the correct answer in the space provided.

9. **What do the following terms mean?**

GUI ______________

HTML ______________

URL ______________

HTTP ______________

Icon ______________

NCSA ______________

10. **Explain in your own words how to enter a URL or Location name. Include information on how to key URLs or Locations correctly.**

Manipulating Your GUI Browser

Introduction

GUI Browsers, like Mosaic and Netscape, make it easy to explore the World Wide Web and other Internet sites. In this exercise, you will learn to use several key features found in GUI Browsers.

Objectives

Start your GUI Browser client

Explore your Home Page

Experience hypertext and hypertext links

Navigate with your GUI Browser

Return home

Use the Back Button

View your history

Use the Home Button

Enter URLs like NCSA, the Jet Propulsion Lab, and Cal Tech

Explore multimedia Home Pages

README file 19

FAQ's: What is a "Failed DNS Lookup" or a "Unable to Locate Host" error?

You will often run into the error message, "Failed DNS Lookup," or the "Unable to Locate Host" error. DNS is short for Domain Name System. In the DNS, a Domain Name Server is a computer that converts names to addresses and finds resources on the Net. If the "Failed DNS Lookup" error appears, it means the DNS server could not find the address you requested.

A host is a remote server or computer. If you are unable to locate your host, either the URL address is wrong, or your host is down. *

RESOURCE TABLE

CLIENT	GUI Browser
RESOURCE LOCATION	Locate the NCSA Demo Page: Browser: Enter **http://www.ncsa.uiuc.edu:80/demoweb/demo.html** Locate the Jet Propulsion Lab: Browser: Enter **http://www.jpl.nasa.gov/** Locate the Cal Tech Home Page: Browser: Enter **http://www.caltech.edu/**
SPECIAL ADVICE	BE PERSISTENT. If something doesn't work, try again later. If some of the connections fail, try these alternatives: Locate the Disney Home Page: Browser: Enter **http://www.disney.com/** Locate the MIT Home Page: Browser: Enter **http://web.mit.edu/** Locate National Parks on-line: Browser: Enter **http://www.infowest.com/soutah/nationalparks/index.html**

inter-steps

1. Start Netscape, Internet Explorer, Mosaic or other GUI Browser.

STEP 1A

Double-click on your Browser icon.

STEP 1B

When your GUI Browser starts, it looks for your Home Page. It may take a few seconds for your Home Page to load.

Mosaic Browser icon

Netscape Browser icon

2. Explore your Home Page.

Internet Explorer Browser icon

README file 20

SOFT NOTE: View your Address or Location windows

It will be easier to record URLs if you turn on the Show Current URL or Show Locations option.

Mosaic for Windows:

Select Show Current URL from the Options pull-down menu.

Mosaic for Macintosh:

Select Show URLs from the Options pull-down menu.

Netscape:

Select Show Locations from the Options pull-down menu.

Internet Explorer

Select Address Bar from the View pull-down menu. *

STEP 2A

Click on any hypertext link on your Home Page.

STEP 2B

Record the URL address, the title of the Home Page, and a brief description of each selection in Cyber Log 4-1-1.

Throughout Sector 2, you will see notations such as *Cyber Log 4-1-1*. In such a notation, the first two numbers (*4-1*) refer to the Cyber Log number, which is always the same as the activity number; for example, Cyber Log 4-1 is in Activity 4-1. The third number (*-1*) refers to the part of the Cyber Log; for example, Part 4 of Cyber Log 4-1 would be referred to as *Cyber Log 4-1-4*.

STEP 2C

Repeat steps 2A and 2B two more times.

3. You are probably halfway around the Cyberspace world by now. There are three ways to return to your original Home Page.

STEP 3A

You can retrace your steps by clicking on the Back Button.

The slow way home

STEP 3B

In Mosaic, you can retrace your steps by clicking on the Navigate menu and selecting History.

In Netscape, select Go; then select the Home Page you want to go to from the History list.

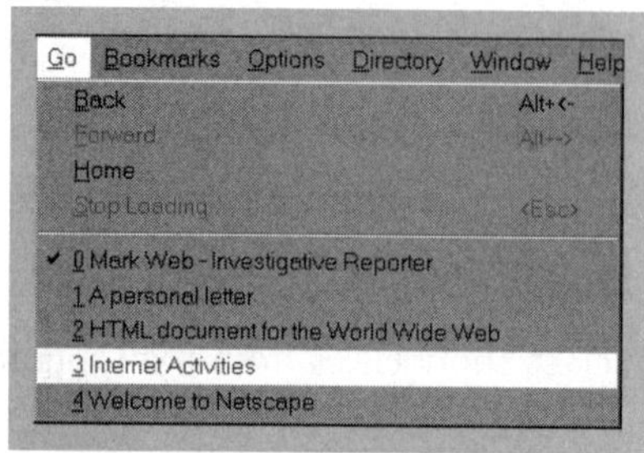

Select Go; then select from the list

In Internet Explorer, select Favorites; then select your Home Page from the list.

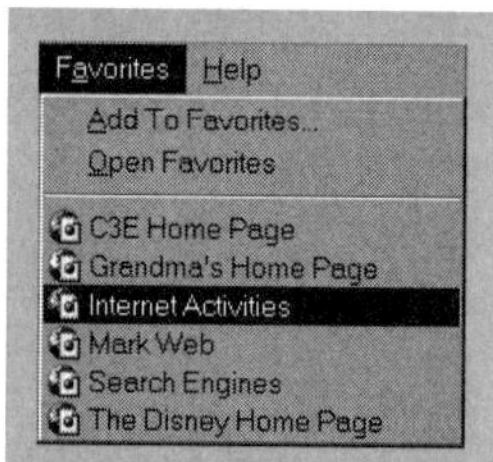

Select Favorites; then select from the list

file 21

SOFT NOTE: Browser hints

Popular Home Pages take lots of **hits**. A hit is recorded every time someone connects to a Home Page. There is so much traffic on the Net, you may get "Timed Out" on popular sites. Keep trying, or try a different hypertext link.

Sometimes you may select a hypertext link that requests a Home Page, graphic, or file that is simply too big for your connection or computer to handle. If a selection takes too much time, click on the spinning world icon in Mosaic, or click on the Stop Button in Netscape.

If your text or graphics doesn't look correct on your screen, try clicking on your Reload Button.

STEP 3C

You can also return to your Home Page by clicking on the Home Icon.

The fastest way home

Return to your Home Page any way you like.

4. Find the Internet Activities Home Page.

STEP 4A

Click on the Open button on your Browser's toolbar.

Note: You may also select Open or Open Location from the File menu.

The Netscape Open button

The Internet Explorer and Mosaic Open button

STEP 4B

Enter the Internet Activities Home Page URL into the open window. Key the URL exactly as it is written, then click the Open or OK button.

Enter the following URL address and select OK or OPEN:

http://www.thomson.com/swpco/internet/wq50ab1.html

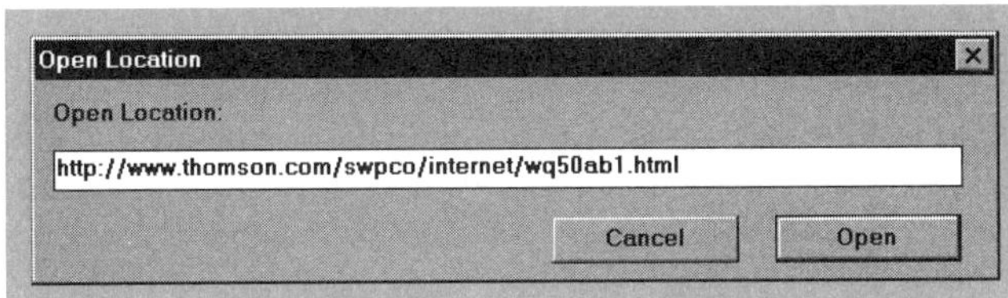

URL entered in the Netscape Open Location window

Note: you can also enter an URL directly into the Location or Address window on your Browser.

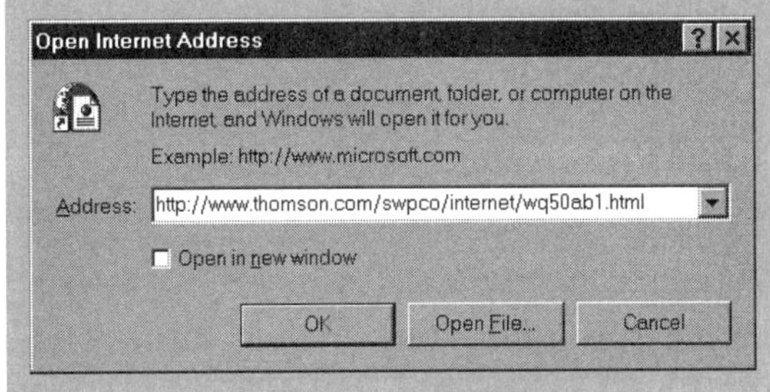

URL entered in The Internet Explorer Open Internet Address window

5. Wait a few seconds for the Internet Activities Home Page to appear, then explore the Home Page.

STEP 5A

Scroll down until you can see the Activity 4-1 link in the Table of Contents. Click on the Activity 4-1 hypertext link.

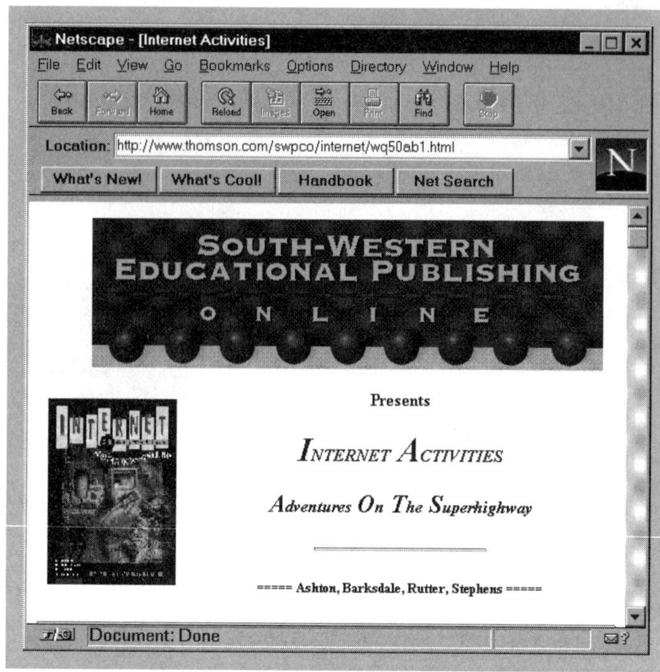

The Internet Activities Home Page

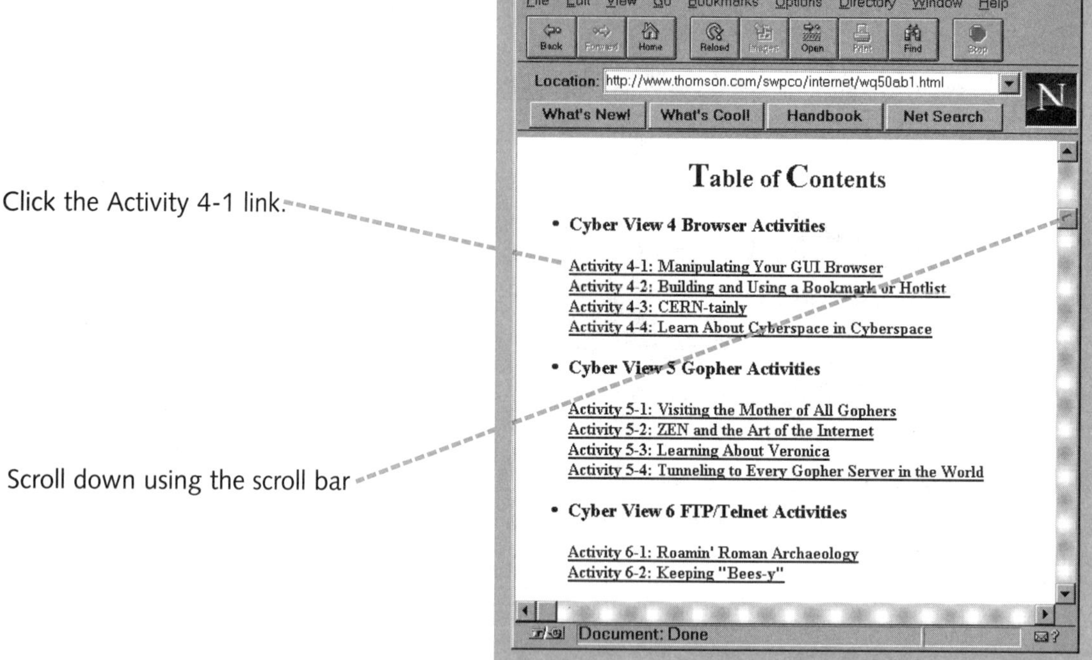

The Table of Contents

6. There are three Resource Locations listed under Activity 4-1. Click the three hypertext links: NCSA, the Jet Propulsion Lab, and Cal Tech. Enter the URL, Title, and a description of each page in the space provided in Cyber Log 4-1-1. Return to each of the three Home Pages using your Forward and Backward buttons. Complete the questions in Cyber Log 4-1-2, 4-1-3, and 4-1-4.

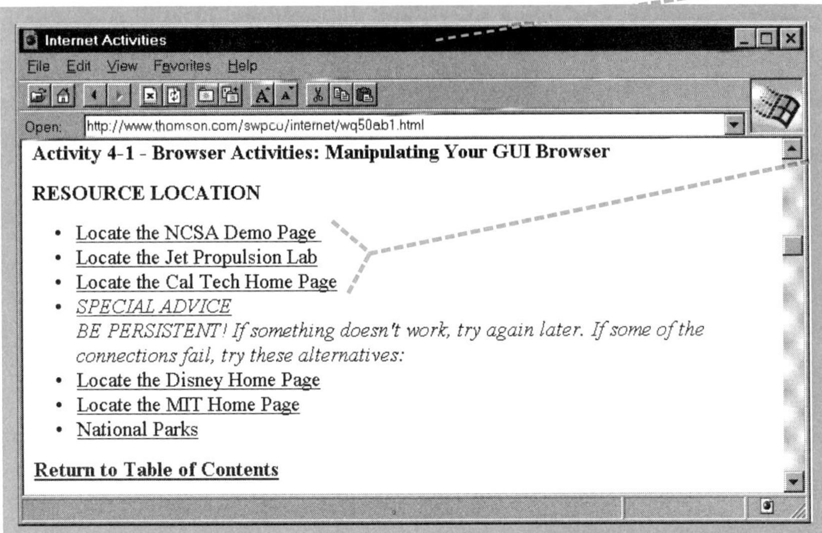

The Activity 4-1 Resource Locations as seen in The Internet Explorer Browser

Note: If any hypertext links don't work, try the alternative links below the Special Advice message. If, for any reason, you can't reach the Internet Activities Home Page, enter the URLs that appear in the Resource Table on page 36 by hand, as described in Step 4.

Hint! When Answering the questions in Cyber 4-1-1, remember that the Home Page Title appears in the Title Bar at the very top of the Browser.

7. Take a few hypertext jumps on your own. Try selecting some pictures or graphics. Some graphics are hot spots and work like hypertext links. Click on them.

Record your path in Cyber Quest 4-1-5. Don't forget to return home when the bell rings at the end of the class. See inter-step 3 if you forget how to return home.

8. Exit or Quit your GUI Browser when you are finished for the day.

STEP 8A

Select File, then Exit in Windows, or

STEP 8B

Select File, then Quit on the Macintosh.

9. Review your Cyber Log and select your three favorite URLs / Locations. Record your choices in Cyber Quest 4-1-6. Give a reason why you like each.

CyberLog 4-1

1. **Record three new URL addresses you have discovered by clicking on hypertext links. For example:**

   URL / Location: **http://www.ncsa.uiuc.edu/demoweb/demo.html**
   Home Page Title: *NCSA Mosaic Demo Document*
   Description: *Talks about the World Wide Web*

URL / Location: ______________________
Home Page Title: ______________________
Description: ______________________

URL / Location: ______________________
Home Page Title: ______________________
Description: ______________________

URL / Location: ______________________
Home Page Title: ______________________
Description: ______________________

2. **The NCSA Mosaic Demo Document (If the connection to NCSA fails, use the alternative URL for Cal Tech found in the Resource Table. List five key hypertext options on the Cal Tech Home Page.)**

   Where is NCSA? ______________________

   List five of the Exemplary Applications Categories listed on this Home Page.

A. ______________________
B. ______________________
C. ______________________
D. ______________________
E. ______________________

3. **The Jet Propulsion Laboratory Home Page (If the connection to JPL fails, use the alternative URL for MIT found in the Resource Table.)**

   Select several hypertext links from this Home Page. List the three URLs / Locations you selected.

URL / Location: ______________________
Home Page Title: ______________________
Description: ______________________

URL / Location: ____________________
Home Page Title: ____________________
Description: ____________________

URL / Location: ____________________
Home Page Title: ____________________
Description: ____________________

4. **Thc Cal Tech Home Page (If the connection for Cal Tech fails, use the alternative URL for O'Reilley and Associates, Inc. found in the Resource Table.)**

Take notes on what you read while visiting this Home Page. List some of the facts and statistics mentioned. Try some of the hypertext links to dig deeper and to learn more about the topics discussed.

____
____
____
____
____
____
____

CyberQuest 4-1

5. **Surf the Net. Select several new hypertext links. Record each URL and a brief note about each. Surf until you drop!**

URL / Location: ____________________
Home Page Title: ____________________
Description: ____________________

URL / Location: ____________________
Home Page Title: ____________________
Description: ____________________

URL / Location: ____________________
Home Page Title: ____________________
Description: ____________________

HOT HOME PAGES

6. **Make a list of your top three Home Pages. Use your notes in your Cyber Log to create this list. This list can be used in Activity 4-2 to create your own Bookmark or Hotlist.**

   Three Favorite Home Pages:

URL / Location: ______________________________
Home Page Title: ______________________________
Why is it hot? ______________________________

URL / Location: ______________________________
Home Page Title: ______________________________
Why is it hot? ______________________________

URL / Location: ______________________________
Home Page Title: ______________________________
Why is it hot? ______________________________

Building and Using a Bookmark or Hotlist

Introduction

Now that you have learned to use your GUI Browser, it is time to find and save some of your favorite Home Pages.

GUI Browsers allow you to create lists of URLs you like to return to over and over. These lists are called: Hotlists in Mosaic, Favorites in the Internet Explorer, or Bookmarks in Netscape. Be careful that you keep your list to a reasonable number. A long Hotlist will make it hard to find your top selections.

Objectives

Start your GUI Browser

Locate several new hot Home Pages

Create a Hotlist

Use your Hotlist

Save your Hotlist

RESOURCE TABLE

CLIENT	GUI Browser
RESOURCE LOCATION	Locate the NCSA's Starting Points For Internet Exploration Home Page: Browser: Enter **http://www.ncsa.uiuc.edu/SDG/Software/Mosaic/StartingPoints/NetworkStartingPoints.html** Locate the Sendai National College of Technology: Browser: Enter **http://www.sendai-ct.ac.jp/**
SPECIAL ADVICE	Use Yahoo as an alternative starting point for Cyber Log 4-2-5. Browser: Enter **http://www.yahoo.com**

inter-steps

1. Start Netscape, Internet Explorer, Mosaic, or other GUI Browser.

2. Connect to the Internet Activities Home Page.

Internet Activities Home Page

http://www.thomson.com/swpco/internet/wq50ab1.html

3. Place an entry into your Hotlist, Bookmark list, or Favorites list.

STEP 3A

In Netscape: Click Add Bookmark from the Bookmarks pull-down menu.

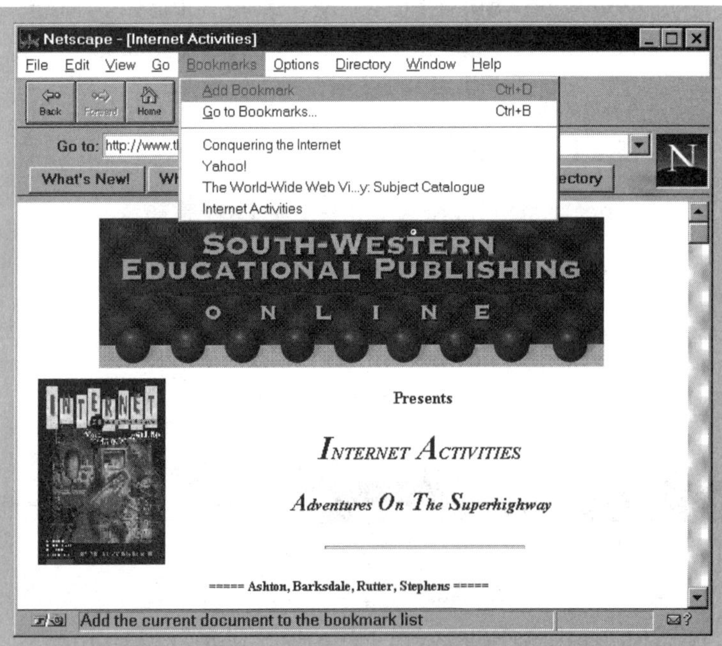

Add Bookmark option

STEP 3B

In Mosaic for Macintosh: Click on the Hotlist pull-down menu, then choose Add This Document. (In some versions of Mosaic you can also click on the Hotlist button.)

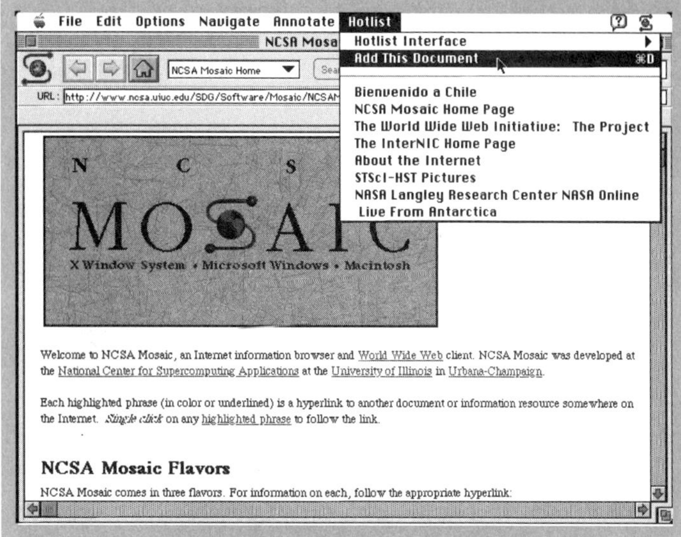

Add This Document option

STEP 3C

In the Internet Explorer: Click on the Favorites pull-down menu, then choose Add to Favorites.

4. Add the NCSA Network Starting Points Home Page and the Sendai National College of Technology to your Hotlist, Bookmark list, or Favorites list. Hint! You can select the links from the Activity 4-2 on the Internet Activities Home Page, or you can enter the URLs by hand as shown in the previous activity. The URLs you need are listed in the Resource Table.

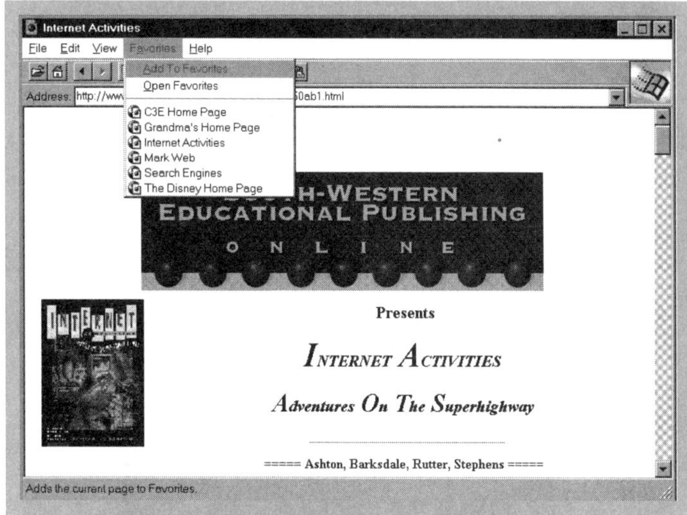

The Favorites option

STEP 4A

Connect to the NCSA Networks Starting Points Home Page. Add the entry to your Hotlist, Bookmark list, or Favorites list as learned in Step 3. Read the disclaimer on this Home Page, then answer the questions in Cyber Log 4-2-1.

STEP 4B

Connect to the Sendai National College of Technology in Japan and add it to your Hotlist, Bookmark list, or Favorites list. Review the English version of this Home Page.

5. Access the Internet Activities Home Page from your Bookmark list, Favorites list, or Hotlist.

STEP 5A

In Netscape: Click Internet Activities from the Bookmarks pull-down menu.

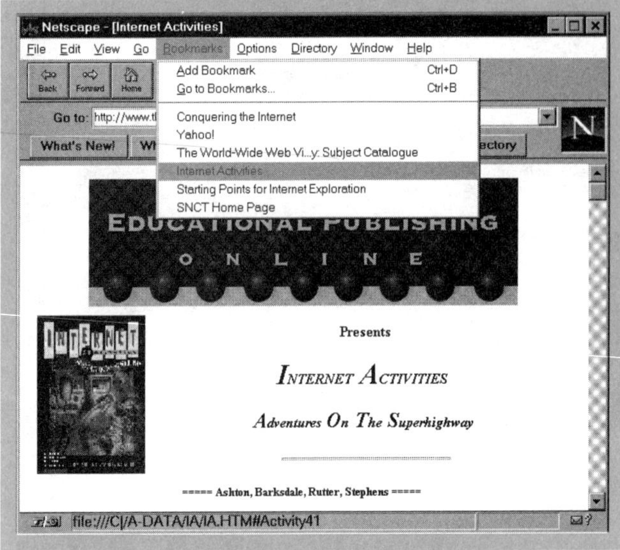

Select Internet Activities from the Bookmarks menu

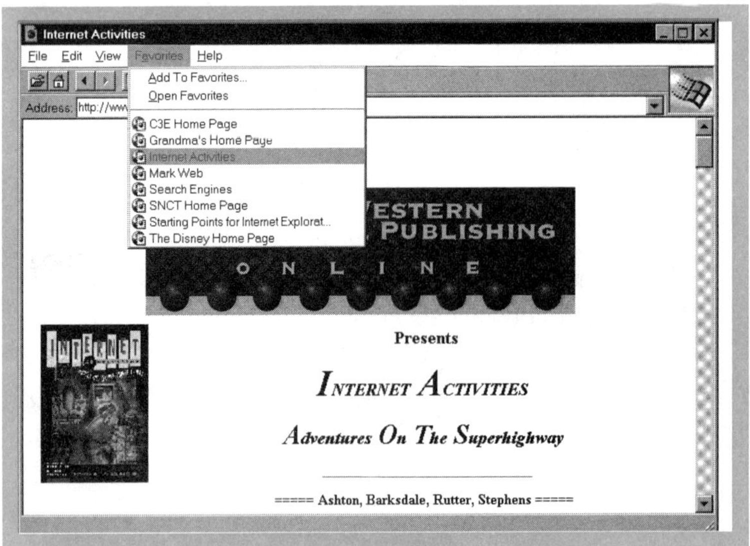

STEP 5B

In Internet Explorer: Click Internet Activities from the Favorites menu.

Select Internet Activities from the Favorites menu

STEP 5C

In Mosaic for Macintosh: Click the Hotlist pull-down menu, then pick the Internet Activities link.

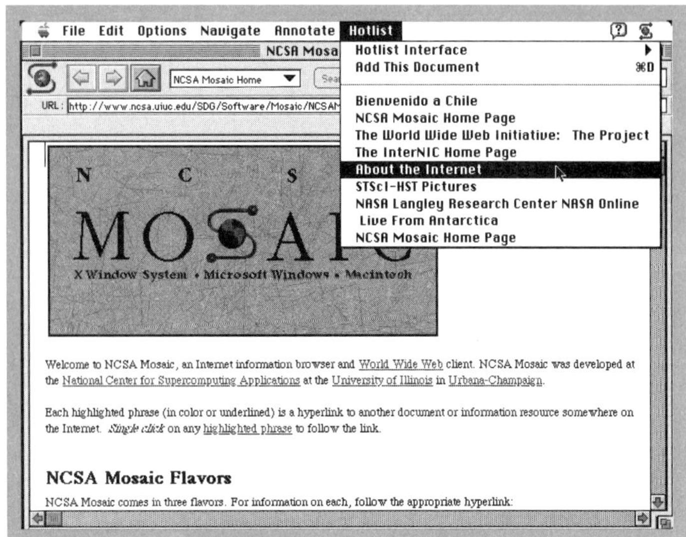

Mosaic Hotlist

6. After the Internet Activities Home Page appears, scroll down and click on the Activity 4-2 hypertext link. There you will find five URLs. Select and bookmark each one of them. Enter the URL and the Title of each Home Page in the space provided in Cyber Log 4-2-2. When you are finished, rank the Home Pages 1 to 5. Let number 1 be your favorite and place a 5 by your least favorite.

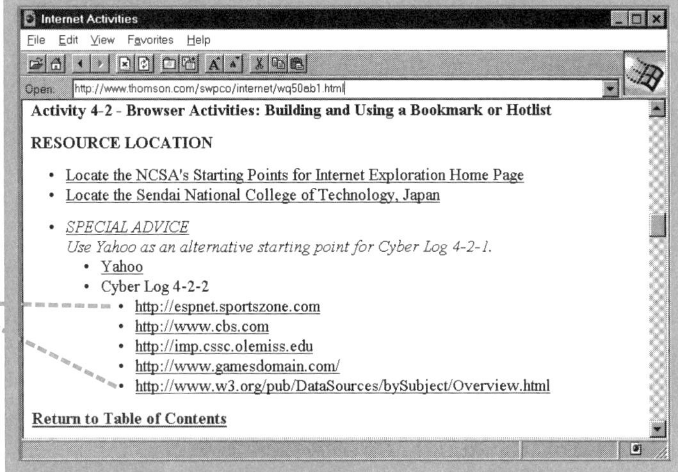

Select and bookmark these URLs

Use Activity 4-2 to finish Cyber Log 4-2-2

7. In Cyber Log 4-2-3, record the steps you take in order to add a Home Page to your Hotlist, Bookmark list, or Favorites List

8. Exit or Quit your GUI Browser.

9. Complete the activities in Cyber Quest 4-2 on page 51.

READ ME file 22

SOFT NOTE: Hotlist at risk

Sometimes your Network Administrator will protect the start-up files for your computer system. This protects everyone from losing the basic network services. However, this also means that you may not have the network rights to save your Hotlist.

CyberLog 4-2

1. **After reading the disclaimer in the NCSA Network Starting Points Home Page, answer the following questions: (If you used the alternative URL, return later to the NCSA Network Starting Points Home Page and fill out this portion of the Cyber Log.)**

A. Why was it necessary for NCSA to write this disclaimer?

____

B. What can you do to help keep the Net open to other users?

____

C. Why is it that you cannot always reach your favorite Home Page on the Net?

____

2. **Enter the URL and title of each new Hotlist entry you make during this lesson. Rank your five new entries. Let number 1 be your favorite Home Page, and number 5 be your least favorite.**

Ranking ___ Hotlist URL: _______________________
Title of Home Page: _______________________

Ranking ___ Hotlist URL: _______________________
Title of Home Page: _______________________

Ranking ___ Hotlist URL: _______________________
Title of Home Page: _______________________

Ranking ___ Hotlist URL: _______________________
Title of Home Page: _______________________

Ranking ___ Hotlist URL: _______________________
Title of Home Page: _______________________

3. **Record the steps you take in order to add a Home Page to your Hotlist.**

____
____
____
____
____

CyberQuest 4-2

4. **Start your GUI Browser again. Check and see if your Hotlist or Bookmark list has been saved properly. If it is gone, what could be the reason your Hotlist has not been saved? (See README file 22.) Try each selection in your Hotlist, or in the Hotlist or Bookmark list that is provided.**

5. **Surf the Net and look for five new Home Pages you like and add each one to your Hotlist, Bookmark list, or Favorites list. Write the title of each new Home Page in the place provided. Write a brief description of each. Rank these Home Pages. Have number 1 be the best, and number 5 be the least interesting to you. (Hint! Use Yahoo. You can find it on the Internet Activities Home Page. Click the Activity 4-2 hypertext link.)**

Home Page Title: ____________________
Description of Contents: ____________________
Ranking: _____

Home Page Title: ____________________
Description of Contents: ____________________
Ranking: _____

Home Page Title: ____________________
Description of Contents: ____________________
Ranking: _____

Home Page Title: ____________________
Description of Contents: ____________________
Ranking: _____

Home Page Title: ____________________
Description of Contents: ____________________
Ranking: _____

CERN-*tainly*

Introduction

What better way to understand something, than to visit the people that built it? Take a transatlantic trip to CERN in Switzerland, the home of the World Wide Web.

Objectives

Trace the origins of WWW

Learn about CERN

Analyze electronic towns

RESOURCE TABLE

CLIENT	GUI Browser
RESOURCE LOCATION	Locate The World Wide Web Home Page of CERN in Switzerland: Browser: Enter **http://www.w3.org/hypertext/WWW/TheProject.html**
SPECIAL ADVICE	CERN is a very reliable connection. However, here is an alternative URL you can try for Cyber Log 4-3-1 if the connection goes down. If you cannot connect to CERN at this time, be sure to return later. It is a must for all Web travelers. Locate the Netscape Welcome Page, then arrow down and select Exploring the Internet: Browser: Enter **http://home.mcom.com/home/welcome.html**

inter-steps

1. Start your GUI Browser.

2. Select the Internet Activities Home Page from your Bookmark, Favorites, or Hotlist.

3. Visit the World Wide Web project Home page. Select the 4-3 hypertext link from the Internet Activities Home Page. Click on the *Locate the World Wide Web Home Page of CERN in Switzerland* hypertext link or enter the URL below:

   http://www.w3.org/hypertext/WWW/TheProject.html

   You will be taken to the World Wide Web Home Page of CERN in Switzerland.

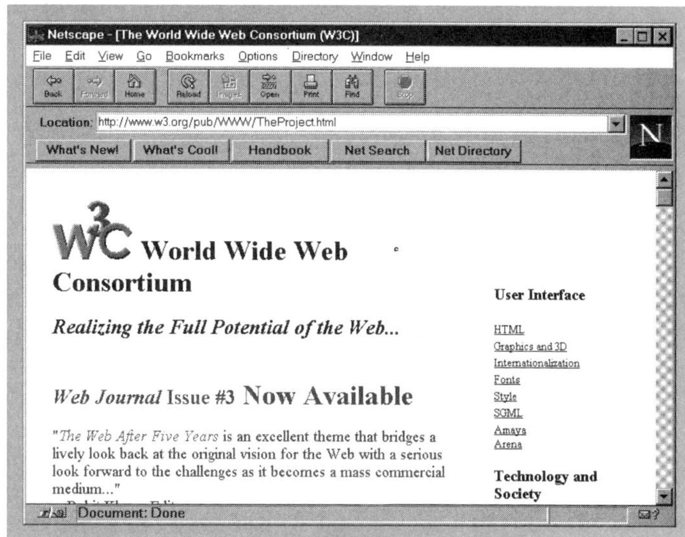

The World Wide Web Home Page

4. ALTERNATIVE: Complete the questions in Cyber Log 4-3-1. If the URL does not load, the connection may be down. Try the alternative URL listed in the Special Advice section of the Resource Table.

CyberLog 4-3

1. **Visit CERN in Switzerland (Alternative: Visit Netscape), then answer the following questions:**

A. What is the WWW? (Or explain your alternative selection.)

____

B. What is CERN? (Or explain your alternative selection.)

____

C. Where is CERN? (Or where is your alternative selection?)

____

D. Why was CERN formed? (Or why was your alternative selection developed?)

____

CyberQuest 4-3

2. **You have been asked by a major computer manufacturing company to find a location for a new, high-tech manufacturing plant. The plant will produce a new line of computers and will employ about 2,000 new workers. You are looking for a community that will provide the new plant with a well-educated, computer-literate workforce. You also want to locate your new manufacturing plant in a safe community, with a low crime rate and with excellent schools. Following are four URLs. One entry is for Champaign County, Illinois. The second and third entries are from Ottawa, and Vancouver, Canada. The last entry is for CERN in Switzerland. Investigate these communities. Pick one, and build a case why your company should locate a multimillion dollar facility in this location. Give reasons why you are excluding the other cities. Take notes on each location, then go to your word processor and complete your proposal.**

Note: Make sure you use your Internet Activities Home Page to complete this assignment. There are 5 cities listed for you to use. Click the Activities 4-3 link and look for the Cyber Quest cities.

3. Try to locate five other electronic towns on the Net. Make a list of these cities and their URLs / Locations. Start your search with City Net: Enter **http://www.city.net/**

Learn about Cyberspace in Cyberspace

Introduction

Some of the best information on the Net is not found in books. It is found on the Net itself. In this activity, you will be introduced to dynamic resources on the Net. The word **dynamic** means constantly changing. Internet resources are always being updated. In a couple of months, if you return to these same Home Pages, the information will be different, updated, and improved.

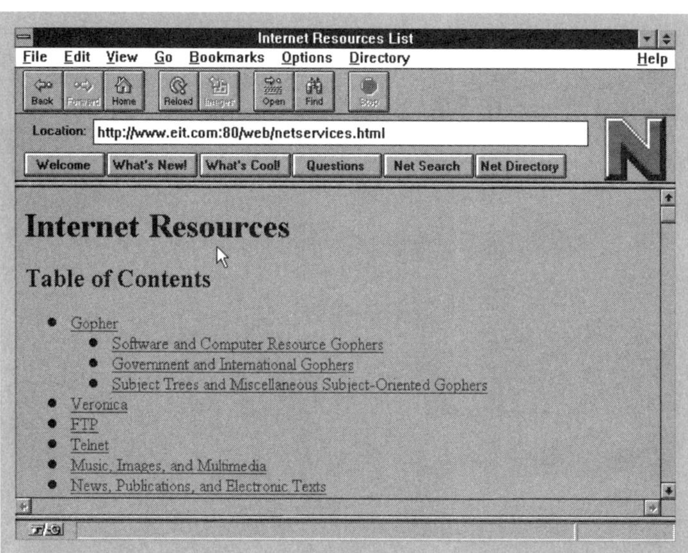

Internet Resources

In this lesson, you will be given three URLs that point to locations that teach about the Internet and the World Wide Web. As you search, look at Cyber Views 4, 5, 6, 7, 8, and 9 to compare your answers with those you have found on-line.

Objectives

Search three URLs for information about the Net

Investigate the tools of the Internet

Learn more about the World Wide Web

RESOURCE TABLE

CLIENT	GUI Browser
RESOURCE LOCATION	Locate Internet Resources: Browser: Enter **http://www.eit.com:80/web/netservices.html** Browser: Enter **http://yahoo.com/Computers/Internet** Browser: Enter **http://www.eit.com/help/search.html**
SPECIAL ADVICE	If one of the locations is down, try the next location and return to the previous URL at a later time. Don't forget to visit the Internet Activities Home Page for all the activities in this book. The Internet Activities Home Page is updated frequently with new and better URLs or addresses to help you complete your work. Browser: Enter **http://www.thomson.com/swpco/internet/wq50ab1.html**

CyberLog 4-4

1. **Start your GUI Browser.**

2. **Enter the URLs found in the Resource Table. Write a short explanation of each of the tools and resources found in Cyber Log 4-4. Compare your descriptions of each tool with the information found in Cyber Views 4, 5, 6, 7, 8, and 9.**

Hypertext ______________________________

Hypermedia ______________________________

WWW ______________________________

Mosaic ______________________________

HTML ______________________________

Uniform Resource Locators ______________________________

Archie ______________________________

Veronica ______________________________

E-mail ______________________________

Anonymous FTP ______________________________

WWW Browsers ______________________________

Internet Relay Chat ______________________________

Gopher ______________________________

Telnet ______________________________

News ______________________________

CyberQuest 4-4

3. **Using the URLs you have just used as a starting point, find other locations that talk about the Internet. (HINT: Look in the Special Advice section of the Resource Table.) List any new locations you find here.**

URL: ______________________________

Home Page Title: ______________________________

Description: ______________________________

URL: ______________________________

Home Page Title: ______________________________

Description: ______________________________

URL: ________________________________
Home Page Title: ________________________________
Description: ________________________________

4. **Which resources did you find the most valuable in answering the questions in Cyber Log 4-4-2?**

URL: ________________________________
Home Page Title: ________________________________
Description: ________________________________

Why was this resource the most valuable?

5. **In Cyber View 3, you learned a little about the history of the Internet. However, much of the story is still untold. Write a brief report on the history of the Internet or on the development of the Web. You may also select one of the key elements of Cyberspace, like Archie or Jughead, and prepare a report on one of them.**

Gopher Activities

This Cyber View will teach you the basics of the Internet Gopher and its rodent friend, Veronica. Gopher and Veronica make it easy to dig and tunnel through the endless mounds of Internet data.

Burrow through the following topics in this Cyber View:

- Gopher's goal
- The Elements of Gopherspace
- The Gopher menu system
- Veronica
- Various platforms

Following this Cyber View, there are four activities:

Activity 5-1: Visiting the Mother of All Gophers
Activity 5-2: Zen and the Art of the Internet
Activity 5-3: Learning about Veronica
Activity 5-4: Tunneling to Every Gopher Server in the World

README file 23

NET NOTE: Surfing with a Gopher

Once you go on-line with a Gopher, you can **surf the Internet**. Surfers are people who explore the Net looking for information, data, activities, games, friends, opportunities, and ideas.

If you are going to surf with a Gopher, you had better learn a little bit about the Internet's most famous rodent. Watch the README boxes for more Gopher tales from Gopher lore. *

Solving a Big Internet Problem

One of the biggest Internet problems is the unbelievable amount of information on its numerous hosts. The Internet is often accused of "information overload." There is so much data that you can surf the Internet eight hours a day, every day for the rest of your life, and not come close to exploring all the possible resource hosts.

This is where Gopher comes in. The Gopher is an easy-to-use, menu-driven program that helps you locate Internet resources.

Go Golden Gophers!

The Gopher started at the University of Minnesota, the home of the Golden Gophers. Researchers and students at the University of Minnesota faced the same dilemma we all face:

READ ME file 24

FAQ's: What is Gopherspace?
The Internet pathways available with Gopher are called *Gopherspace*. Since everything in Gopherspace is reduced to menus or lists, you must burrow or tunnel from one list to the next until you find your prize—the file of your choice.

How do you find what you want over the Internet quickly and easily?

Their solution was to come up with a menu-driven software client called Gopher.

Gopherspace

Gopherspace is made up of several elements:

- Gopher Servers
- Gopher Clients
- Directories
- Files

Gopher Servers

The first element in Gopherspace is a collection of host computers called **Gopher Servers**. Gopher Servers display their computer information in the form of a series of menus. A **menu** is a listing of the contents of the host computer. If you have Gopher Client software, you can read these menus and select the information you need from the lists that appear.

Gopher Clients

The Gopher software you run to visit Gopherspace is called **Gopher Client** software. Gopher Servers serve information to Gopher Clients. If you have a direct, SLIP, or PPP connection, you can run your own copy of the Gopher Client. If you have a dial-in connection, your dial-in provider must be running a Gopher Client.

Figure 5-1 shows a menu listing several available Gopher Servers you can visit with your Gopher Client. If you are running DOS or UNIX Gopher Clients, your screens may look slightly different; however, the words in the menus will be the same.

Directories

A **directory** is a storage location, like a file folder, where related data is kept. For example, data on football may be found in a Football directory. Data on basketball could be found in a Basketball directory. Data on basketball and football may be found inside a Sports directory.

Files

At the end of any Gopher search is a file. In fact, the goal of a Gopher is to help you find the file you want quickly, even if you don't know the specific name of the file. Files are collected in directories; for example, a directory on social studies may have files on history and geography.

Gopher filenames are easy to understand; for example, the file *data.tur* may be called *Data on Turtles* in Gopherspeak.

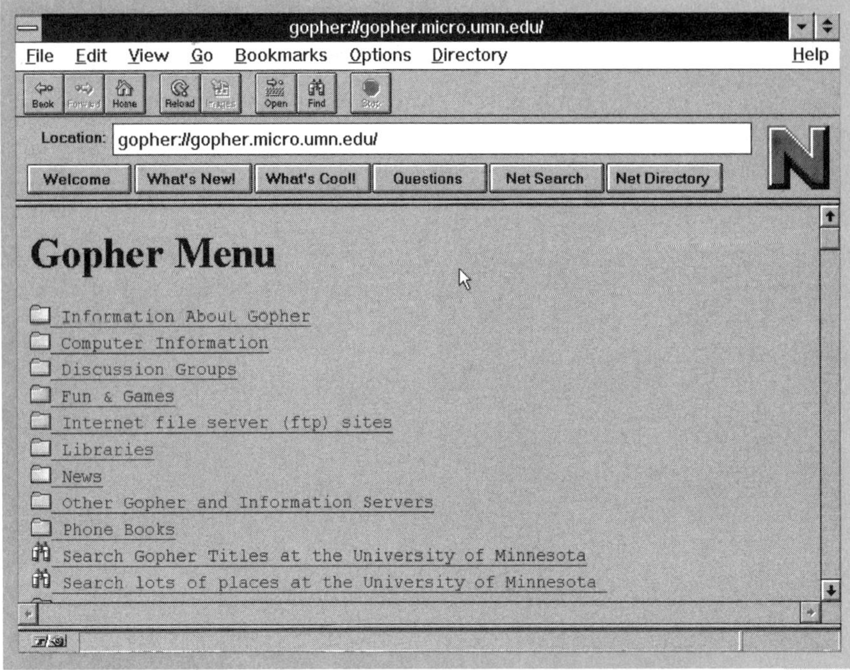

f 5-1 Gopher Servers

Files may be of any size and come in many forms. A file may be a letter, report, book, article, picture, video clip, sound bite, or any other collection of data you can read, view, or hear.

To summarize, you can compare a Gopher Server to a library, with every book becoming a directory. A book on sports may have several files, or chapters, devoted to your favorite sports.

Following are seven examples of files you can find in Gopherspace:

- FAQ's on the Mother of All Gophers
- Veronica help files
- Humor files
- Zen and the Art of the Internet
- White House briefings
- Travel information guides
- NASA News

file 25

NET NOTE: The Gopher's strange name
Many think that Gopher really stands for "go for," as in *Go for an Internet file.* Gophers actually take this insult personally.

file 26

FAQ's: Where can I get the FAQ's?
All over the Net you will find directories and files called FAQ's. FAQ's is Netspeak for Frequently Asked Questions. The FAQ's files are always a good place to start learning about a new service, Gopher Server, or Internet location.

The Gopher Menu System

The Gopher allows you to jump from menu to menu until you find what you are looking for. With the Gopher, you start by selecting general topics first, then narrow down your choices until you find the specific menu topics that interest you most.

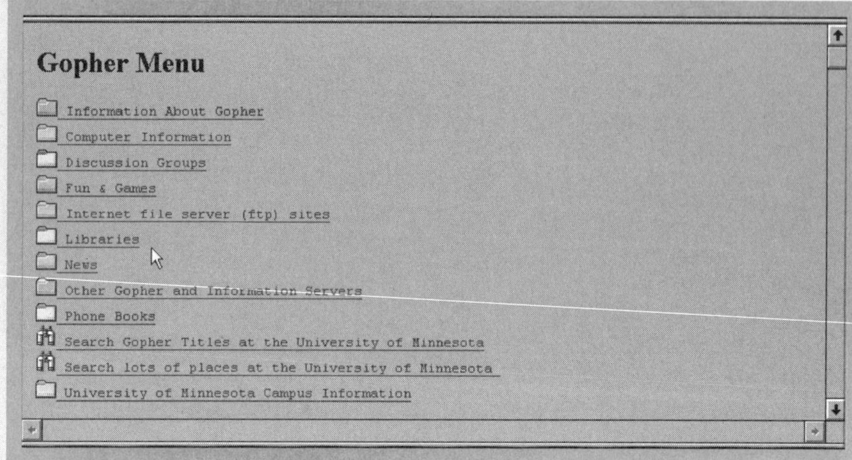

f 5-2 University of Minnesota Gopher menu

Figure 5-2 shows an example of a Gopher menu from the ancestral home of all Gophers, the University of Minnesota.

Pick any selection from this menu, and you will be taken to another sub-menu that further narrows down the topics. If you select the ***News*** directory, you come to a News menu. Notice that there are additional directories that you can select. In Figure 5-3, there is only one file. It is called ***NASA News***.

Select the ***NASA News*** file and you come to a text file that tells you more about exploring NASA (see Figure 5-4).

Gopher could not be easier to use.

Gopher Menu
AMInews Ski Reports
Cornell Chronicle (Weekly)
French Language Press Review
IT Connection (University of Minnesota)
Minnesota Daily
NASA News
National Weather Service Forecasts
Other Newspapers, Magazines, and Newsletters
Purdue University News
Technolog (Institute of Technology, University of Minnesota)
The Bucknellian Student Newspaper at Bucknell University
The Daily Illini (University of Illinois)

f 5-3 *NASA News* is a file in the News menu.

Veronica's Virtue

Even with the help of Gopher, the Net can be a bit mind-boggling. Veronica was developed to make it even easier to find the Gopher files you need most.

Developed by the University of Nevada, Veronica does keyword searches in Gopherspace. Veronica looks at Gopher Servers, creates an index, then lets you search the index based on your keyword choices.

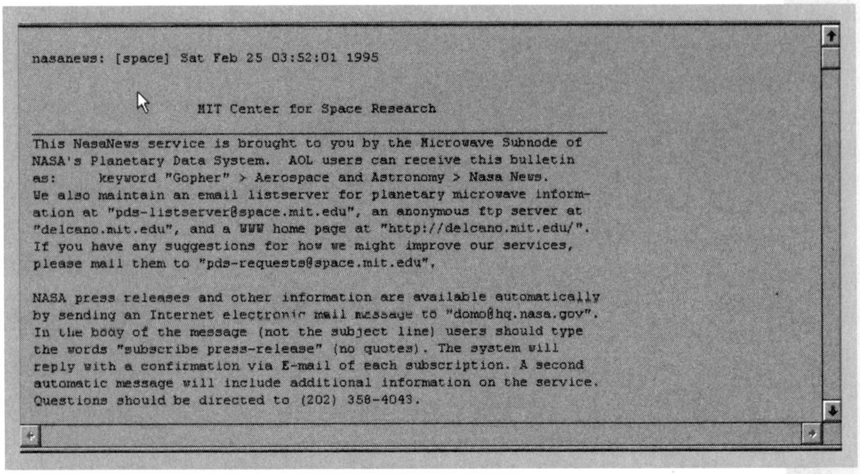

```
nasanews: [space] Sat Feb 25 03:52:01 1995

              MIT Center for Space Research

This NasaNews service is brought to you by the Microwave Subnode of
NASA's Planetary Data System.  AOL users can receive this bulletin
as:     keyword "Gopher" > Aerospace and Astronomy > Nasa News.
We also maintain an email listserver for planetary microwave inform-
ation at "pds-listserver@space.mit.edu", an anonymous ftp server at
"delcano.mit.edu", and a WWW home page at "http://delcano.mit.edu/".
If you have any suggestions for how we might improve our services,
please mail them to "pds-requests@space.mit.edu".

NASA press releases and other information are available automatically
by sending an Internet electronic mail message to "domo@hq.nasa.gov".
In the body of the message (not the subject line) users should type
the words "subscribe press-release" (no quotes). The system will
reply with a confirmation via E-mail of each subscription. A second
automatic message will include additional information on the service.
Questions should be directed to (202) 358-4043.
```

f 5-4 *NASA News* file

For example, if you select the keyword *frog*, Veronica would find every menu item that has *frog* in its listing. If *frog* is not in the menu, even if the article is about frogs, Veronica will not find it.

Pick a Platform

There are many different kinds of computers and computer software available for Internetting. These different computer systems and the software that runs on them are called **platforms**.

All platforms require specialized Internet Server and Client software to communicate effectively with an Internet host. Following are the four most popular Internet platforms:

- Windows®
- Macintosh®
- UNIX®
- DOS®

There are many versions of Gopher for each platform. Some are new and easy to use. Some are older and not so user-friendly.

Generally, all Gopher Clients are similar to each other. The following examples should provide you enough information to help you run your version of Gopher. Pick the platform you will be using to run your Gopher Client. Skip any of the platforms you will not be using.

READ ME file 27

NET NOTE: Veronica's secret

Rumor has it that Veronica's real name is Very Easy Rodent-Oriented Net-wide Index to Computerized Archives. She has made us promise not to tell, so please, keep her secret.

READ ME file 28

NET NOTE: Platform competition

For years people have watched IBM and Apple compete for computer sales. These two platforms never could talk together without a lot of additional software and equipment.

Modern communications have required that competitive platforms communicate with each other. Recently, Apple and IBM formed a partnership to produce computers that can run the same software. These computers are called the Power PC and the Power Macintosh.

Windows and Macintosh GUI Browsers

A whole new group of GUI Browser clients has become available that makes Gopher exploration much easier than it was in the past. With GUI Browsers like Netscape and Mosaic, finding Gopher is as easy as entering a Gopher URL. Gopher URLs are easy to spot. The characteristic **http://** is replaced with **gopher://**; for example, **gopher://gopher.micro.umn.edu:70/1**. Review Cyber View 4 on how to enter URLs.

After you key your Gopher URL, you will come to a Gopher menu.

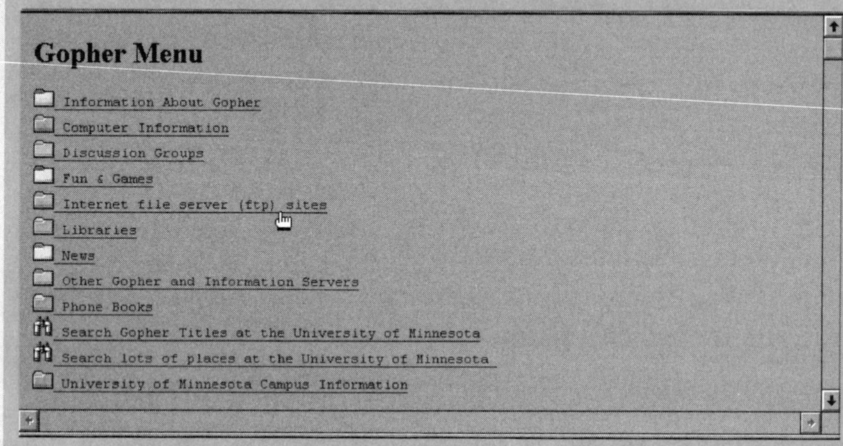

f 5-5 University of Minnesota Gopher menu

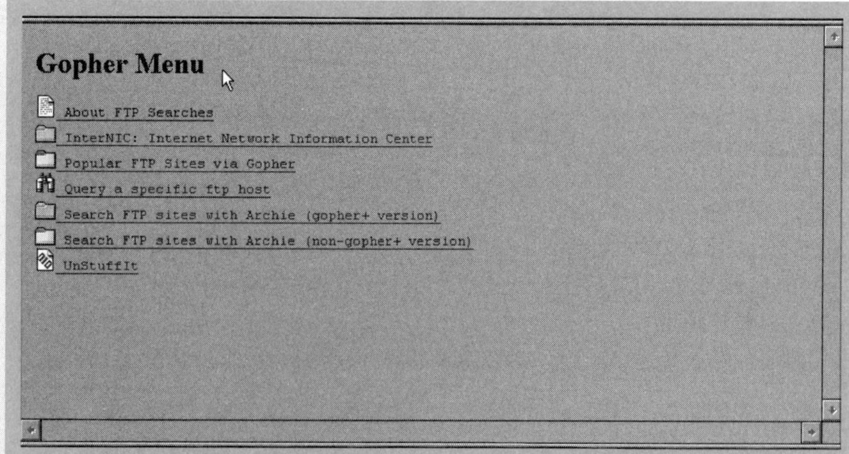

f 5-6 Internet File Server menu

STEP A Double-click with your mouse on the menu item of your choice. If you select the fifth menu item in Figure 5-5 ...

STEP B ... you will come to the menu shown in Figure 5-6.

STEP C To back up, click on the Back Button, or reenter a new Gopher URL to go to a different Gopher location.

Other Macintosh and Windows Gophers

There are Gopher Clients that specialize in Gopher.

f 5-7 Gopher icon

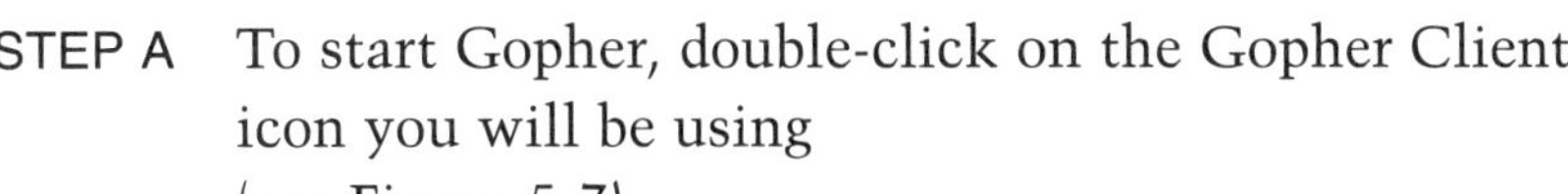

STEP A To start Gopher, double-click on the Gopher Client icon you will be using (see Figure 5-7).

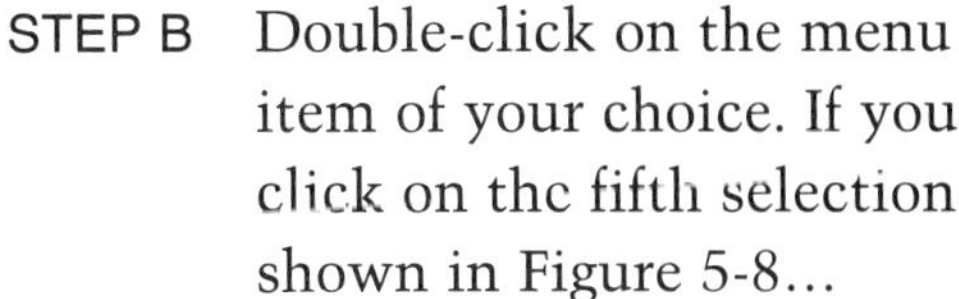

STEP B Double-click on the menu item of your choice. If you click on the fifth selection shown in Figure 5-8...

You will come to the menu shown in Figure 5-9.

Your teacher will help you through the specific start-up steps for your unique Gopher.

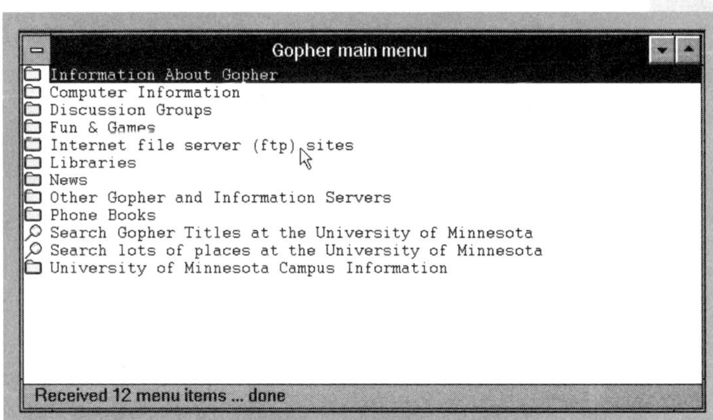

f 5-8 Gopher menu

f 5-9 Internet File Server menu

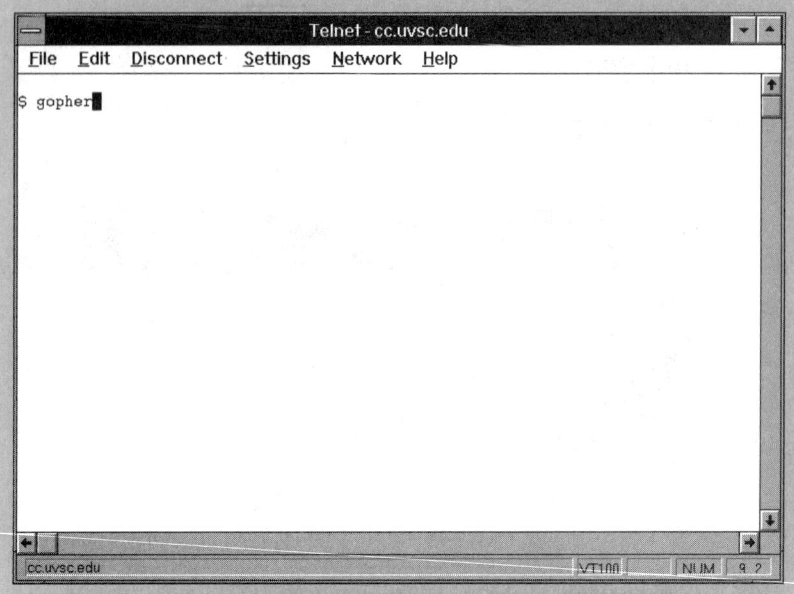

f 5-10 Key *Gopher* at the UNIX prompt.

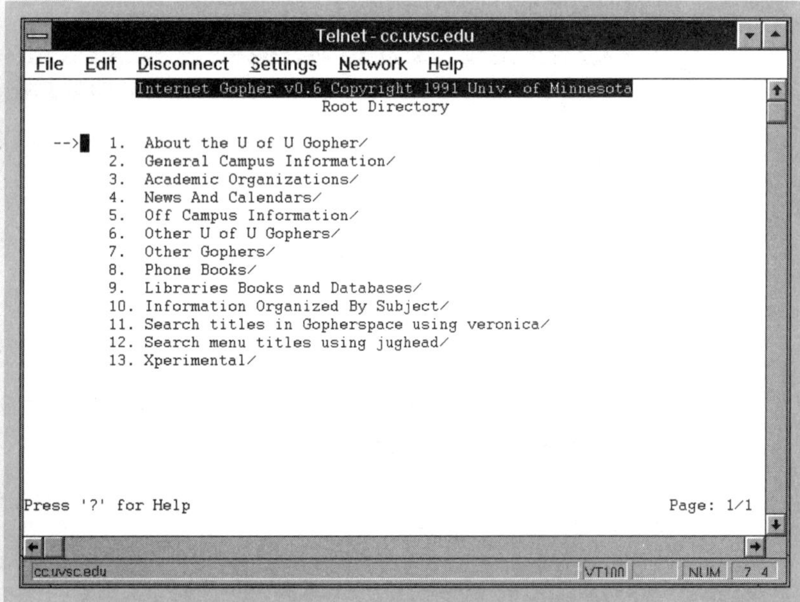

f 5-11 UNIX Gopher menu

UNIX

If you are connected to a UNIX host, connecting to a Gopher is as easy as keying the word Gopher at the UNIX prompt (see Figure 5-10).

A Gopher menu will appear like the one shown in Figure 5-11.

Select the number of the menu item you want Gopher to find. For example, press 5, then press ENTER. Continue in this fashon to burrow to your destination.

When you are done with Gopher for the day, you will have to know how to quit. UNIX usually lets you quit by pressing *CONTROL +Q*. However, there are many local variations. Read your UNIX help files for further instructions.

DOS

DOS clients can be run by keying the Gopher Client software command at the DOS prompt. DOS clients have proven very reliable, and are faster for Gophering than their Windows and Macintosh counterparts. A program called Minuet has a whole host of excellent Internet tools, including Gopher. Minuet is published by the University of Minnesota and is used in the example that follows.

To start a DOS Gopher:

STEP A At the DOS prompt, key the name of your DOS Gopher.

STEP B After Minuet loads, hold down the *Alt* key while pressing the *A* key to open the Activities menu (see Figure 5-12).

STEP C Select Gopher+ from the pull-down menu. You will see a menu like the one shown in Figure 5-13.

STEP D Arrow down to your menu selections and press ENTER. If you select the fifth menu item, you will come to the menu shown in Figure 5-14.

STEP E When you want to back up, press *Shift+Tab* or select the menu level you want with your mouse, then continue on your path.

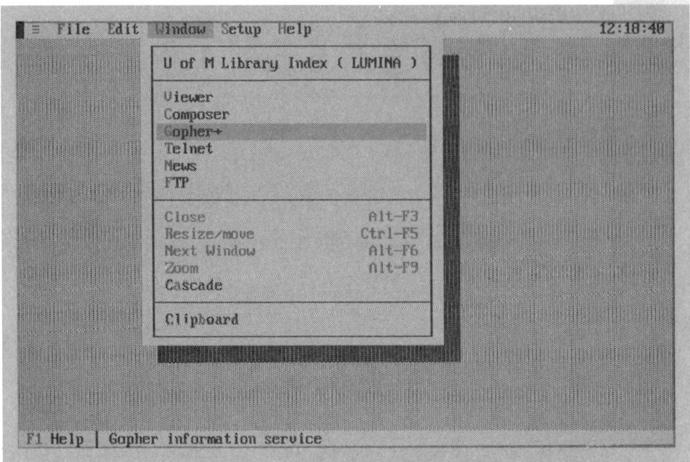

f 5-12 Minuet Activities menu

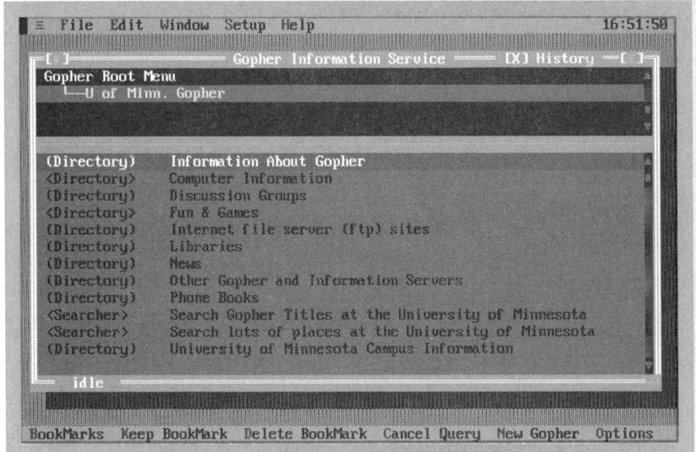

f 5-13 Minuet Gopher menu

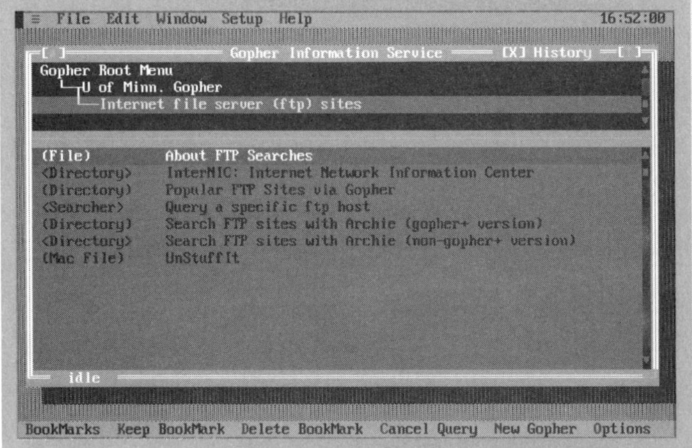

f 5-14 Internet File Server menu on Minuet

CyberQuiz 5

On a separate piece of paper or on a handout provided by your teacher, answer the following questions.

Circle Yes if the statement is true or No if the statement is false.

1. **Yes or No** The Gopher started at the University of Minnesota.
2. **Yes or No** The Internet pathways available with Gopher are called FAQ's.
3. **Yes or No** Gopher allows you to jump from menu to menu until you find your file.
4. **Yes or No** Veronica does keyword searches in Gopherspace.
5. **Yes or No** The Internet is often accused of not having enough information.

For questions 6 through 8, circle the letter that corresponds to the best answer.

6. **If you go "surfing with a Gopher" you are**
   a. a Gopher Server
   b. doing a keyword search
   c. exploring the Net in search of information
   d. planning to attend the University of Minnesota

7. **Gopherspace is comprised of**
   a. Gopher Servers and Clients
   b. files
   c. directories and menus
   d. All of the above

8. **Veronica**
   a. was developed at the University of Nevada
   b. looks at Gopher Servers, creates an index, then lets you search the index that is based on your keyword choices
   c. lets you select a keyword like *frog*, letting you find every menu name with the word *frog* in it
   d. All of the above

For questions 9 through 10, write the correct answer in the space provided.

9. **Define the following:**

FAQ's ____________________

Veronica ____________________

Gopher ____________________

Directories ____________________

Menus ____________________

Files ____________________

10. **Describe briefly how Veronica can make it easier for you to find the Gopher file you need.**

____

____

____

README file 29

FAQ's: The Mother of All Gophers?
The University of Minnesota's Gopher Server is often called *The Mother of All Gophers*, and rightly so. This is where Gopherspace began. The initial development and implementation of Gopher as a user-friendly, Net-surfing program began at the University of Minnesota.

Visiting the Mother of All Gophers

Introduction

In this activity, you will launch your Gopher Client and go for a dig at the University of Minnesota, the heartland of Gopherspace. The University of Minnesota is well-known for its early development of Gopher. The Gopher Client is famous world-wide. Its ease of use and simplicity has helped make the Net accessible to users. This activity will give you a chance to become more familiar with the University of Minnesota and the Gopher Server that got it all started.

Objectives

Launch your Gopher Client

Become familiar with on-line Gopher resources

Tunnel the Net for NASA News

Learn more about The Mother of All Gophers and the University of Minnesota

RESOURCE TABLE

CLIENT	GUI Browser or Gopher Client
RESOURCE LOCATION	Locate the Mother of All Gophers at the University of Minnesota with one of the following tools: Browser: Enter **gopher://gopher.micro.umn.edu/** or enter **gopher://gopher.micro.umn.edu:70/1** Gopher: Key the following in your Gopher's entry box: **gopher.micro.umn.edu:70/1**, or select the University of Minnesota or The Mother of All Gophers from your Gopher's main menu. Some hosts abbreviate the name U of Minn. Gopher, or UMN Gopher. Look around. You may have to search for a menu item called Other Gophers. As a last resort try All the Gopher Servers in the World. You will find it somewhere on your host's main Gopher menu.
SPECIAL ADVICE	If you run into problems finding the University of Minnesota, try the following URL: Browser: LC MARVEL (Library of Congress MARVEL Gopher): Enter **gopher://marvel.loc.gov/** MIT (the 0 in front of NASA News is a zero): Enter **gopher://space.mit.edu:79/0nasanews**

inter-steps

1. Run your Gopher Client software.

2. If you are using a GUI Browser as your Gopher Client, enter the following URL or Location, then skip to inter-step 4:

Enter **gopher://gopher.micro.umn.edu/** or
Enter **gopher://gopher.micro.umn.edu:70/1**

If you are using another Gopher Client, you should already be able to see your Gopher menu. Search your main Gopher menu for The Mother of All Gophers or The University of Minnesota Gopher Server. Your host may call it by other names. Following are names that have been observed in Gopherspace:

- U. of Minn. Gopher
- UMN Gopher
- Original (UMN) Gopher
- The Mother of All Gophers
- The University of Minnesota Gopher

If that doesn't work, try looking under the following:

- Other Gophers
- All the Gopher Servers in the World

3. Select the University of Minnesota's Gopher menu item. You will be taken to a menu that looks something like this ….

If you see a totally different menu, keep looking for the main Gopher menu at the University of Minnesota.

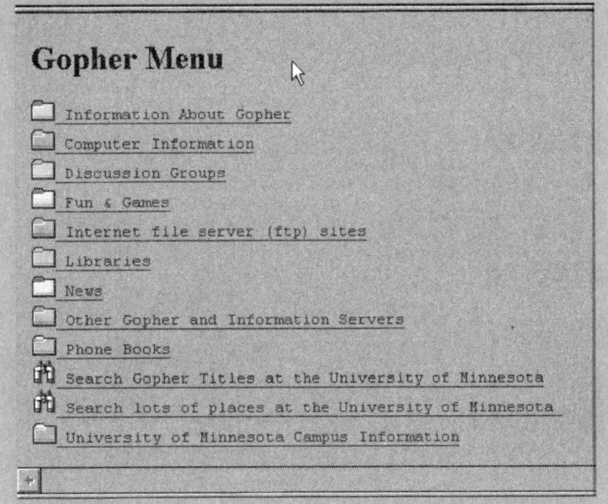

Gopher menu

4. Tunnel through the University of Minnesota's menus by selecting or clicking on the following menu items as you see them:

STEP 4A

Select University of Minnesota Campus Information. (You may have to select All the University of Minnesota
Gopher Servers first.)

STEP 4B

Select Admission Services.

STEP 4C

Select Admission Contacts.

Gopher Menu

How to find entries which have moved
All the University of Minnesota Gopher servers
University Planning
Academic Staff Advisory Committee
Academic, Administrative & Financial Policies
Access to Grades and Course Information (from Student Access System)
Admissions Services
CLA Student Board
Campus Events
Campus Services
College Bulletins (University of Minnesota)
Council on Liberal Education

gopher://spinaltap.micro.umn.edu:70/11/providers/admissions

Select Admission Services.

5. Open the file *Admissions Contacts*. Look for the electronic mail address of the admissions contact. Write it down in the space provided in Cyber Log 5-1-1.

6. Return to the first, or main, University of Minnesota Gopher Server menu.

7. Choose the following menu items from the main UMN Gopher menu:

STEP 7A
Select News.

STEP 7B
Select NASA News.

8. Take notes in Cyber Log 5-1-2 on the main events written about in the latest issue of the NASA News. Some likely news articles that you will find include:

- Space Stations
- Launch Notices
- Astronaut Profiles

Gopher Menu

How to find entries which have moved
All the University of Minnesota Gopher servers
University Planning
Academic Staff Advisory Committee
Academic, Administrative & Financial Policies
Access to Grades and Course Information (from Student Access System)
Admissions Contacts
CLA Student Board
Campus Events
Campus Services
College Bulletins (University of Minnesota)
Council on Liberal Education

Select Admission Contacts.

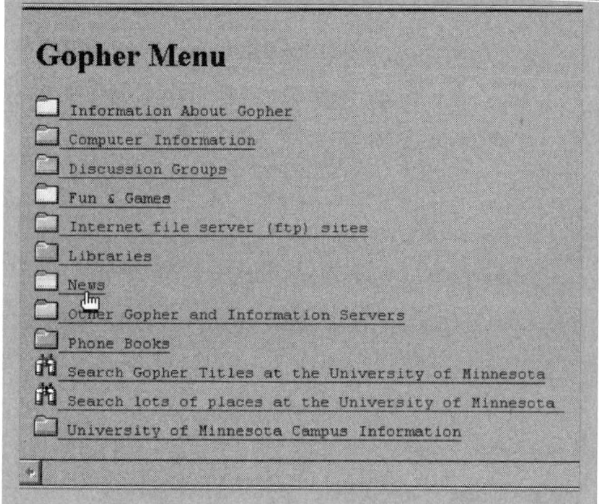

Select News.

README file 30

NETIQUETTE: Save paper, disk space, and login time.
There are lots of people trying to use the same network resources. If you find a file you want like the NASA News, you can save it by selecting your Save option on your Gopher Client. A good name for this file might be *NASANEWS*.

However, ask permission before you save anything. These files are often very large, and will take up a lot of space on either your host or your personal computer. Make sure there is room to store the files you want to keep. It might be a better idea to keep one copy at your school for everyone to use.

You may also print the NASA News by selecting your File, Print option. However, that can take a lot of paper. Ask permission before you print. You could tie up your network printer for ages.

CyberLog 5-1

1. **Record the E-mail address of the admissions officer at the University of Minnesota.**

   ____

2. **NASA News**

   Summarize four pieces of information in the NASA news release. Highlight specifically the technical innovations that are discussed. (Use the alternative URL in the Resource Table for MIT's NASA News.)

   1. ______________________________
   2. ______________________________
   3. ______________________________
   4. ______________________________

CyberQuest 5-1

3. **Return to the University of Minnesota's News section, and find three other files containing news. Write down the path you followed to tunnel to this information. Separate each menu item by a forward slash (/). For example:**

0. *GOPHER / University of Minnesota Gopher / All University of Minnesota Gopher Servers / University of Minnesota Campus Information / Admissions Services / Admissions contacts*

A. GOPHER / ______________________________

B. GOPHER / ______________________________

C. GOPHER / ______________________________

4. **Prepare a news release that you think could be accepted for posting on your Gopher Server. Pick a topic like Events at Your School or An Overview of Your Community. Create a short report in a word processor, and save it for future use.**

READ ME file 31

NET NOTE: Quote from Zen

The author of Zen and the Art of the Internet gives the Internet newbie this important warning:

"One warning is perhaps in order; this territory we are entering can become a fantastic time-sink. Hours can slip by, people can come and go, and you'll be locked into Cyberspace. Remember to do your work. With that, I welcome you, the new user, to the Net."

In this activity, you will learn who is the author of the above quotation.

Zen and the Art of the Internet

Introduction

Zen and the Art of the Internet is one of the legendary resources on the Net. Zen is a respected source of wisdom, an official guide to the Internet traveler. You can't really be an Internet expert without finding and reading at least part of Zen and the Art of the Internet.

Objectives

Launch your Gopher Client

Search for and find a specific file

Search for and categorize information

Become familiar with a few contributors that help make the Net possible

RESOURCE TABLE

CLIENT	GUI Browser or Gopher Client
RESOURCE LOCATION	Locate Zen and the Art of the Internet with either of the following tools: Browser: Enter **gopher://gopher.tc.umn.edu:70/11/Libraries/Electronic%20Books**; and follow the path in inter-step 3. Gopher: Enter **gopher.tc.umn.edu:70/11/Libraries/Electronic%20Books;** and follow the path in inter-step 3.
SPECIAL ADVICE	If your connection fails, or proves flaky, you may need these alternative URLs to access Zen and the Art of the Internet: Browser: Enter **http://www.cs.indiana.edu/docproject/zen/zen-1.0_toc.html** This has a very extensive Table of Contents and is easy to use. Browser: Enter **http://www.tlc-systems.com/dir.html**

inter-steps

1. Run your Gopher Client software.

2. Enter the URL or Gopher address found in the Resource Location section of the Resource Table.

3. Select *By Title*.

4. Arrow down to Zen and the Art of the Internet and select it.

5. Zen is divided into chapters and appendices.

STEP 5A

Scroll through the table of contents and record each chapter heading of Zen in Cyber Log 5-2-1.

STEP 5B

As you scroll through the table of contents, identify three topics from three different chapters that you are interested in. Record the chapter section and name of each topic in Cyber Log 5-2-2.

STEP 5C

As you scroll through the preface, identify and record in Cyber Log 5-2-3 the main author's name and his E-mail address.

STEP 5D

List five contributors the author feels are responsible for the creation of Zen and the Art of the Internet. Record this information in Cyber Log 5-2-4.

READ ME file 32

SOFT NOTE: Keyword Zen

Some Gopher Clients allow you to search by keywords. A program that is often used to search Gopher menu titles is called Veronica. You will learn more about Veronica in Activity 5-3. With Veronica you can search the words *Zen* and *Art* and locate additional copies of Zen.

README file 33

NETIQUETTE: Be kind to Internet hosts

Everyone on the Net must remember that we are constantly using someone else's computer and modem for our benefit. Be kind to your Internet host. Log in only long enough to get the resources you need, then get off and let someone else have a turn.

With popular documents like Zen, it might make a good project to download a copy to your local file server for access by students at your school (see Cyber View 6 on FTP). This way, requests for copies can be provided by the school, keeping Internet traffic to a minimum. This will give more opportunity to others, and reduce the impact on your remote hosts. Your remote hosts will thank you. *

CYBERLOG 5-2

1. **Record the chapter headings for Zen and the Art of the Internet below:**

1. ____________________
2. ____________________
3. ____________________
4. ____________________
5. ____________________
6. ____________________
7. ____________________
8. ____________________
9. ____________________
10. ____________________
11. ____________________
12. ____________________
13. ____________________

2. **List three topics you are interested in. Record the chapter, section numbers, and the name of each topic in the chart below:**

CHAPTER HEADINGS	SECTION #S	NAME
Example: *Network Basics*	*1.1*	*Domains*

3. **Record the name of the author of Zen and the Art of the Internet, and record his E-mail address.**

Author: ________________________ E-mail address: ______________

4. **List at least five contributors responsible for the creation of Zen and the Art of the Internet.**

1. ______________________________
2. ______________________________
3. ______________________________
4. ______________________________
5. ______________________________

CyberQuest 5-2

5. **ZEN'ALYSIS: Explain how Zen can help you in your future Net cruising.**

____

____

____

____

____

6. **Find the section on Network Basics and arrow down to the heading Domains. What do the following abbreviations mean?**

.au ______________________________

.ca ______________________________

.fr. ______________________________

.uk ______________________________

FQDN ______________________________

MIT.EDU ______________________________

apple.com______________________________

7. **From what you read in Zen, Network Basics, Domains, what is a Domain?**

____

____

____

____

____

8. **As you look over Zen, what do you think is missing? Is there a need to constantly update Zen? What suggestions would you write to the author?**

____

____

____

____

____

9. **RESEARCH CHALLENGE: Who can say how many copies of Zen there are on the Net? If you find any additional copies in your surfing, return to this Cyber Log and write down your Gopher search paths. For example:**

0. *The Mother of All Gophers / Documents / Zen and the Art of the Internet.*
1. ______________________________
2. ______________________________
3. ______________________________

README file 34

NET NOTE: Most Used Gopher Words

At the University of Minnesota Gopher, there is a file that lists the 1,000 most-used words in Gopherspace. If you search one of these words, you could get 50,000 or 75,000 entries, too many to be of any help to you.

It is important to learn to use Veronica effectively. The list of most-used words can help you avoid long, unproductive searches. The list is copyrighted by Steven I. Foster, and can be shared free of charge as long as you do not change anything.

Learning about Veronica

Introduction

As you probably know by now, there are many Gopher Servers and thousands upon thousands of menus, directories, and files. It is often hard to know where to search for the exact information you may need. Veronica can help.

Veronica lets you use keywords to find Gopher files you may want to read.

Objectives

Learn more about Veronica using your Gopher Client

Find the 1,000 most commonly used words in Gopherspace

Develop information retrieval skills with Veronica

Save Gopher files

RESOURCE TABLE

CLIENT	GUI Browser or Gopher Client
RESOURCE LOCATION	Locate Veronica with either of the following tools: Browser: Enter **gopher://gopher.micro.umn.edu** then follow the path in inter-step 3. Gopher: Enter **gopher.micro.umn.edu:70/1** then follow the path in inter-step 3.
SPECIAL ADVICE	This activity uses Gopher to learn more about Veronica. Depending on your Internet Access, Veronica may not be effective. There are other search systems explored in Activity 11 of Sector 3.

inter-steps

1. Run your Gopher Client software.

2. Search your main Gopher menu for The Mother of All Gophers or The University of Minnesota Gopher Server and select it.

3. Find the 1,000 most frequently used words in Gopherspace. Tunnel through the University of Minnesota's menu, selecting the following menu items:

STEP 3A
Select Other Gopher and Information Services.

STEP 3B
Select Search Titles in Gopherspace using Veronica.

STEP 3C
Select More Veronica: Software, Index Control Protocol, HTML Home Page.

STEP 3D
Select Statistics on Gopherspace and Veronica.

README file 35

SOFT NOTE: The Veronica alternative
Beware that Veronica is very popular. The number of people accessing Veronica may make it difficult to connect to the service. You may have to try several sites, and try again and again on different days.

Because Veronica is so popular, only use Veronica when you need it. Log in and log out quickly. *

STEP 3E
Select the file *Top 1,000 most-frequent "words" in Gopherspace.*

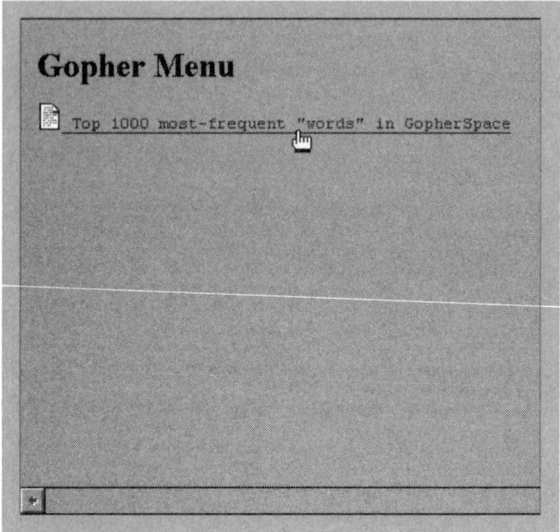

Select Top 1,000 ...

STEP 3F
Save this file to a local drive and name it *top1000.*

4. Find the most frequently asked questions (FAQ's) about Veronica. Find the file by tunneling through the University of Minnesota's menu system.

STEP 4A
Return to the top level of the University of Minnesota's Gopher Server menu.

STEP 4B
Select *Search Titles in Gopherspace using Veronica.*

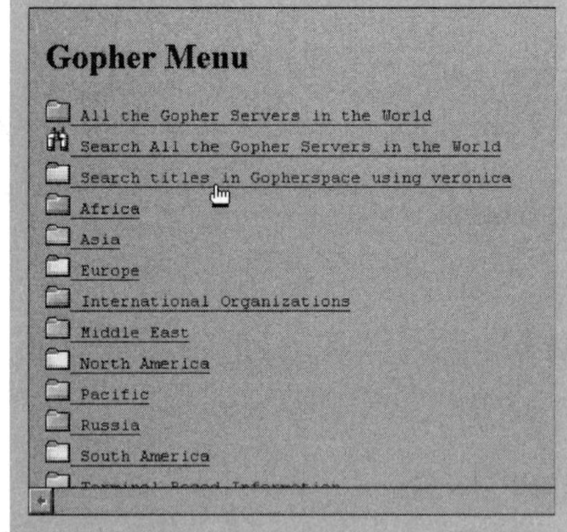

Search using Veronica.

STEP 4C
Select the file *Frequently-Asked Questions (FAQ) about Veronica.*

STEP 4D
Save this file to a local drive and name it *faq.*

STEP 4E
Select the file *How to compose Veronica Queries.*

STEP 4F
Save this file to a local drive and name it *compose.*

5. Close your Gopher Client.

6. Retrieve the three files you have just saved into your word processor one at a time, and respond to the questions in Cyber Log 5-3.

CyberLog 5-3

1. **Open the file *top1000* in your word processor. There is no need to print this file. Read it electronically on your screen and save a few trees from extinction.**

   Record the top ten most frequently indexed words on Gopher Servers and the frequency of use for each word.

WORD	FREQUENCY OF USE

2. **After reading the file *compose*, what two major methods are used for searching resources with Veronica?**

A. ____________________

B. ____________________

3. **After reading the file *faq*, summarize the top four most frequently asked questions about Veronica and the corresponding answers.**

Question 1

Answers

Question 2

Answers

Question 3

Answers

Question 4

Answers

CyberQuest 5-3

4. **Test your knowledge of Veronica. Select a Veronica search from the University of Minnesota Veronica search options and try some searches.**

   Suggestions:

   veronica software search

   veronica training

   veronica bugs

   veronica help

   zen

   zen internet

   zen art internet

education internet

education internet newsgroups

usenet groups

usenet groups business

usenet groups business stock market

5. **Try some combinations of your own. List your search combinations below:**

____

____

____

____

____

____

____

____

READ ME file 36

FAQ's: Can you really tunnel every Gopher Server in the world? Yes, you can. But beware of Gopher traps.

As you burrow through Gopherspace, you will run into problems. Some machines are password-protected, while other machines might simply be down (that is, off). There may also be some incompatibility problems with your software and the software of the host server you are trying to reach.

Still, the Gopher is normally very reliable. If you run into a snag, try tunneling in a different direction. *

activity 5-4

Tunneling to Every Gopher Server in the World

Introduction

One of the best sources for information on the Net is the Library of Congress. But don't feel limited to that one site. You can dig a new tunnel anytime you like and examine what might be interesting to you on any Gopher Server in the world.

In Gopherspace, you can tunnel and tunnel and tunnel until you are not sure where you are or how to get back home. Simply start over if you get lost beyond hope.

Once you know how to find the Library of Congress MARVEL server (LC MARVEL for short), you'll find much more to explore on your own. It's time for some serious tunneling!

Objectives

Find additional Gopher resources

Tunnel to the Library of Congress

Tunnel foreign Gopherspace

Access congressional databases

RESOURCE TABLE

CLIENT	GUI Browser or Gopher Client
RESOURCE LOCATION	Visit the Library of Congress using one of these tools: Browser: Enter **gopher://marvel.loc.gov/** then start with inter-step 3. Gopher: Search for the Library of Congress (LC MARVEL) Gopher Server (see inter-step 2).
SPECIAL ADVICE	Continue selecting directories until you come to a file of interest. Remember, a file is the end goal of a Gopher search.

inter-steps

1. Run your Gopher Client software.

2. Search your main Gopher menu for The Library of Congress Gopher Server or LC Marvel. If Library of Congress Marvel is not listed, search for it on The University of Minnesota Gopher Server.

STEP 2A

Select List of US Government Gophers.

STEP 2B

Select Library of Congress MARVEL.

3. Once you find The Library of Congress Gopher Server, or LC Marvel, tunnel through the following menus:

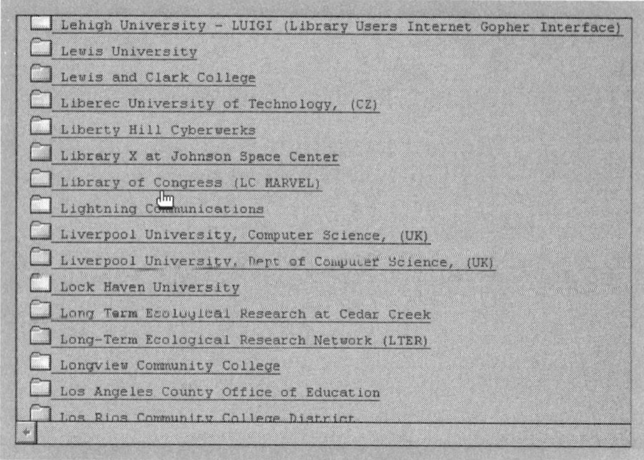

Library of Congress Gopher Server

STEP 3A
Select U S Congress.

STEP 3B
Select Congressional Directories.

STEP 3C
Select Congressional Directory.

STEP 3D
Select Senate Directory.

Record the phone number, fax number, and E-mail address (if available) for the two senators from your state in the space provided in Cyber Log 5-4-1.

4. Return to the U S Congress main menu.

STEP 4A
Select Congressional Gophers.

STEP 4B
Select Senate Gophers.

STEP 4C
Select Available Documents Distributed by Member.

STEP 4D
Select any available state and record two senators, the titles, and a brief description of what they have to say in their latest press releases in Cyber Log 5-4-2.

README file 37

FAQ's: What is MARVEL?
An acronym is a word made up of the first letters of other words. The acronym MARVEL stands for Machine-Assisted Realization of the Virtual Electronic Library. Only on the Net can you come up with an acronym so MARVELous. *

CyberLog 5-4

1. Record the phone number, fax number, and E-mail address (if available) for the two senators from your state.

SENATOR'S NAME	PHONE	FAX	E-MAIL ADDRESS

2. Record the names of two senators and give a brief description of the context of their press releases.

SENATOR'S NAME	STATE	PRESS RELEASE SUMMARY

CyberQuest 5-4

3. Investigate the voting record of your two senators. This can be done by selecting the menu Project Vote Smart from the Congressional Gophers menu. Find your senators and see how they voted on key controversial issues like abortion, taxes, military spending, education, welfare, and many other issues.

SENATOR'S NAME	STATE	ISSUE	VOTING RECORD ON KEY ISSUE

4. **Go exploring in Gopherspace. Go anywhere in the world in search of good sources of information. Look for Gopher Servers in foreign countries. Keep a written record of your exploration below:**

FTP AND TELNET ACTIVITIES

The reward for surfing the Internet with Gopher or a GUI Browser is finding a file that contains the data you need. But after you locate it, how do you retrieve it? The File Transfer Protocol (FTP) was one of the early tools developed for moving files over the Net. Today we can use FTP to bring important files home.

Telnet allows you to log in and operate a remote host computer from your keyboard. With Telnet, your computer becomes a terminal, sometimes called a **dumb terminal**, attached to your host. The phrase *dumb terminal* simply means your computer processing is being done by your host, not by your desktop computer.

Learn the following concepts in this Cyber View:

- FTP — the copy machine of the Net
- Various FTP clients
- Anonymous FTP
- Understanding the Telnet environment
- Starting your Telnet client
- Operating a dumb terminal

Following this Cyber View, there are two activities:

Activity 6-1: Roamin' Roman Archaeology
Activity 6-2: Keeping "Bees-y"

Introducing FTP—the Copy Machine of the Net

FTP is the Internet's copy machine. FTP makes a copy of a file located on a remote host and gives it to you. Be careful. The file you choose may be extremely large and chew up the storage space on your computer or on your network host. Ask your teacher's permission before copying files.

FTP has been one of the most useful tools on the Internet for many years. Before FTP, transferring files was a difficult thing to do. Files would get lost because of incompatible software, incompatible filenames, and incompatible directory structures. FTP helped solve many of these problems.

READ ME file 38

FAQ's: What is an anonymous FTP?

Anonymous FTP allows you to pass through the security system of a remote host. Anonymous means nameless. Key *Anonymous* to log in to the FTP computer you are attaching to, and you can have access to the computer's files.

Thousands of computers allow people to use anonymous logins to gain access to FTP files. It is considered polite to leave your Internet name as the password.

Starting Your FTP Client

FTP can be used with any platform: DOS, UNIX, Windows, or Macintosh.

Text-Based FTP

Using FTP in UNIX and DOS is as easy as keying *ftp* at the system prompt and entering the host name where your file is located. For example, *ftp nic.merit.edu* will connect you to the Merit database (see Figure 6-1).

With some DOS programs, like Minuet, starting FTP is as easy as selecting a menu item from the Window pull-down menu (see Figure 6-2).

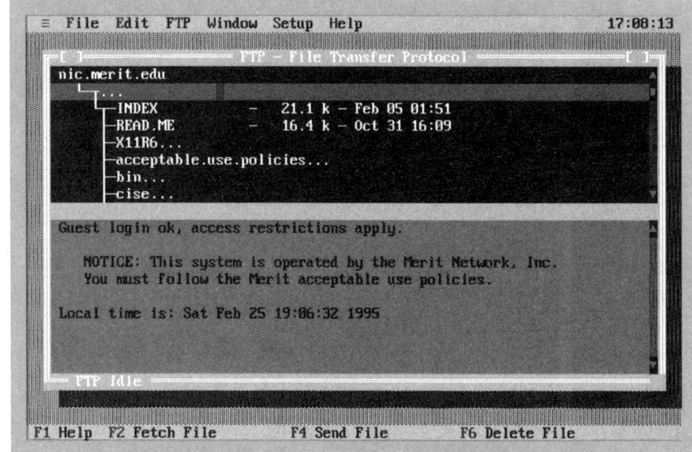

f 6-1 Merit database

GUI Browsers and Gopher Clients for Windows and Macintosh

FTP is so easy with GUI Browsers and Gopher Clients that you may not even know you are doing it. GUI Browsers and Gophers have FTP built into their save options. You can download a file simply by selecting Save from the File pull-down menu.

You can direct your Browser to an FTP site by entering the FTP address as a URL. For example:

ftp://ftp.lib.virginia.edu

If you know the name and path of the file, you can enter the entire address, path, and filename as the URL. For example:

ftp://ftp.lib.virginia.edu/pub/alpha/vat/archeology/arch08.jpg

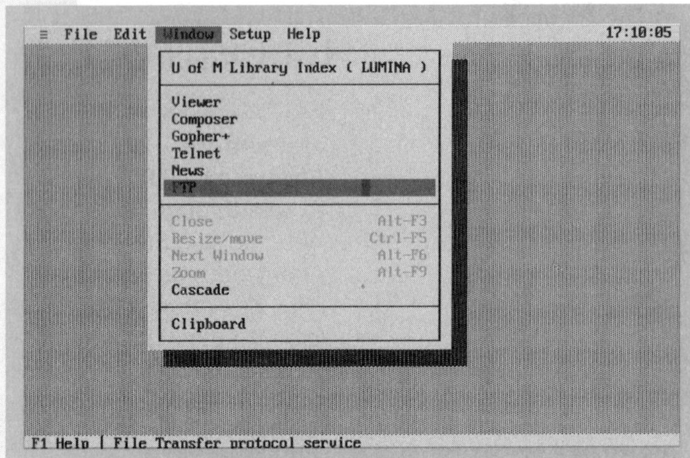

f 6-2 Selecting FTP with Minuet

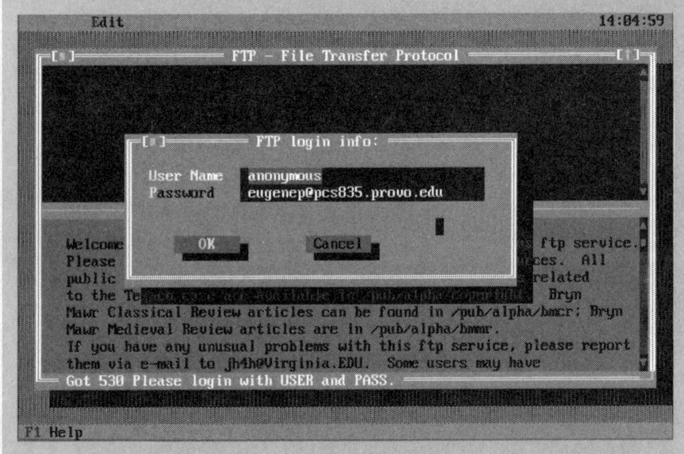

f 6-3 Anonymous login and E-mail password

```
A:\>exit
ftp> help
Commands may be abbreviated.  Commands are:

!               delete          lls             prompt          send
?               dir             lpwd            put             sendport
append          exit            ls              pwd             statistics
bell            force           mdelete         quit            status
bye             get             mdir            recv            user
cd              hash            mkdir           remotedir       verbose
close           help            mls             rename
copy            lcd             mget            rget
debug           lexec           mput            rmdir
defaults        ldir            open            rput
ftp>
```

f 6-4 Available FTP commands

To save the files on your machine, simply select the File menu, then Save.

An Old-Fashioned Anonymous FTP Session

This example walks you through a sample FTP session on a text-based client. UNIX is the oldest form of FTP available. If you can FTP in UNIX, you will truly be a master of the Net, a wizard of FTP.

After you open your FTP client and enter an FTP address, your remote host will normally ask you for your user name. Many servers will allow you to log in as *anonymous,* which means unknown user. When you log in with anonymous, you are having an anonymous FTP session.

After you log in, most hosts will ask for a password. While not totally necessary, it is considered polite to enter your Internet E-mail address as the password (see Figure 6-3).

Getting Help

FTP is like a file transfer toolbox with many tools. One of the FTP tools is the *help* command. By using the *help* command, you can see a list of all the available FTP commands, like the list shown in Figure 6-4.

You can learn more about specific commands by keying *help* and the name of the command, such as *help send.* You can exit the help screens by pressing ENTER.

Once you are connected to your remote host, the *dir* and *ls* commands will help you find the file you need. If you key *dir*, you will see a list of directories or folders and the files in the current directory (see Figure 6-5).

Filenames are on the left side of the screen.

As shown in Figure 6-6, the command *ls* will list only the filenames in the current directory.

Getting a File

Find the file you are interested in and key the *get* command, followed by the name of the file you want. You also have to key a destination for your file. In the following example, the file will be saved on your C:\ drive:

get zen.txt c:\zen.txt

You can change the name of the file by simply keying a new name; for example: *get zen.txt c:\mycopy.txt.* Press ENTER and zap, you have FTP'd your file. Now you can pull the file into your word processor.

Introducing Telnet

Telnet was an important Internet tool, designed to give access to large mainframe computer programs that only existed on remote hosts. Telnet sites are disappearing as fast as new World Wide Web sites can be set up. However, there are still some Telnet sites out there. Your Browser has Telnet capabilities built into its software. If you suddenly find yourself in an old-fashioned Telnet session, these hints should help you survive the experience.

Telnet connects your computer screen and keyboard to a remote computer. Your machine will **emulate**, or imitate, the commands of the host machine. Your computer becomes a dumb terminal.

One of the most common dumb terminals is the Vax Terminal Model 100 (VT100). More often than not, you will emulate a VT100 terminal. If you have a hard time reading your screen or if your keyboard does not respond correctly, you may have the wrong terminal emulation and will have to try another.

README file 39

FAQ's: What are the most common FTP commands?

cd	Changes directories on your remote host
close or *quit*	Ends your FTP session
dir	Displays a list of the contents of a directory
get	Gets your file for you
help	Gives information on FTP commands
ls	Lists filenames
open	Connects you to a remote host *

```
H:\TEMPFTP  exit
ftp> dir
ftp.exe          96714   2-01-94    4:12   A
ftp.msg           6581   2-01-94    4:12   A
ftpd.exe         74056   2-01-94    4:12   A
ftpd.msg          4339   2-01-94    4:12   A
ftpserv.bat        863   2-01-94    4:12   A
ftp.pif            545   2-01-94    4:12   A
ftpd.pif           545   2-01-94    4:12   A
tcpip.exe        41188   2-01-94    4:12   A
lwp.msg           7995   2-01-94    4:12   A
serveftp.exe     89120   2-01-94    4:12   A
lsl.com          18313  10-11-94   10:03   A
lsl.msg           3571   8-16-94    9:21   A
rapfiler.exe    113440   2-01-94    4:12   A
net.cfg            457   3-04-95   12:42   A
wlodi.com        64132   1-27-95    0:00   A
wlodi.wlc          458   1-27-95    0:00   A
wlink.exe       389664   1-27-95    0:00   A
dump0000.pcx      5313   3-03-95   21:35   A
vtcpip.386       10557   2-01-94    4:12   A
wlink.ini          144   3-03-95   21:32   A
 20 File(s)
ftp>
```

f 6-5 Results of the *dir* command

```
ftp> ls
command.com
smc_odi.bat
nostop.sys
non-stop.com
netx.exe
ipxodi.com
logemon.bat
himem.sys
gmouse.com
emm386.exe
lsl.com
config.sys
smcplus.com
autoexec.bat
rplodi.com
net.cfg
ftp>
```

f 6-6 Results of the *is* command

README file 40

NETIQUETTE: Be kind to your host

Remember, when you use Telnet, you are using someone else's computer. Don't stay connected any longer than you have to. This way your remote host can give someone else a turn.

Many of these computers have timers that will disconnect you after a length of time. Some hosts are smart enough to know when you haven't touched your keyboard for a while and will boot you off. Don't be upset if you are logged out prematurely. Your host may think you have gone home for the day.

Remember, you are a guest, and someone else is paying the bills for maintaining the resource. You can always log in again later.

VT100 is usually a good place to start. With VT100 you can operate a CRAY Supercomputer, a UNIX computer, or the biggest IBM mainframe computer. When you connect to a remote host with Telnet, you start a **Telnet session**. When you disconnect from your host, your session is over.

Telnet access has been available from the earliest days of the Net. Telnet made the NSF supercomputers accessible to you, even if you did not live anywhere near a supercomputer center (see Cyber View 3).

The Backbone of the Net

The Internet was created before most people had even heard of the personal computer. The Net was created by connecting powerful mainframe computers.

When the Internet started, these mainframe and minicomputers were the only processors powerful enough and fast enough to support all of the Internet resources. Today, they still form the backbone of processing power on the Internet.

With the birth of personal computers in the early 1980s the dominance of the mainframes began to wane. Most desktop and portable PCs today have more computing power than the early mainframes that occupied entire rooms. Gradually, these mainframe systems are being replaced by more efficient computers, but many of the old systems remain. Telnet and FTP are tools that are still in use by these early computers.

Starting Your Telnet Client

Telnet is an Internet tool that you can run from a text-based platform or a GUI-based platform.

Text-Based Telnet

Using Telnet in UNIX or DOS is as easy as keying *telnet* at the system prompt. Follow your Telnet command with the host and port numbers to which you are trying to attach. For example: **telnet camms2.caos.kun.nl 2034** (see Figure 6-7).

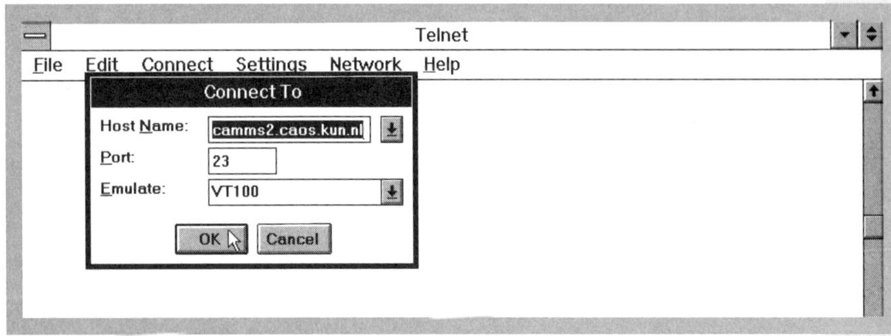

f 6-7 Beginning a text-based Telnet session

GUI Telnet

To begin the Telnet session from your Browser, select File, then Open URL, and enter the protocol and address. For example: **telnet://camms2.caos.kun.nl 2034**.

Operating a Dumb Terminal

Once your session starts, however, you will not get much help remembering the Telnet commands you need to use. The most important Telnet command is *help*. (By the way, all commands must be in lowercase.) Key *help* to learn what all the other commands are, and what they do. Two other important commands are *close* and *quit*. Both terminate or end your session. You can also escape by pressing the Control key followed by [. Whenever you get frustrated and nothing else works, press *Control-[* to escape.

When Telnetting, you will find yourself on new, unfamiliar computers. Pay attention to any special instructions you are given. When running a Telnet session, it is always helpful to have a piece of scratch paper nearby to write down any commands or instructions that you may need later.

README file 41

NET NOTE: UNIX

UNIX was developed by AT&T's Bell Laboratories in the late 1960s. This simple and elegant operating system became a favorite of universities—in part because they could get it free from AT&T. UNIX was improved over time and continues to dominate mainframe computing.

There are other operating systems, like IBM's VM and MVS systems and Digital Corporation's VMS, but UNIX became the most popular.

Modern PC users often find UNIX a difficult and cumbersome language to learn. Most people avoid it today. However, in the history of computing, few computer languages and operating systems have had as much impact and been as reliable as UNIX.

CyberQuiz 6

On a separate piece of paper or on a handout provided by your teacher, answer the following questions.

Circle yes if the statement is true or No if the statement is false.

1. **Yes or No** Anonymous means nameless.
2. **Yes or No** Telnet allows you to operate a computer other than your own.
3. **Yes or No** UNIX was developed by NASA in the late 1960s.
4. **Yes or No** You cannot FTP files while working in a GUI Browser.
5. **Yes or No** Many modern personal computers are more powerful than the early mainframe computers.

For questions 6 through 8, circle the letter that corresponds to the best answer.

6. **FTP is**
   a. the Internet's copy machine
   b. the way to move files from one computer to another
   c. File Transfer Protocol
   d. All of the above

7. **You can FTP with the following platforms**
   a. DOS
   b. Windows
   c. UNIX
   d. Macintosh
   e. All of the above

8. **One of the most common dumb terminals is**
   a. LAX
   b. a UNIX mainframe
   c. VAX Terminal Model 100
   d. a CRAY Supercomputer

For questions 9 through 10, write the correct answer in the space provided.

9. **Define the following terms**

dir	________________
VT 100	________________
get	________________
help send	________________
Telnet	________________
FTP	________________

10. **Why is FTP an important tool?**

____

____

____

Roamin' Roman Archaeology

Introduction

Interest in Roman archaeology began to grow around the middle of the 1500s. For hundreds of years, the work of excavating and understanding the old civilization continued. Educated people around the world waited years for news of new discoveries. Today, you can research the work of archaeologists as soon as they post it on the Internet, often within days of major discoveries.

Objectives

Connect to a remote FTP server

Log in to an FTP server

Enter an E-mail address as a password

Download several files on archaeology

Read about Leon Battista Alberti and Flavio Biondo

RESOURCE TABLE

CLIENT	GUI Browser or other FTP client
RESOURCE LOCATION	Search for Leon Battista Alberti and Flavio Biondo with either of the following tools: Browser: Enter **ftp://ftp.lib.virginia.edu/pub/alpha/vat/archeology**, then search for the following files: **archintro.txt** **arch08.txt** **arch08.jpg** **arch09.txt** **arch09.jpg** Other FTP: At the FTP prompt key **ftp.lib.virginia.edu**, search down the directories **/pub/alpha/vat/archeology**, then look for the following files: **archintro.txt** **arch08.txt** **arch09.txt**
SPECIAL ADVICE	*Note:* Be sure to key *archeology* exactly as shown in the Resource Table. Login name: anonymous Password: Your E-mail address With your Browser you can view the graphic files without downloading a .jpg viewer. Browsers make FTP a lot easier.

inter-steps

1. To log in to a remote FTP server:

STEP 1A

Open your FTP client and start FTP.

Browser: Enter **ftp://ftp.lib.virginia.edu.** You will connect to the University of Virginia's FTP server. (NOTE: If you enter **http://lib.virginia.edu**, you will be connected to their Web server and will not be abse to access the same information.) Skip to inter-step 2.

Other FTP: Start your FTP client by keying *ftp* (lowercase letters only) at the command prompt, or by selecting the FTP option in your FTP client.

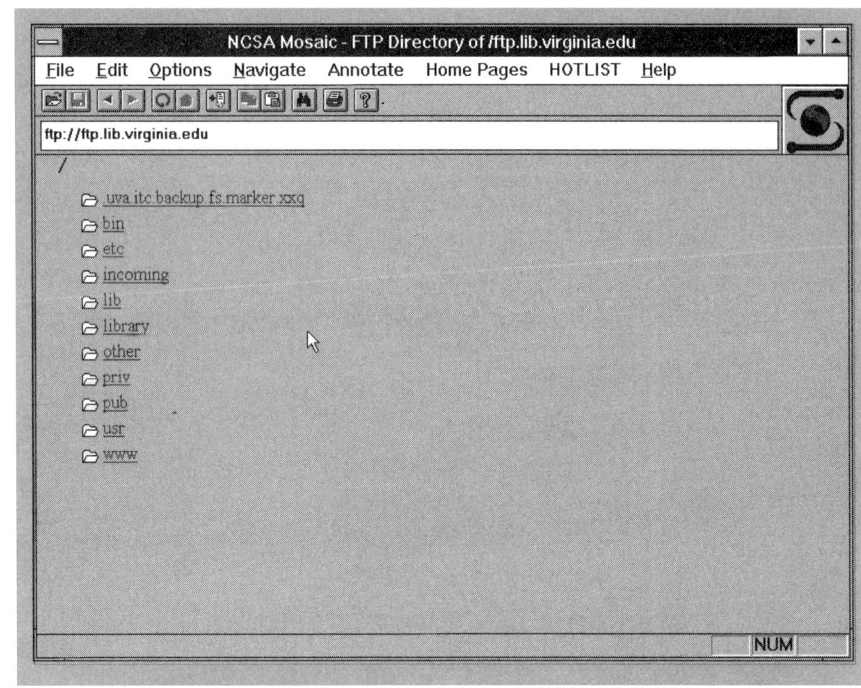

University of Virginia's FTP server

STEP 1B

Enter the following FTP address:

ftp.lib.virginia.edu

You will be connected to the remote host at the University of Virginia. You may combine steps 1A and 1B. For example:

ftp ftp.lib.virginia.edu

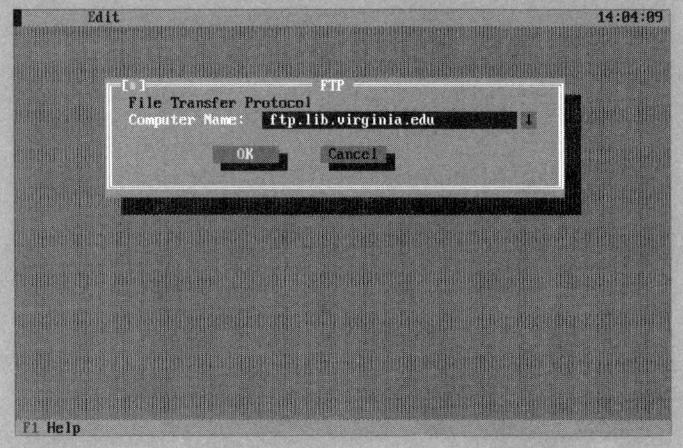

Minuet FTP client

STEP 1C

Enter the login name anonymous when prompted.

STEP 1D

Enter a password. It is proper Netiquette to enter your E-mail address or the E-mail address of your school provided to you by your teacher.

2. Dig down into the directory structure of University of Virginia's Anonymous FTP server. This is a lot like going down layers of Gopher menus.

Browser: To move down the directory structure, simply click on the desired subdirectory as it appears in the graphical window.

Select *pub*

Select *alpha*

Select *vat*

Select *archeology*

Other FTP: To move down the directories to */pub/alpha/vat/archeology*

Key *cd* then *pub*

Key *cd* then *alpha*

Key *cd* then *vat*

Key *cd* then *archeology*

3. Find the files you will need to complete Cyber Log 6-1.

Browser: Scroll down the window to locate the desired files. You are looking for:

archintro.txt

arch08.txt

arch09.txt

arch08.jpg

arch09.jpg

Other FTP: Use the dir or the ls commands to see the names of the files in the directory. You are looking for:

archintro.txt

arch08.txt

arch09.txt

4. Transfer or work with the desired files.

Browser: Highlight the desired file. Select File on the menu bar, then Save. Enter the drive and filename you want the file stored under on your system. But why save it? With the Browser, you can double-click on the filename and view the file without downloading it to your system. This is true for text files as well as many graphical files. The .jpg files in this directory are viewable with your Browser. You can complete Cyber Log 6-1 at this point.

Other FTP: Use the get command to begin the file transfer. You will only be able to transfer one file at a time. This example assumes that you will save the files on your C:\ drive with the filenames given.

get archintro.txt c:\intro.txt

get arch08.txt c:\arch08.txt

get arch09.txt c:\arch09.txt

After you have downloaded the files and terminated the session (Step 5), you will need to retrieve the files in your word processor to view them. You will not be able to view the graphical files (those that have an extender of .jpg) without a graphical viewer (see Cyber Quest 6-1).

5. When the transfers are complete, key *quit* if you are using an FTP client, or select File, Exit if you are using a GUI Browser to terminate the session.

6. Retrieve the text files in your word processor to complete the Cyber Log. If you have a GUI Browser, you have already completed your work and can proceed to the next activity.

CyberLog 6-1

1. **Answer the following questions based upon what you have studied:**
When did Renaissance scholars begin to take an interest in Roman archaeology?

___

What was Leon Battista Alberti's occupation?

___

What was Flavio Biondo's occupation?

___

Alberti helped what pope study Roman architecture?

___

On the work of what Greek mathematician did Alberti model his rigorous maps of Rome?

___

What was the title and purpose of Biondo's work?

___

CyberQuest 6-1

2. **Included in the directory with the three files you downloaded are other image files. The image files have the last three characters .jpg. If you do not have a GUI Browser, you will need a graphics viewer to view these graphics. You will need to complete the following four steps:**

STEP 2A Locate and download the graphic viewer software. Often it is compressed and will require a decompression tool such as PKUNZIP.EXE.

STEP 2B Install or set up the graphics software. For instructions on how to prepare the software, look for a README file in the directory with the viewer file.

STEP 2C Download the image files using FTP.

STEP 2D After you have everything on your machine, start the viewer software and load the image files.

Keeping "Bees-y"

Introduction

Many of the rich data resources of the Internet are conversations among people interested in the same topic. In this activity, we will study the conversation among various people about bee pollen. We will download the conversation from an archive. Most Newsgroup conversations are recorded and stored or archived for future research.

Objectives

Operate an FTP client

Follow the strands of an on-line conversation

Evaluate the quality of the data presented

README file 42

NET NOTE: Bee Newsgroup extract
In this activity, you will get an extract from a conversation in a Newsgroup. You can follow the changes in speakers. That explains the irregular formatting.

RESOURCE TABLE

CLIENT	GUI Browsers or other FTP client
RESOURCE LOCATION	Search for information on bees with either of the following tools: Browser: Enter **ftp://sunsite.unc.edu**, search the directories **/pub/academic/agriculture/sustainable_agriculture/beekeeping**, then look for the filename **bee-pollen.production-storage-use** Other FTP: At the FTP prompt key **sunsite.unc.edu**, search down the directories **/pub/academic/agriculture/sustainable_agriculture/beekeeping**, then look for the filename **bee-pollen.production-storage-use**
SPECIAL ADVICE	Locate information on Bees in the SURWEB: Sandbox Browser URL: **http://www.surweb.org/surweb/sandbox/bees/bee.htm** Try the following locations if the above site is not available: Browser: Enter **http://www.colostate.edu/Depts/Entomology/courses/en507/student_papers_1995/sears.html** Browser: Enter **http://weber.u.washington.edu/~jlks/bee.html**

inter-steps

1. To log in to a remote FTP server, start FTP and connect to the remote server.

Browser: Select File on the menu bar, then Open URL, enter the site address, **ftp://sunsite.unc.edu**, and connect.

Other FTP: Key **ftpsunsite.unc.edu**

Enter your login name, anonymous, and password when prompted.

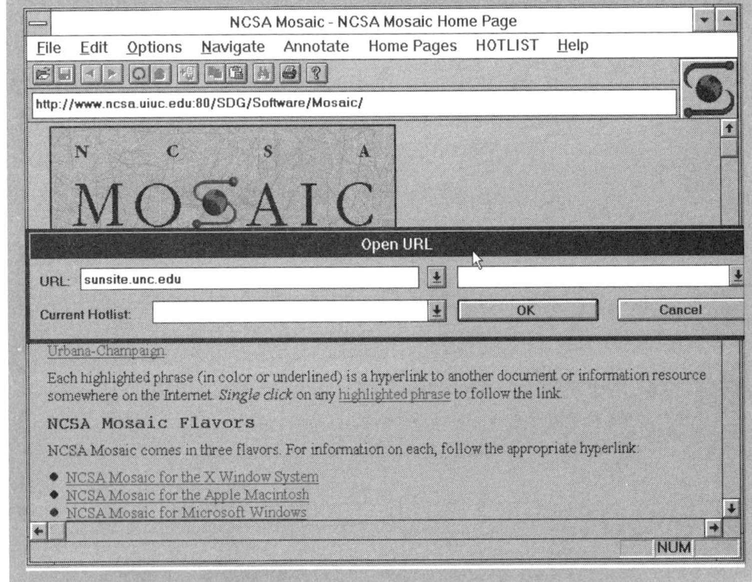

Starting FTP on a Browser

2. Locate the files you need to complete Cyber Log 6-2 by digging down through the directory structure

Browser: Scroll through the listed subdirectories and select the desired subdirectory as it appears on the window by double-clicking on it. First find *pub*, then *academic*, next *sustainable_agriculture*, and finally, *beekeeping*.

Other FTP: To move down the UNIX directories */pub/academic/sustainable_agriculture/beekeeping*

Key *cd* then *pub*

Key *cd* then *academic*

Key *cd* then *sustainable_agriculture*

Key *cd* then *beekeeping*

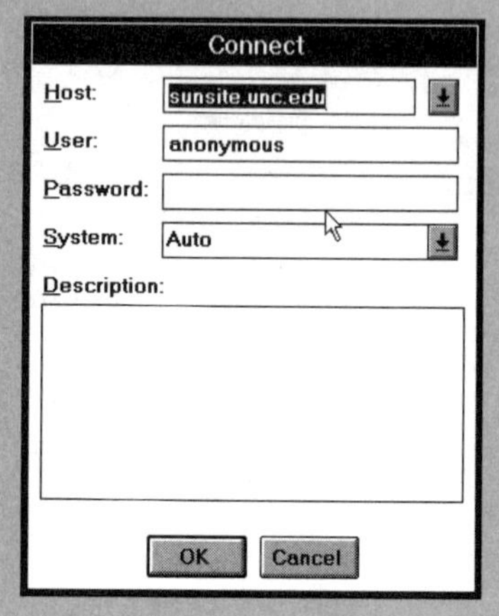

Starting an FTP client

3. Find the file you will need to complete Cyber Log 6-2-1. Look for the following file:

Browser: Scroll through the files shown on the file manager window until you locate *bee_pollen.production-storage-use*.

Other FTP: You are looking for the file *bee_pollen.production-storage-use*. Yes, that is the filename. UNIX permits much longer filenames than DOS or Windows. Locate the file with the dir or ls command.

4. Transfer or work with the desired files.

Browser: Highlight the file *bee_pollen.production-storage-use*. If you desire to save it on your system, select File on the menu bar, then Save. Enter the filename and path when prompted. You do not need to download the file. You may view it while still connected by double-clicking on the highlighted filename. You may complete Cyber Log 6-2-1 at this point.

Other FTP: Begin the transfer with the FTP command get.

get bee_pollen.production-storage-use c:pollen.txt

5. Close the session by selecting File then Exit, in your GUI Browser. In your text-based UNIX FTP client, the command is quit.

6. If you downloaded the file in the Text mode, you will need to retrieve the file in your word processor to view it and to answer the questions in Cyber Log 6-2-1.

CyberLog 6-2

1. **Answer the following questions based upon what you have studied:**

What country does this information come from?

What is bee pollen?

Why do bees collect it?

What is the potential good of pollen?

How do critics counter the claims of pollen?

What are the author's credentials?

Can the author's credentials be verified on the Net?

Do you know that the author is who he/she claims to be?

How reliable are these data?

CyberQuest 6-2

2. **What other information can you find about animals? Find five other resources on the Net about animals. Prepare five questions like those in Cyber Log 6-2. Give your questions to another student with the appropriate FTP or URL so that the other student can research and answer your questions.**

E-Mail Activities

Electronic mail, or E-mail, is the most widely used resource on the Internet. For many Internet users, E-mail is the most useful network service. In this Cyber View, we will investigate how to send and receive E-mail.

ReadMe file 43

NET NOTE: The end of the post office?
If everyone started using E-mail, would there be a need for a traditional post office? Would you stop writing letters on paper if you knew you could write to all of your friends and family over the electronic superhighway?

The post office is one of the true bargains left in America. It is nothing short of remarkable, that for less than 50 cents you can have your letter hand-delivered to a friend's front door in another state in just a few days.

However, you can send E-mail for pennies. You don't need a stamp or envelope and your mail can arrive in a matter of seconds. *

Browse the following topics in this Cyber View:

- Electronic mail
- E-mail on the Net
- Various E-mail software options
- The parts of an E-mail message
- E-mail features and commands
- Mailing lists
- Managing E-mail

This Cyber View includes the following three activities:

Activity 7-1: Who Can I Send E-Mail To?
Activity 7-2: Subscribing to a List
Activity 7-3: The Great Equalizer

Electronic Mail

E-mail allows you to send personal messages, notes, or letters to individuals or groups over the electronic highway. The most important part of any E-mail is the message you write. Most E-mail messages should be brief and to the point. Long, rambling E-mail messages are hard to follow. Practice communicating a clear message whenever you write E-mail.

E-mail is a vital activity in most businesses today. From the CEO's office to the administrative assistant on the shop floor, E-mail has proven to be an effective communications tool. In addition, E-mail is becoming increasingly important in homes and schools.

Internet E-Mail

Internet E-mail is organized a little like the postal system. Everyone on the Internet has a different mailing address. The Net is also like the phone system, with each location having its own number. However, that is where similarities stop.

To send E-mail on the Internet, you need to know a person's address. Currently, there is no phone book or directory to help you find an Internet address. There is no information service to call, like 411 or 555-1212, if you need another person's number. You may have to call your friends and get their addresses before you can send them E-mail.

READ ME file 44

NET NOTE: The future of E-mail

The E-mail software of today will seem outdated when people are able to send voice and video mail to each other. Live video mail may replace the traditional phone and current E-mail when the price of the technology comes down.

E-Mail Software

Older programs are usually text-based; that is, users must enter memorized commands with the keyboard before the E-mail programs can work. These earlier systems can be a little frustrating to learn, but they work very well once you understand all of the commands.

Most of the text-based programs were developed years ago in the early days of the Net. Their advantage is cost. Most of these older packages are free and can be downloaded over the Net. However, there is very little support or personal assistance for these programs. If something goes wrong, you will be on your own to figure things out.

Most modern, up-to-date E-mail software has a GUI, or Graphical User Interface. Pictures, called icons, replace text commands. These icons help E-mail users send commands with the click of a mouse. GUI software runs on Macintosh, Windows, and OS2® computers. GUI makes E-mail much more user-friendly.

Commercial E-Mail Software

Up-to-date commercial E-mail software is now widely available. Several programs offer **gateways** to the Internet. A gateway is a tool that allows commercial software to speak the language of the Internet. Novell® GroupWare, Lotus® cc:Mail®, and Microsoft Mail are all good examples of easy-to-use, commercial GUI E-mail programs.

READ ME file 45

NET NOTE: Your personality and your signature

Once you start sending lots of E-mail, you will develop certain habits. For example, do you double-space before your name? Do you end with "Sincerely," "Goodbye," or "See you later"? Do you sign your full name or just your first name? Do you use your nickname? Do you end with a quote or slogan of some kind?

The signature is where you can really reflect your personality. Be careful. Many of the people you write to may not have met you, or may not know your sense of humor. What you think is funny or interesting, others may take as being silly or arrogant.

Commercial E-mail service is also provided by many on-line companies. America Online, CompuServe, Prodigy, GEnie®, Delphi, AT&T, and MCI offer E-mail service to the Internet. These **service providers** often provide their own E-mail software tools to their subscribers. Each of these companies charge a fee to use their E-mail systems.

Eudora

There are several free E-mail packages available on the Internet. The most famous of these is Eudora. Some versions of Eudora have been updated with a GUI interface. Versions of Eudora can run under Microsoft's Windows, IBM's OS2, or Apple's System 7.X.

Parts of an E-Mail Message

All E-mail messages can be divided into the following three parts:

- heading
- body, or text
- signature, or sign-off

Heading

As shown in Figure 7-1, the *heading* normally has four parts.

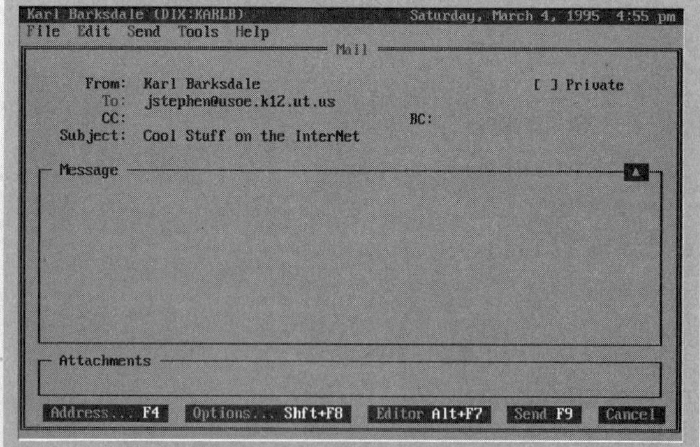

f 7-1 E-mail heading

To: The Internet address of the person or persons you are mailing to

From: Your Internet address

Subject: A brief, expressive title explaining the contents of your message

Date: The date your message was sent

Body or Text

The *body*, or *text*, of your E-mail message contains the information that you are sending (see Figure 7-2).

Signature

Your *signature,* or *sign-off*, reflects your personality and ends your message, as shown in Figure 7-3.

Common E-Mail Features

Communication is the goal of E-mail. Modern E-mail packages have several features that can help you communicate more effectively. However, not all the features explained here appear in every E-mail program.

In and Out Boxes

As shown in Figure 7-4, E-mail software usually provides both In and Out boxes. Mail intended for you comes to your In box. A copy of E-mail you have sent goes into your Out box. It is important to delete old, unwanted messages from both your In and Out boxes. Each message takes up a little bit of space on someone's hard drive. If you do not delete your unnecessary messages, the hard drive could fill up, and mail service would stop. Also, keeping lots of extra messages in your In and Out boxes will make it harder to find the messages you really need.

Address Book

Most E-mail packages provide a place for you to store your most commonly used addresses. Companies and schools often provide a list of E-mail users for their companies, in a company directory. Finding an address in this situation can be as easy as keying the name of the person you hope to mail to.

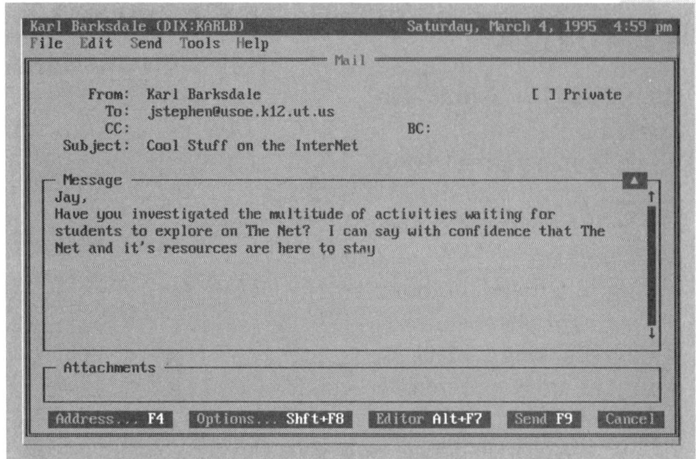

f 7-2 E-mail body

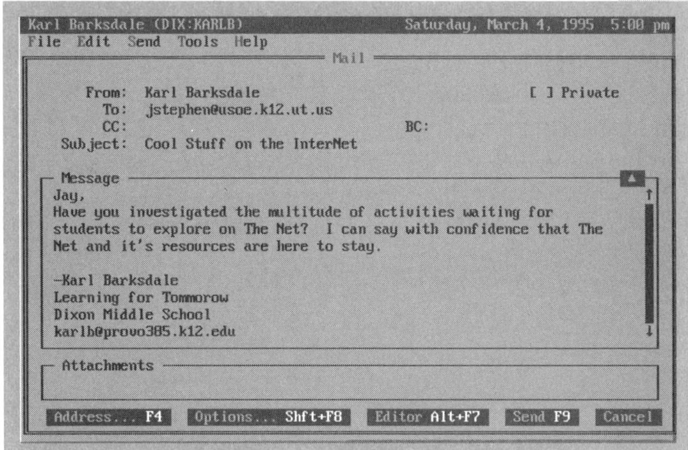

f 7-3 E-mail signature

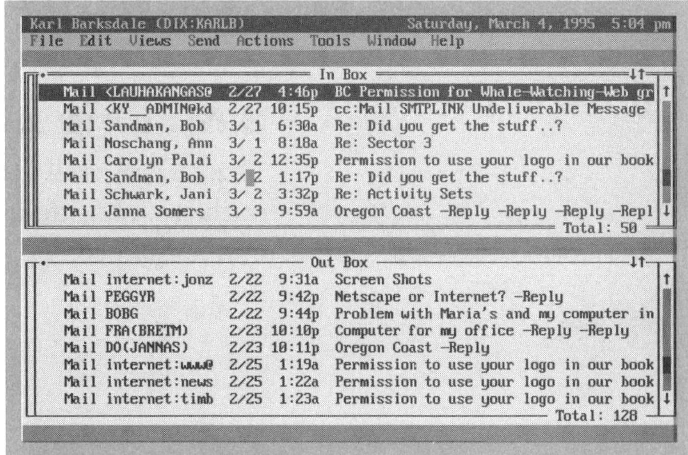

f 7-4 In and Out boxes

READ ME file 46

NETIQUETTE: E-mail etiquette

When sending E-mail, try to keep your E-mail short and to the point. Of course, when you are writing to a friend, go on as long as you like. But, in business, long E-mail messages are considered rude. Also, avoid capitalizing every word. THIS IS CONSIDERED SHOUTING! DON'T SHOUT UNLESS YOU MEAN IT.

Also, joining and not reading a mailing list is in bad taste. So is subscribing to and cancelling a mailing list on the same day. *

Common E-Mail Commands

Following are some common E-mail commands:

SEND	Allows you to send E-mail to others on the Net
READ	Allows you to read E-mail sent to you
REPLY	Allows you to respond quickly to a message without having to rekey the header of the sender's message
FORWARD	Allows you to send, or *forward*, a message originally sent to you by another person
CC	CC is short for carbon copy. This command sends a copy of a message to another person at the same time you send your message to your target recipient. In business, you may send a message to another employee, and cc a copy to your boss.
SAVE	Allows you to save a copy of the E-mail for use later. Important E-mail should be saved.
DELETE	Allows you to clean up and empty your E-mail In and Out boxes
ATTACHMENT	Allows you to send additional documents or files with your E-mail message. If your E-mail software permits, these files can be anything from text files to multimedia graphics.

Mailing Lists

There are literally thousands of mailing lists that you can subscribe to. Mailing lists allow a single E-mail to be sent to any number of people. Mailing lists are easy to set up and can be private. Some mailing lists allow advertising. In fact, there are mailing lists that are maintained by businesses just for business purposes.

Managing Your E-Mail

It's not unusual for E-mail and Internet mailing lists to generate lots of E-mail. You can become swamped in unanswered E-mail. For this reason, it is important that you manage your mailbox. Most systems will not allow an endless accumulation of E-mail. Therefore, it is necessary to SAVE critical messages and DELETE the rest. It is important to know what your E-mail system will allow in terms of:

- total number of messages stored
- how long messages can be stored
- maximum on-line storage capacity for all messages, attachments, and files

Following are some additional suggestions that will help keep your E-mail effectively organized:

- Set a time to read your E-mail every day.
- Actively monitor your In and Out boxes.
- Keep your E-mail Address Book up to date so that you only send valid messages. (Remember, if the message is sent to an invalid address, it will come back to you and you will have to delete it.)
- Don't subscribe to a mailing list unless you are going to read the messages.
- Learn how to cancel a mailing list, so if you change your mind about its value, you can keep it from filling up your In box with unwanted mail.

CyberQuiz 7

On a separate piece of paper or on a handout provided by your teacher, answer the following questions.

Circle Yes if the statement is true or No if the statement is false.

1. **Yes or No** Everyone on the Internet has a different mailing address.
2. **Yes or No** You need a stamp and an envelope to send E-mail.
3. **Yes or No** E-mail software usually provides In and out boxes.
4. **Yes or No** To send someone E-mail, all you need to know is the person's name.
5. **Yes or No** Capitalizing your E-mail message is considered shouting.

For questions 6 through 8, circle the letter that corresponds to the best answer.

6. **A gateway allows commercial software to**
   - a. replace the telephone and telegraph with voice mail
   - b. send video mail to your television
   - c. speak the language of the Internet
   - d. lose the mail
7. **E-mail software with a Graphical User Interface has**
   - a. icons
   - b. text commands
   - c. Telnet built into its interface
   - d. eliminated the need for the post office
8. **E-mail messages contain**
   - a. a heading
   - b. a body or message
   - c. a signature
   - d. All of the above

For questions 9 through 10, write the correct answer in the space provided.

9. **Give the meanings of the following:**

heading ________________

body ________________

signature ________________

Eudora ________________

cc ________________

mailing list ________________

10. **In your opinion, why do you think E-mail is the most widely used Internet resource? Do you think E-mail will totally replace the current postal system for everything but packages? Explain your opinions.**

____
____
____
____
____
____
____
____
____
____
____
____
____
____
____
____
____

Who Can I Send E-mail To?

Introduction

The absolute most common activity on the Net is E-mail. To send or receive E-mail from an E-mail list or group, you need to locate a mailing list you will be interested in. This activity will help you identify a list of mailing lists, which in turn you will subscribe to in Activity 7-2.

Objectives

Launch your E-mail program

Perform the basics of sending a simple E-mail message

Understand the great number of mailing lists available

Be self-sufficient in cruising the Net for mailing lists

README file 47

NET NOTE: Alternative methods for accessing E-mail lists other than E-mail

PAML: Publicly Available Mailing Lists are posted to the USENET Newsgroups *news.newusers* and *news.groups* (see CyberView 8 for Newsgroups).

NEW-LIST: Serves as a clearinghouse for all new mailing lists that are created. Available through FTP at **vm1.nodak.edu**.

THE WELL: Whole Earth Lectronic Link. For information about The Well, send a message to **info@well.com.** *

RESOURCE TABLE

CLIENT	E-mail program
RESOURCE LOCATION	E-mail address to retrieve list of lists: **Listserv@bitnic.educom.edu**
SPECIAL ADVICE	There are other ways besides E-mail to obtain address lists. See the README in this activity for more detail.

inter-steps

HINT: Realize you must have access to the Internet for this activity to work properly.

1. Launch your E-mail program. Depending on your system, it may look like the following screen shots:

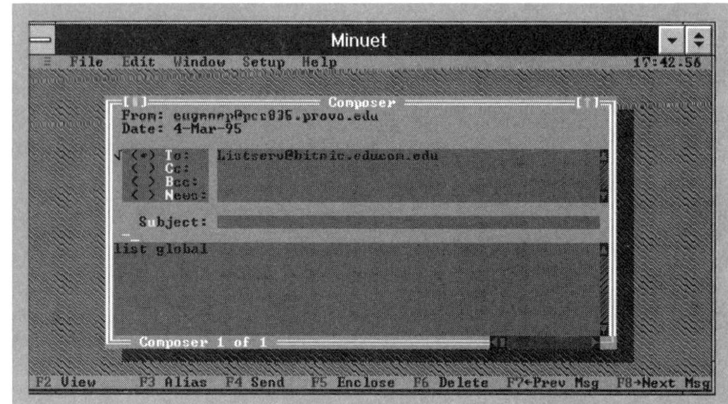

Minuet E-mail screen

2. You need access to the Internet. Therefore, make sure your teacher or Network Administrator has provided you with the proper addressing sequence to gain Internet access.

3. Send an E-mail note with the two message fields below containing precisely the information you see bolded.

   To: **Listserv@bitnic.educom.edu**

   Body: **list global**

   HINT: The To: field may require additional addressing information in order to gain access to the Internet. Remember to leave the subject field blank. Wait for at least one day for a return reply. If your mail server is not currently functioning, it may take some time.

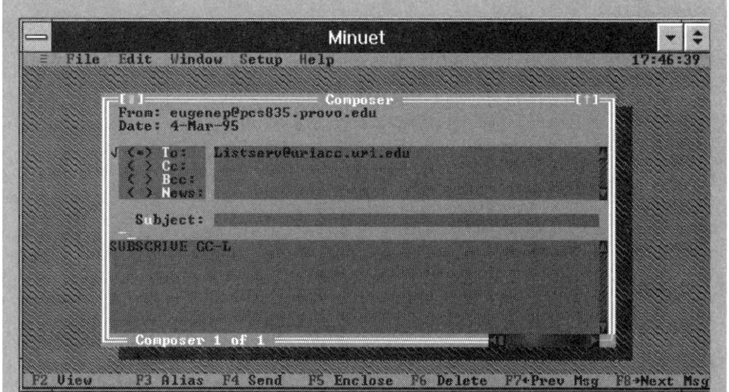

E-mail request to an automated list server

4. Once you have received your E-mail Address list of lists, do the following:

STEP 4A

Take note of how long it took to receive a reply to your request. Enter time in the nearest number of whole hours in Cyber Log 7-1-1.

STEP 4B

Save the list as *niclist* (If necessary, ask your teacher how to save an E-mail message.)

STEP 4C

Select three lists you would like to participate with.

STEP 4D

In Cyber Log 7-1-2, enter the addresses of where these lists can be retrieved, along with any specific instructions.

STEP 4E:

Indicate the reason you are interested in participating in each list.

5. Close your E-mail program.

CYBERLOG 7-1

This activity provides a straightforward way to start E-mail activities on the Net, as well as shows you ways to find an almost limitless supply of mailing lists that you can participate in through sending and receiving E-mail. Soon you will be cruising and surfing the Net via E-mail.

1. **It took _______ hours to receive a reply to my subscription request.**
2. **Complete the following table for three different E-mail address lists:**

E-MAIL ADDRESS LIST	WHY ARE YOU INTERESTED IN THIS LIST?

CyberQuest 7-1

3. After all of your subscription requests come in, write a short report on each, discussing the value of each. Discuss what they cover and how well they cover their topics. Then rank them one to three, with one being the highest.

4. Locate three lists related to any continent you choose other than North America. Record the address and the topic of each list.

____

____

____

Subscribing to a List

ReadMe file 48

SOFT NOTE: Don't get overwhelmed!
As the old saying goes, practice makes perfect. This activity provides you with a means to practice until you can do the process in your sleep. Subscribing to mailing lists is a very straightforward process. *Realize that you can receive literally hundreds of mail messages per day by subscribing to just a few popular mailing lists.* ✻

Introduction

In Activity 7-1, you found that mailing lists are readily available. This activity will help you subscribe to a few of those lists. The first mailing list we want to subscribe to distributes announcements of new public mailing lists on the Internet. The second is a group that discusses and debates the concept of a "global classroom." Many international student viewpoints can be discovered here. There should be no concern in finding groups that have common interests with you.

Objectives

Launch your E-mail program

Get started in E-mail discussions

Know a way to receive updated lists of lists

Know what the necessary components for subscribing to a mailing list are

RESOURCE TABLE

CLIENT	E-mail program
RESOURCE LOCATION	How to subscribe to two different lists: **Listserv@vm1.nodak.edu** **Listserv@uriacc.uri.edu**
SPECIAL ADVICE	When subscribing to an E-mail list, there is certain information you need to enter exactly for your subscription request to be fulfilled in a timely manner.

inter-steps

1. Launch your E-mail program.

2. Send an E-mail note with the two message fields below containing precisely the information you see bolded:

   To: **Listserv@vm1.nodak.edu**

   Body: **SUBSCRIBE NEW-LIST** *first-name last-name*

HINT: The italicized reference to first-name last-name means to key your own first and last name. Also, remember to leave the subject field blank. (It may take more than a day for a return reply if the mail server is not currently functioning.)

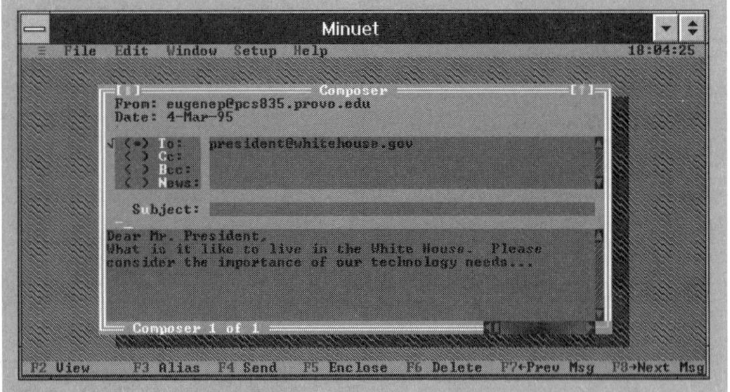

Subscribing to a mailing list

3. Send an E-mail note with the two message fields below containing precisely the information you see bolded:

   To: **Listserv@uriacc.uri.edu**

   Body: **SUBSCRIBE GC-L** *first-name last-name*

4. Close your E-mail program.

5. Complete a report on each subscription request and include it in Cyber Log 7-2-1 and 7-2-2. In the report, indicate the length of time taken before your request was officially completed. As you begin to receive messages from each subscription list, indicate the average daily number of messages over a five-day period, the tone (factual, opinionated, personal, etc.) of the messages, as well as any other important facts or problems you are made aware of as a new subscriber to the list.

CyberLog 7-2

1. **Report for subscription request to Listserv@vm1.nodak.edu.**

2. **Report for subscription request to Listserv@uriacc.uri.edu.**

CyberQuest 7-2

Consider subscribing to additional E-mail lists. You may want to subscribe to the three additional lists that interested you in Activity 7-1. You can find those addresses entered in your Cyber Log 7-1-2.

HINT: Just one final reminder that the number of messages you receive might be difficult to keep up with, and might also overload your system. Therefore, use good judgment in the number of E-mail lists that you subscribe to.

The Great Equalizer

Introduction

Cruising the Net puts you in touch with all kinds of people, common folks to royalty and everything in between. We all get equal treatment and consideration over the Net. The Net becomes a great equalizer of status and worldly position. This activity will provide you an avenue to connect with two better known people; namely, the president of the United States and Rush Limbaugh.

Objectives

Launch your E-mail program

Recognize electronic forms of communication are a great equalizer

Realize access to groups and individuals never thought possible

Develop skill in constructing complete and effective messages

README file 49

NETIQUETTE: Spelling

When making requests of anyone, observing the rules of Netiquette and common courtesy can make your experience much more successful.

As you construct the E-mail messages, make sure you accurately spell names and check all spelling very carefully.

RESOURCE TABLE

CLIENT	E-mail program
RESOURCE LOCATION	E-mail addresses of two prominent, well-known people: **president@whitehouse.gov** **70277.2502@compuserve.com**
SPECIAL ADVICE	Notice in the second address above, that oftentimes numbers are used for E-mail addresses. This particular address is assigned to the individual by a private electronic E-mail service called CompuServe.

inter-steps

1. You are going to send an E-mail note to the president of the United States, expressing your interest in the Net and asking for his maximum support of this communications network. Enter the entire body of your message in Cyber Log 7-3-1 and get approval from your teacher before you send the message.

2. Similarly, you are going to send an E-mail note to Rush Limbaugh, asking him to encourage the president to continue supporting the growth and improvement of the Information Highway, or the Net as we call it. Once again, enter the entire body of your message in Cyber Log 7-3-2 and get approval from your teacher before you send the message.

3. Launch your E-mail program.

4. To send your E-mail message to the president, enter the following address in the To field:

   To: **president@whitehouse.gov**

5. To send your E-mail message to Rush Limbaugh, enter the following address in the To field:

   To: **70277.2502@compuserve.com**

6. Close your E-mail program.

7. If no reply is received, wait at least two weeks before you send any kind of follow-up.

READ ME file 50

NETIQUETTE: What's in a message?

1. A salutation or greeting.
2. A body which is divided into three sections: first, an introductory paragraph, secondly, a paragraph making your request, and finally, a summary paragraph recapping your points.
3. A concluding comment expressing your sincere desire to see something happen with your request.
4. End the message with a cordial comment, followed by your name, address, and phone number.

CyberLog 7-3

1. **Construct your message to the president below. Take note of the Netiquette box in the inter-steps for help in constructing your message. Get approval from your teacher before sending.**

2. **Construct your message to Rush Limbaugh below. Take note of the Netiquette box in the inter-steps for help in constructing your message. Get approval from your teacher before sending.**

CyberQuest 7-3

3. **Evaluate the responses you receive in a short summary. Are the responses form letters? Who is answering the E-mail messages you sent? How valuable are these responses? Do they provide adequate information on the issues you raised?**

NEWSGROUP ACTIVITIES

Newsgroups are the second most widely used Internet resource next to E-mail. Newsgroups can be created whenever people wish to share information about a common topic. Many topics in this Cyber View also apply to the E-mail Cyber View. Things like post, subscribe, thread, and moderated are all terms that the Net surfer will see and learn more about as E-mail and Newgroup activities are pursued.

Investigate these newsworthy topics:

- What USENET is
- What USENET is not
- Reading Newsgroups
- Newsgroup threads
- Moderated and unmoderated groups
- Local screening

Following this Cyber View, there are four Newsgroup activities:

Activity 8-1: Believe It or Not
Activity 8-2: Off-Line Newsreaders
Activity 8-3: Starting a Newsgroup
Activity 8-4: Participating in Newsgroups

READ ME file 51

NET NOTE: USENET culture

The USENET is probably the best place to get a feel for the culture of the Net. USENET and the Internet in general have often been described as electronic anarchy. Anarchy is defined as the absence of government, a state of disorder and confusion.

The reality is, order is maintained by group members who set the rules for their discussions. If you step out of line, members will let you know it with a flame.

There are also some very interesting characters on USENET. **Wizards** are experts. **Flamers** send flames, or written rebukes. **Saints** help **newbies**, or new users, and **lurkers** are those who read groups but don't post their own articles.

USENET

USENET is a huge collection of computers that allow you to **post** (distribute or publish) and read discussion news items with the help of a software tool called a **newsreader**.

The USENET is not technically part of the Internet. However, it is so interwoven with the fabric of the Net that most people consider it to be an Internet service.

USENET started as a joint project between students and professors at Duke University and the University of North Carolina. The early USENET allowed a group at Duke and a group at UNC to discuss important aspects of their research on-line. From these beginnings, it grew into the USENET we know today.

Following are some of the groups aimed at new users:

- ***news.newusers.questions*** - a place to ask questions about USENET
- ***news.announce.newusers*** - contains articles on USENET
- ***news.answers*** - has FAQ's about USENET
- ***alt.internet.services*** - a place to ask questions about Internet resources

Posting to USENET

The USENET is like a huge bulletin board where you can publish or post information, ideas, and comments called **articles**. USENET Newsgroups, or **groups** for short, are shared by millions of **subscribers**, or participants, over the Net.

USENET allows many people to talk about an issue at the same time. You can read any group and post to any group.

How Big Is USENET?

No one knows how big USENET really is. There is no central list of services or groups and no way to track all the activities on USENET. There may be more than 6,000 active USENET groups that publish and share information every day.

What USENET Is Not

For new users, USENET is one of the more confusing parts of the Internet. Even the name, *USENET Newsgroups*, creates misconceptions. It is a good idea to look at some of the things USENET is not.

USENET Is Not an Electronic Newspaper

The USENET is often misunderstood. Many people think that USENET is like a giant electronic newspaper. In reality, Newsgroups are more like discussion groups than electronic versions of newspapers. Traditional news services are now available on-line for a fee, but these services are not the same as USENET Newsgroups (see Cyber View 9).

READ ME **file 52**

NETIQUETTE: Avoiding flames

Flames are rebukes sent to people who violate Netiquette. To avoid flames:

- read a new Newsgroup for a few days before you begin to participate
- get a feel for the group before you post
- stick to the topic of the group, and be brief in your postings
- be considerate and thoughtful. Your posting may be read by millions of people.
- if you are responding to a message, quote the key points of the original message so others can follow the conversation
- sign your login name. This is a sign to group members that you are responsible for what you write.
- don't repeat yourself
- use descriptive titles for your postings

READ ME file 53

FAQ'S: What does *alt* stand for?

USENET divides the major Newsgroups into categories. Some of the most recognizable categories include the following:

alt.	=	alternative (topics or subjects)
comp.	=	computers
biz.	=	business
misc.	=	miscellaneous
news.	=	USENET News
rec.	=	recreation
sci.	=	science
soc.	=	social issues
talk.	=	talk and debate12.
K12.	=	education

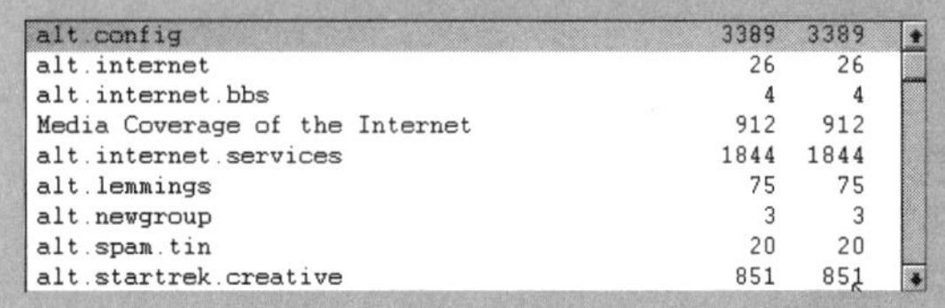

f 8-1 List of Newsgroups

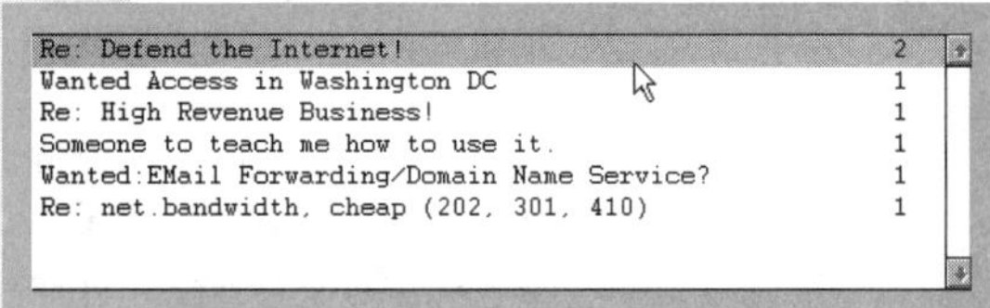

f 8-2 List of Newsgroup subject lines

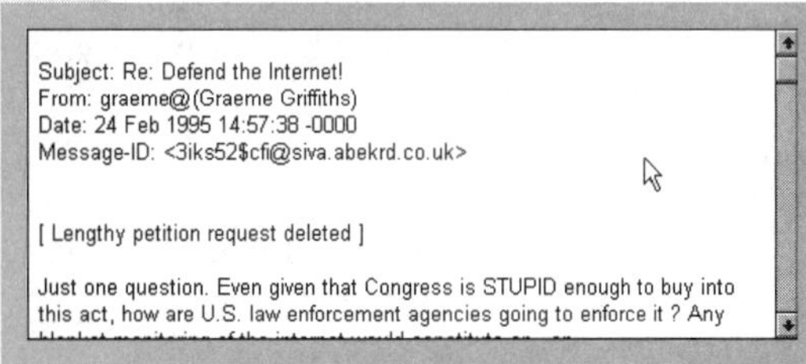

f 8-3 Text of Newsgroup article

USENET Is Not for Advertising

If you look at any newspaper, you realize that advertising is very important to the survival of a paper. The USENET is not meant for advertising. If you advertise in a Newsgroup, you will be accused of spamming, so prepare to be flamed.

USENET Is Not a List of Groups

Many people think that USENET is a list of Newsgroups. USENET is an interconnected group of computers that understand the USENET names and addresses. These computers are able to store and send you the Newsgroups you subscribe to. They can also send your postings to anyone who may be a member of your Newsgroups.

USENET Is Not Guaranteed to be Accurate

Just because you read something in a Newsgroup does not mean it is true. The USENET does allow freedom of speech, but it does not guarantee the truth.

How to Read Newsgroups

Newsgroups use software tools called readers to view Newsgroup postings. There are many newsreaders available over the Net; for example, rn, trn, nn, tin, news, vnews, pcnews, and many more. You can also read Newsgroups with GUI Browsers.

All Newsgroup readers share something in common. They start by looking at the Newsgroup **category** and Newsgroup **title**. For example, in the group *alt.internet*, *alt* is the category, and *internet* is the group title (see Figure 8-1).

Each Newsgroup posting or article has a title, or **subject line**; for example Re: Cool Stuff on the Internet (as shown in Figure 8-2).

After you pick an article you like, the reader displays text like the text shown in Figure 8-3.

Threads

Good newsreaders allow you to follow the **thread** of a discussion. A thread is a series of messages on the same theme or topic. This saves lots of time and allows you to avoid threads that do not interest you. Most quality on-line commercial services offer readers that allow you to follow threads (see Cyber View 9).

Moderated and Unmoderated Groups

There are two kinds of groups available on USENET:

- moderated
- unmoderated

A **moderated** group has a person or group that screens anything going into the group for distribution to its readers. Moderators cut out unnecessary postings and articles that do not fit the topic of the group.

Unmoderated groups do not have anyone moderating the group. Therefore, group members must be more aware of what is and is not appropriate for the group.

Local Screening

USENET is like the Internet in that there is no central authority. No one is directly in charge of how it works. USENET groups can be created by nearly anybody and can cover any topic.

Much USENET chatter may be uninteresting and of little value to you. However, every now and then you can follow a thread, or conversation, that is very interesting, insightful, or just plain fun. These conversation threads make USENET valuable to Net users.

Your local USENET administrator may restrict the groups you have access to. This kind of local screening does help keep out groups that would offend many people (see Cyber View 9). It also protects the local computers from being swamped with Newsgroup mailings that people do not want or need.

READ ME **file 54**

NET NOTE: Most famous flames

The most famous flames ever sent were targeted at a law firm advertising their services over the Net. These lawyers (who specialize in green card or immigration law) were accused of spamming the Net; that is, posting garbage or spam where it wasn't wanted. The lawyers became known in Internet lore as "The Green Card lawyers."

Do you think advertising should be allowed on the public Internet or in your favorite Newsgroup?

CyberQuiz 8

On a separate piece of paper or on a handout provided by your teacher, answer the following questions.

Circle Yes if the statement is true or no if the statement is false.

1. **Yes or No** USENET is a huge collection of computers that allows you to post and read news.
2. **Yes or No** Newsgroups are a more popular Internet resource than E-mail.
3. **Yes or No** USENET is an electronic newspaper.
4. **Yes or No** You should feel free to advertise for your business on USENET.
5. **Yes or No** There are both moderated and unmoderated groups on USENET.

For questions 6 though 8, circle the letter that corresponds to the best answer.

6. **Information, ideas, or comments on USENET are called**
   a. resources
   b. subscriptions
   c. articles
   d. spam
7. **A thread is a series of messages that are**
   a. unrelated
   b. on the same theme or topic
   c. moderated
   d. just plain fun
8. **To view postings, Newsgroups use**
   a. flames
   b. Netiquette
   c. subject lines
   d. readers

For questions 9 through 10, write the correct answer in the space provided.

9. **Describe the following:**

news. ____________________

misc. ____________________

biz. ____________________

comp. ____________________

alt. ____________________

10. **List several ways you can avoid being flamed when you post information to a Newsgroup.**

____

____

____

READ ME file 55

SOFT NOTE: Configure, Access, and Help on Newsgroups

Configure: Ensure that your Network Administrator has properly configured a common newsreader program and correct client interface for your network and operating system platform.

Access: Depending on your access provider, you will run your newsreader program with point and click (i.e., Window/Mac) or text-based input (UNIX emulation).

Help: Most Newsgroups have README or INTRO files that provide information such as the owner's E-mail address and how to actively post to a given Newsgroup. *

Believe It or Not

Introduction

A bundle of information is available through the USENET Newsgroups, but some of it tends to be inaccurate. In this activity, you will find three Newsgroup entries on three different Newsgroup hosts which you believe to be unjustified statements. You will record your reasoning and why you believe each case to be inaccurate in the Cyber Log.

Objectives

Launch your Newsgroup reader

Become acquainted with several Newsgroups

Identify points of Netiquette

Develop Newsgroup searching skills

Successfully close a Newsgroup session

RESOURCE TABLE

CLIENT	Newsgroup reader
RESOURCE LOCATION	Various Newsgroup addresses: **news.misc** **news.admin.misc** **misc.answers** **alt.best.of.internet** **rec.arts.tv**
SPECIAL ADVICE	**news.future** **http://www./w3.org/hypertext/datasources/news/news.html#125** **http://Info.cern.ch/hypertext/www/newsgroups/html**

inter-steps

1. Access your newsreader and choose any one of thousands of Newsgroups to evaluate.

   Following are a few potential Newsgroups to surf and cruise:

   news.misc

   news.admin.misc

   misc.answers

   alt.best.of.internet

   rec.arts.tv

README file 56

SOFT NOTE: Read, post, and perform keyword searches on thousands of Newsgroups
Reading: This is usually as simple as highlighting, scrolling, or using a keyword search to find the desired file.

Keyword Searches: Some newsreaders provide a way for you to search entries in a Newsgroup based on common groups of keywords.

Post: This is similar to sending an E-mail message and it provides a way for you to participate in the Newsgroup.

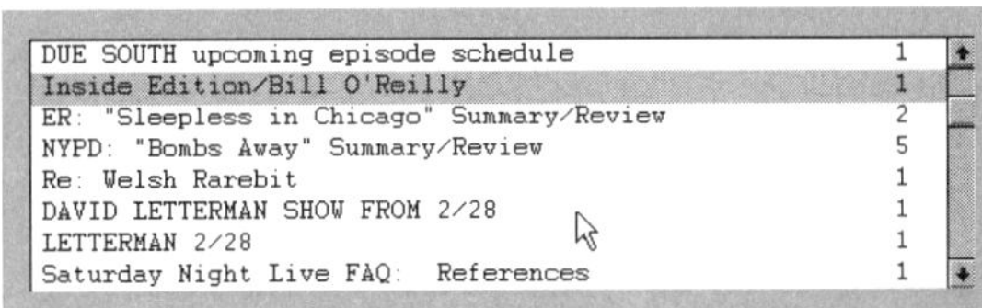

Newsgroup menu

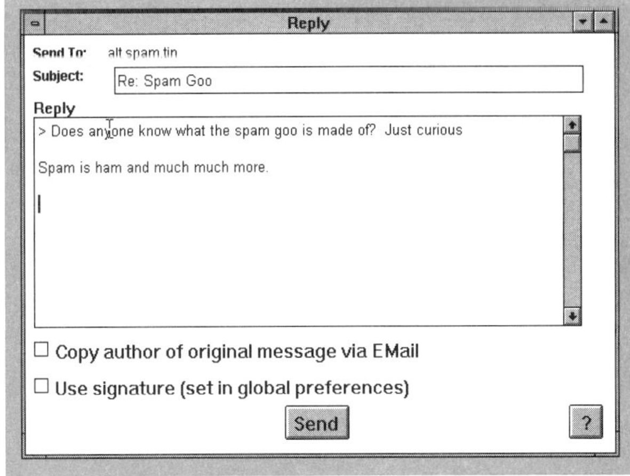

Posting on **alt.spam.tin**

2. Read several entries and state specific reasons why these entries might be inaccurate. Include quotes from these entries on Cyber Log 8-1-1.

3. Prepare your own response to an entry you read and post it to that Newsgroup. Record this entry on Cyber Log 8-1-2.

4. Exit your Newsgroup reader.

CyberLog 8-1

1. **Include both title of entry and a quote from the entry which you believe to be inaccurate in three different Newsgroup comments.**

Entry: ______________________________

Quote: ______________________________

____

____

Entry: ______________________________

Quote: ______________________________

____

____

ReadMe file 57

SOFT NOTE: Integrity of data

Learn to evaluate carefully the information you acquire on the Net. There is a wealth of valuable data, but it needs to be properly sifted and screened if the Net is to become an important tool for you. Netiquette and high standards always come first in your Net cruising. *

Entry: ____________________

Quote: ____________________

____

____

2. **Write your response to an entry above.**

____

____

____

____

____

____

____

____

____

____

____

____

____

____

CyberQuest 8-1

1. **If your newsreader has a keyword search function, then enter one or a group of keywords on various topics of your choice. Realize that you can usually combine related words but they might require an and/or, which will either reduce or enlarge the newsgroups available to search. In the following table record seven word combinations and the number of entries of each combination. You may recognize that this type of searching takes advantage of "Boolean logic operators."**

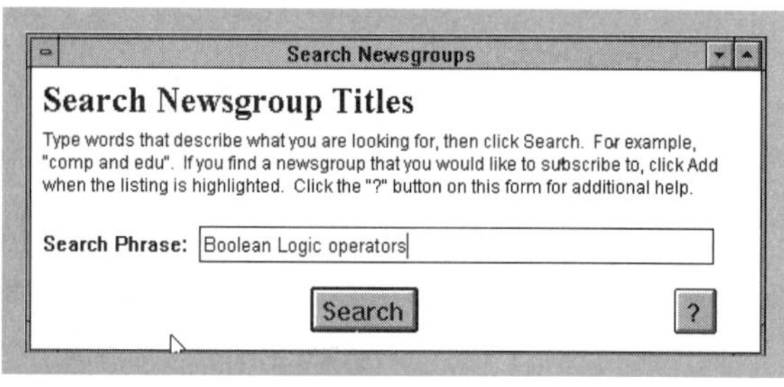

Searching a Newsgroup

Some examples might include:

Single	**Reduce**	**Enlarge**
politics	politics and democrats	politics or weather
travel	travel and Hawaii	travel or sports
recreation	recreation and boating	recreation or exercise
religion	religion and Buddhism	religion or rights
government	government and judicial	government or laws
music	music and hard rock	music or ballet

WORD COMBINATION	NUMBER FOUND

2. **Make some generalizations about your findings here (i.e., the number of entries found when using the Boolean logic operator "and" vs. "or," etc.).**

____

____

____

____

____

Off-Line Newsreaders

Introduction

For this activity, you will need to learn two new terms. *Freeware* means free software. *Off-line newsreader* software is a program that is able to read postings off-line. Based on several Newsgroup entries concerning the best freeware off-line news-reader software, you will be requested to make a suggestion for what you believe to be the best recommendation on each computer platform. The comments you read will not be those of experts, but after reading several entries, you should come to a logical educated decision about which off-line newsreader is most universally accepted for each computer platform.

Objectives

Launch newsreader

Identify the best off-line newsreaders for each platform (Windows, Macintosh, or UNIX)

Enhance knowledge of newsreader software

Increase information retrieval skills

RESOURCE TABLE

CLIENT	Newsgroup reader
RESOURCE LOCATION	Address: **alt.usenet.offline-reader**
SPECIAL ADVICE	Don't spend too long searching for multiple entries on a given computer platform if the entries don't seem to be available.

inter-steps

1. Access your newsreader.

2. Select the **alt.usenet.offline-reader** Newsgroup.

Actually, there is not much I miss in XP (CrossPoint). For features that are not supported by XP itself there is a variety of tools available. (Like sorting incoming mail, tagline-shufflers, automatically handling Nodediffs in Fido, etc).

It is the most popular offline-reader in Germany (and for once Germany shareware worth buying). It does not only handle Usenet very well, but also Fido-compatible nets, plus Maus-Net and Z-Net (Although I think they are German nets, not international ones). Which means it is one program for all. Also it runs very smoothly under both Win and OS/2; and it is very easily configurable.

Reading a comment regarding an off-line newsreader

3. Evaluate as many entries as necessary to gain a thorough understanding of the following platforms: Windows, Macintosh, and UNIX. Enter your summary of these entries on the Cyber Log 8-2-1 table, then fill out Cyber Log 8-2-2, indicating which off-line newsreader you would use for each platform based on the summarized recommendations found in Cyber Log 8-2-1.

   HINT: Take note of and record the off-line newsreader name as well as the good and bad qualities being promoted by that particular Newsgroup entry. Try to be as thorough as possible. A review of the Cyber Log questions that you will be asked might be helpful.

4. Regardless of your recommendations offered in Cyber Log 8-2-2, determine what the majority are saying about a viable solution for Windows, Macintosh, and UNIX. Submit your findings in the form of a statistical report, indicating the number of people you found supporting the most popular newsreader for each computer platform of Windows, Macintosh, and UNIX in this Newsgroup forum (**alt.usenet.offline-reader**). Enter your findings in the Cyber Log 8-2-3 table.

5. Close your Newsgroup newsreader.

README file 58

SOFT-NOTE: Off-line newsreaders can get you back on-line with the Net

As a Net cruiser it can be very helpful to understand as much as possible about the most functional, versatile, and resourceful off-line newsreaders that others are using for a given computer platform.

These readers can keep you effectively informed when properly implemented. *

CyberLog 8-2

1. **Enter your findings about each off-line newsreader entry that you encounter. Some platforms may be discussed more than others. Try to find at least one entry on each platform while filling out the entire table.**

OFF-LINE NEWSREADER	PLATFORM	PROS	CONS

2. After cruising the Net for a while, put together a recommendation based on what you believe to be the best solution for each of the three platforms of Windows, Macintosh, and UNIX.

PLATFORM	RECOMMENDATION	WHY?
WINDOWS		
MACINTOSH		
UNIX		

3. Enter statistical findings regarding how many recommended a given newsreader in the following table:

PLATFORM	OFF-LINE NEWSREADER	HOW MANY RECOMMENDED
WINDOWS		
MACINTOSH		
UNIX		

CYBERQUEST 8-2

4. Optional: FTP a freeware off-line newsreader from a location you might have read about and set it up (or get your Network Administrator to help) so it will filter selected entries within selected Newsgroups. Refer to Activity 8-1 for ideas on various keyword search methods you could use.

Starting a Newsgroup

Introduction

People just like yourself cruise the Net all the time. When they have a common interest, they often submit that interest for adoption as a Newsgroup. Often the Newsgroup may already exist, and there is then no need to create another. This activity will help you to think seriously about some unique interest and the possibility of starting your own Newsgroup. It could be almost anything, but it does have to be significantly different and desirable to others if it is going to be successful and seriously considered for acceptance as another Newsgroup.

Objectives

Learn the bias that exists as a new group is considered

Acquire analytical information retrieval skills regarding the Net and Newsgroups

Recognize that starting a new group is not normally accepted unless some unique and usually redeeming values are promoted within the Newsgroup

Stimulate creativity and critical thinking

README **file 59**

FAQ's: Is a Newsgroup for you?

The most widespread kind of Newsgroup contains the prefix **alt.** It stands for *alternate,* which is oftentimes a subcategory for unusual or nonconforming Newsgroups.

Within the thousands of alt Newsgroups, there is usually something for everyone. That does not mean, however, the ideas for Newsgroups are totally exhausted. You just have to think a little harder and be a little more imaginative. *

RESOURCE TABLE

CLIENT	GUI Browser
RESOURCE LOCATION	A guide on creating Newsgroups can be obtained at the following URL: **http://www.cis.ohio-state.edu:80/text/faq/usenet/creating-newsgroups/part1/faq.html**
SPECIAL ADVICE	Please consult an experienced Newsgroup news administrator before attempting to set up your own USENET Newsgroup.

inter-steps

1. Newsgroup Interest Voting Game: Following is a list of existing alt Newsgroups. Select five of your favorite titles from the list and write them into the General Category column in Cyber Log 8-3-1. Don't let anyone see your list. When the teacher says, "Vote," find three people who have also listed one or more of the same groups you have listed. Write their first names in the Potential Interest for Alt Newsgroup column. The first student with three names for each Newsgroup wins the game. Here's an example of one winner's list:

Potential Interest for Alt Newsgroup	General Category
Mari, Mike, Cory	alt.food
Fred, Roberto, Betty	alt.historical.what-if
Mike, Mari, Fred	alt.politics.economics
San-Li, Gary, Jay	alt.tv.friends
Lori, Maddie, Steve	alt.meditation

After the game, evaluate the complete list of Newsgroups again. Which three of the Newsgroups listed below should be eliminated due to lack of interest?

alt.disney.disneyland
alt.fan.holmes
alt.fan.monty-python
alt.food
alt.historical-what-if
alt.interview.media-coverage
alt.meditation
alt.music.amy-grant
alt.music.lyrics
alt.politics.economics
alt.radio.network.npr
alt.support.cancer
alt.tv.animaniacs
alt.tv.friends
alt.tv.mash
alt.usage.english

Method B: You can get a copy of it on the World Wide Web at **http://www.math.psu.edu/barr/**

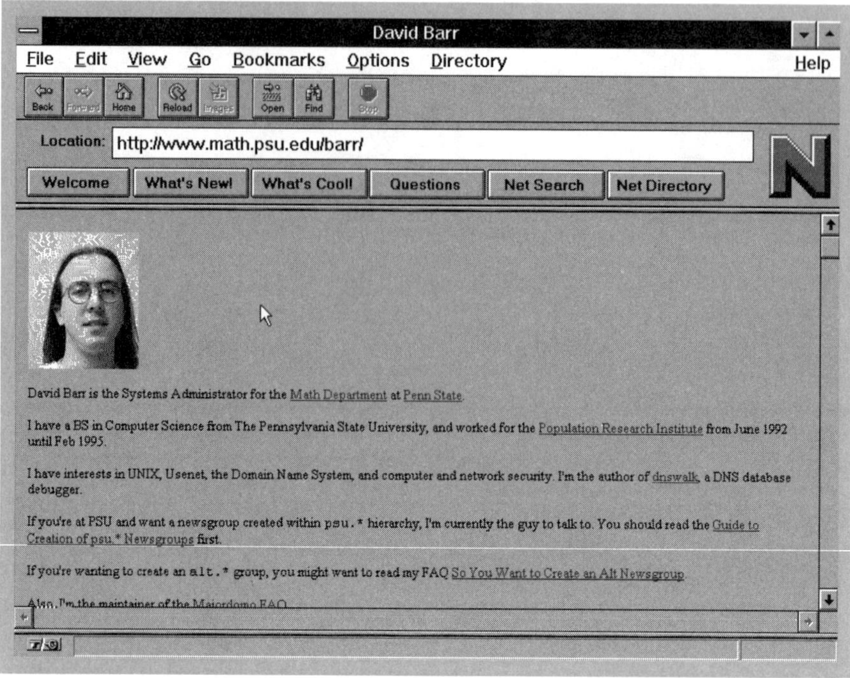

WWW document

or

Method C: You can get a copy using FTP at **ftp://rtfm.mit.edu:/pub/usenet/alt.config/So_You_Want_to_Create_an_Alt_Newsgroup**

5. Close your Net access tool and complete the Cyber Log.

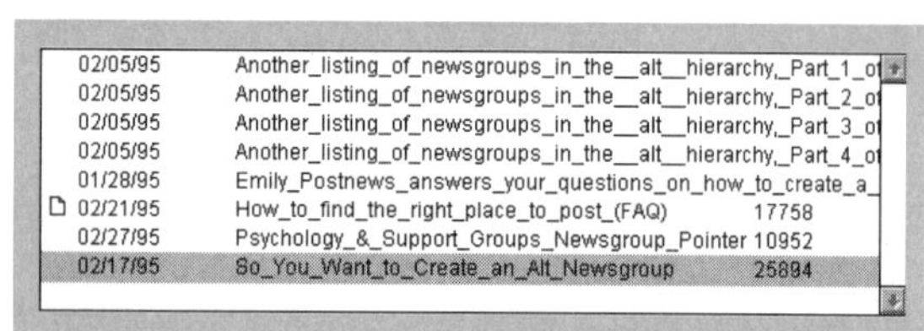

FTP menu

CyberLog 8-3

1. Complete the following table. Be as detailed as possible about each interest area.

POTENTIAL INTEREST FOR ALT NEWSGROUP	GENERAL CATEGORY

2. Summarize with some detail your topic of interest in the following table

POTENTIAL INTEREST FOR ALT NEWSGROUP	GENERAL CATEGORY

3. **Complete with as much detail as possible the steps required to create an alt Newsgroup as outlined in the document *So You Want to Create an Alt Newsgroup*. Numerically itemize the steps.**

CyberQuest 8-3

4. **With your teacher's permission, consider following the steps you have recorded in Cyber Log 8-3-3, and actually make a formal application to start an alt Newsgroup of your own. If you decide to, keep in mind everything you have learned about starting an alt Newsgroup, as well as the following recommendations:**

A. Record the various pros and cons forwarded by system administrators and other concerned parties as your request for a new group is debated.

B. If your request is accepted, make certain that you actively participate in the discussions.

READ ME file 60

NETIQUETTE: There is more than one way to skin a cat!

Remember in activities like this one, differences of opinion are welcomed but a blatant disregard of Netiquette is not. Someone once said, "You catch more bees with honey."

This approach to others is quite appropriate when striving to convince them of your philosophy and ultimately to get your ideas across.

Participating in Newsgroups

Introduction

The Net only works as well as the people who cruise it. If too many people disregard the warning signs, rules, and regulations, then cruising the Net will become a vague memory in our minds. This activity will provide you the opportunity to become more involved with some of the real issues that need to be dealt with regarding the Net.

Objectives

Launch your newsreader

Establish an opinion about future Internet rules, guidelines, and directions

Develop an appreciation for the Internet

Know what Internet stands for

Know where Internet has been

Know where Internet is going

RESOURCE TABLE

CLIENT	Newsgroup reader
RESOURCE LOCATION	**news.misc**
SPECIAL ADVICE	Keep track of any Newsgroups that can help you with your schoolwork.

inter-steps

1. Access your newsreader.

2. Select **news.misc**

3. Examine and evaluate available Newsgroup entries. In Cyber Log 8-4-1, record and summarize five entries which justify and confirm your attitude regarding what you believe the role of the Internet should be in today's culture and political system.

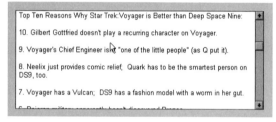

4. Look carefully at the personal views being conveyed in this Newsgroup, and identify three differing opinions which exist regarding a specific issue. If you can't find three different opinions on one issue, then consider more than one issue. Record these opinions in Cyber Log 8-4-2.

5. Close your newsreader.

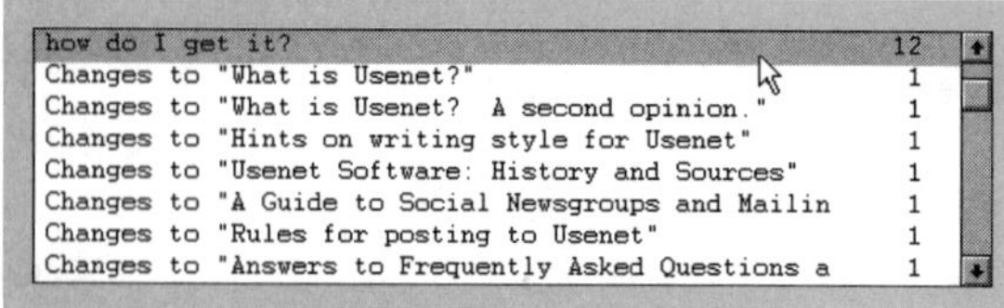

News.misc newsreader in Windows

My (quite limited) experience has been the exact opposite. Since I transferred to a commercial provider, the performance of the Usenet News feed has increased markedly. Of course, the U. of Oklahoma is handicapped by (1) extremely poor connectivity to MidNet and (2) MidNet. The enhanced performance of my commercial ISP has made me more demanding, if anything.

Odd that. You'd think I'd just be happy. Especially since my original Usenet News experience ('84-'86) taught me not to expect followups to articles I posted in no less than about ten days after the date of posting. Longer from sites on the opposite side of hubs like decvax.

Stating an opinion

Top Ten Reasons Why Star Trek:Voyager is Better than Deep Space Nine:

10. Gilbert Gottfried doesn't play a recurring character on Voyager.

9. Voyager's Chief Engineer isn't "one of the little people" (as Q put it).

8. Neelix just provides comic relief; Quark has to be the smartest person on DS9, too.

7. Voyager has a Vulcan; DS9 has a fashion model with a worm in her gut.

Stating another opinion

CYBERLOG 8-4

1. **Complete the table from the instructions found in inter-step 3. It is important to form your own opinion about the Internet and how it should operate before getting too deeply involved.**

NEWSGROUP ENTRY FROM NEWS.MISC	SUMMARY OF ENTRY

2. **Summarize three different opinions found in news.misc in the following table:**

SUBJECT	OPINION

CyberQuest 8-4

3. **Once you have evaluated news.misc entries quite thoroughly, consider doing the following:**

A. Using download or save procedures provided on your system (check with your Network Administrator if you have questions about those procedures), save between five and ten entries which will help you complete the next two steps.

B. Create a report which offers what you believe to be the present and future directions of the Net. Within this report, clearly state your personal views and substantiate those views with entries you've found that support your opinion.

C. Submit the report (no longer than one page) to the **news.misc** Newsgroup.

Commercial On-Line Services

One thing is for sure, when it comes to the Internet, there will always be more to learn, more to explore, more to do, and more new services to come. The Internet is growing at a startling rate. The Net we use today will look primitive to us ten years from now.

Browse the following topics in this Cyber View:

- Commercial On-line services
- Selecting a service
- Smart consumerism
- Limiting access

More to Come

Some of the exciting new resources on the Net are being provided by commercial service providers. Many providers offer access to the Internet, USENET, E-mail, and a GUI Web Browser for a subscription fee.

These service providers have accelerated the growth of the Net into homes and small businesses who could not afford on-line service in the past.

In this Cyber View, we will preview some of the major service providers, as well as look at some of the exciting new services that were unavailable on the Net a few short years ago.

Commercial On-Line Services

Commercial on-line services must compete for customers, so they have been very creative in coming up with new ways to make their on-line service look attractive to new customers. In doing so, many have tried to improve existing Internet online tools. However, be careful. By 1995, not one of the big

README file 61

FAQ's: What is America Online?

America Online, or AOL, is one of the fastest-growing service providers with well over a million subscribers.

AOL was one of the first of the major providers to offer a direct Internet connection. With AOL, getting to the Internet is as easy as clicking a button.

AOL offers news, weather, and ABC Sports. If you want to interact with the crew of Monday Night Football during the game, you can.

AOL also offers a simple E-mail system with access to anyone on the Net. AOL has one of the easiest connections to the Internet. You can use USENET and Internet Relay Chat technology, jump out on the Web, order airline tickets, check stock quotes, rent cars, download software, and a hundred other things.

three services offered access to all of the tools described in Cyber Views 1 through 8. Check the status of their Internet and WWW development efforts before you lay down your cash.

Despite some limitations, commercial on-line service providers create a feeling that the future is just around the corner, and that when you are on-line, you are a part of that future.

Following are the big three on-line providers:

- America Online
- CompuServe
- Prodigy

There are many other companies competing for a piece of the on-line pie, including Delphi, GEnie®, NETCOM®, AT&T, Apple Computer's eWORLD, IBM, Microsoft, Novell, and MCI, to name a few.

ReadMe file 62

FAQ's: What is CompuServe?

CompuServe is the oldest on-line service. CompuServe has the reputation of being the on-line service of business. Certainly, one of CompuServe's strengths is its business offering. But CompuServe offers a much more balanced service than most people realize.

CompuServe has nearly 2,000 services, including news and weather from the Associated Press. Shopping and travel sections are also popular on CompuServe.

CompuServe has some excellent forums, or discussion groups, on a variety of topics. CompuServe continues to be one of the most popular and reliable on-line services. *

Selecting a Service

Each service is a little different from the other. In selecting a service provider, make sure they offer the tools you want and need. Some service providers do not have access to the WWW; others only have E-mail to the Net.

Make a list of the services you consider to be important, and ask each service if they have your list of tools. A basic list of services can include the following:

- E-mail to the Internet
- E-mail attachment capabilities
- USENET reader
- FTP
- Telnet
- WWW GUI Browser
- Internet Relay Chat (IRC or Chat, for short)

- Electronic weather, news, and sports
- Software, graphic, and multimedia download capabilities
- Lockout capabilities
- A security system
- On-line interactive games
- Financial and investment information services
- Travel services
- Shopping services in electronic malls
- Entertainment services, like multimedia comedy sessions
- On-line customer support and help services

Be a Smart Consumer

Many of these service providers will let you try their service free on a trial basis. Be careful, however. If you stay on-line longer than your free trial, you will be charged.

You also have to know how to disconnect. Many of these subscription services bill directly to a VISA or MasterCard. You can run up a large bill very quickly, particularly in the shopping area of the on-line services, and not realize how much you are being charged.

Most on-line services provide a certain number of on-line hours for a set fee; for example five hours for $10. After that, you may be charged $3, $4, or even $5 dollars per hour. When surfing the Net, chatting, or playing games, time can pass rapidly. You can be over your limit quickly; then the dollars really start adding up.

Be sure you understand how you are being billed. For example, some service providers charge extra for E-mail after 50 or 60 E-mail messages. Other services charge you one fee for basic services, and additional fees for any extra services you use. Hidden costs can add up, so be careful.

READ ME file 63

FAQ's: What is Prodigy?

Prodigy is one of the most popular on-line services, with nearly three million subscribers.

Prodigy is oriented toward families. Prodigy was the first of the major service providers to provide a GUI Browser.

Prodigy is easy to use. It has excellent E-mail and other important services. It also has ESPN Sports with ESPNNET.

Key Points to Remember as a Consumer

Following are some tips to remember as you pick and use a commercial on-line service provider:

- Make sure your provider lets you log in with a local phone call. If you have to connect long distance, you will not only pay the on-line service provider, but you will also give additional dollars to the phone company.
- Select a service that allows you to do much of your work off-line. It can take time to compose an E-mail message or to read a Newsgroup. You can save money if your service offers you the ability to compose your mail or read your Newsgroups off-line.
- Check your charges and billing frequently. Make sure you know what services you are being billed for. Ask for a copy of your monthly bill. This way, you have a record of your expenditures.
- Find out if there are any "free zones" on your service. Some services have free areas where you are not charged. For example, are you charged for the time it takes for your service provider to update their software on your machine?
- Make sure you log out. On-line service providers are not like Telnet computers that sense when no activity is taking place and automatically log you out! Instead, if you run off to eat or fall asleep, the meter is still running.

- Check the speed of your on-line connection. Make sure your connection is at least as fast as your personal modem. If your provider does not have a 9,600bps or faster connection, downloading software, multimedia, graphics, or large files can take forever and you pay for that time.

When selecting an on-line service, beware of promises. A promise that your service provider will have a WWW Browser next spring isn't good enough. If a provider does not have the tools or resources you need, look for another provider.

Limiting Full Internet Access

All commercial service providers limit Internet access to members for a variety of reasons. There are many parts of the Internet that are offensive. Some groups allow foul language and pornographic communications. Many people pick an on-line provider because the service can lock out some of the more distasteful parts of the Internet.

There are several other reasons why service providers limit Internet access. Some service providers lack the technical ability to support many Internet services and tools. Other providers limit Internet options they feel are a waste of time for their members.

Another reason to limit access is that the Internet can be a very difficult place for inexperienced newbies. Newbies make Netiquette mistakes and get flamed often.

As a customer, you may appreciate a service that will help you exclude areas that you find offensive, annoying, or of little interest.

CyberQuiz 9

On a separate piece of paper or on a handout provided by your teacher, answer the following questions.

Circle Yes if the statement is true or No if the statement is false.

1. **Yes or No** Commercial service providers give free access to the Internet.
2. **Yes or No** Many people now access the Internet from their homes.
3. **Yes or No** As of 1995, all of the major service providers offered all of the Internet tools to their subscribers.
4. **Yes or No** AOL is the oldest commercial service provider.
5. **Yes or No** Prodigy has ESPNNET as one of its services.

For questions 6 through 8, circle the letter that corresponds to the best answer.

6. **Which of the following is not a commercial service provider?**
   a. CompuServe
   b. America Online
   c. Prodigy
   d. USENET
7. **Find an Internet access provider that**
   a. allows access with a local phone call
   b. allows you to work off-line
   c. allows you to check your billing and charges frequently
   d. has a high-speed connection to your modem
   e. has all of the above

8. **Which service provider is best known for its business offerings?**
   - a. CompuServe
   - b. Prodigy
   - c. eWorld
   - d. America Online

For questions 9 through 10, write the correct answer in the space provided.

9. **Describe the following:**

   America Online ________________

   CompuServe ________________

   Prodigy ________________

   IRC ________________

   Off-line ________________

   Free zones ________________

10. **What key points should you remember if you pick and use a commercial on-line service provider?**

   ____

   ____

   ____

   ____

   ____

   ____

   ____

   ____

   ____

   ____

   ____

   ____

   ____

ON-LINE ACTIVITIES ...

...Instructional Adventures in Cyberspace

In Sector 2, you learned to use the tools of the Internet. You are now ready for the on-line adventures available only to students of Cyberspace.

The activities in Sector 3 will point you to directions that will improve your understanding of the Net. Each activity will give you a little more insight on how the Net can help you in your studies. Try them all!

Sector 3 is a smorgasbord of choices, arranged in alphabetical order by subject area. Your instructor may assign you these lessons in any order, or you may start and finish the lessons in the order that best fits your needs.

These Cyberized subjects appear in the following order:

Archaeology
Art
Astronomy
Business
Careers
Economics
Education
Entertainment
European Studies — Geography
General Resources

Geography — Geophysics
Government and Civics
History
Journalism
Language Arts
Latin American Studies — Geography
Law
Marketing
Mathematics
Meteorology
Music
Photography
Science
Sports
Technology and Computers
Travel and Tourism

When you finish Sector 3, you will be an on-line wizard — a master of the Net.

Archaeology

Qumran and the Dead Sea Scrolls

Introduction

Access to information about the Dead Sea Scrolls has been very limited. In this activity, you will access an exhibit at the Library of Congress and research data and information on these 2,000-year-old documents.

Objectives

Connect to the Ancient Library of Qumran's Welcome Page

Locate historical references on the Dead Sea Scrolls

Read on-line archaeological documents

RESOURCE TABLE

CLIENT	GUI Browser
RESOURCE LOCATION	Locate information on the Dead Sea Scrolls: Browser: URL:**http://sunsite.unc.edu/expo/deadsea.scrolls.exhibit/intro.html**
SPECIAL ADVICE	Select The Qumran Library Home Page to complete Cyber Log question 1. To complete Cyber Log questions 2 through 5, select the Psalms. Return to the Qumran Library Home Page and select Some Torah Precepts to answer questions 6 through 8.

CyberLog 1

Refer to the Resource Table for help in completing this Cyber Log.

QUMRAN LIBRARY

1. **What is the Qumran Library? Why is it such an important electronic archaeological site?**

   ____

   ____

   ____

PSALM

2. **What is the Psalm scroll? Why is it important?**

   ____

   ____

   ____

3. **What material is the Psalm scroll made of?** ______________________

4. **The letters in this scroll are carefully drawn in the Jewish** __________ __________ **style of the** ______________ **period.**

5. **What does Tetragrammaton refer to?** ___________________________

SOME TORAH PRECEPTS

6. What is the title of these fragments? ______________________________

7. What are the four sections of these fragments?
   A. ______________________________
   B. ______________________________
   C. ______________________________
   D. ______________________________

8. How many fragments are there of this scroll? __________

CyberQuest 1

Use your surfing experience to investigate the Dead Sea Scrolls in more detail and find answers to questions on the Qumran community. Take notes on what you find. Prepare a report on the Qumran community and the Dead Sea Scrolls. Make sure you answer some of the following questions: Who were the authors of the Dead Sea Scrolls? Where did they live? When did they write these documents? Why did they write the scrolls? How did they preserve them for such a long time?

Art

The WebMuseum

Introduction

Take a tour of the world-renowned Louvre, visit Paris, wander through the Impressionist gallery, and more. You'll need a GUI Browser, of course. Surf some of the most famous art galleries in the world and select three artists that impress you most. Record your findings in your Cyber Log. Later, pick one of your artists and create an expanded report on his or her work and artistic style.

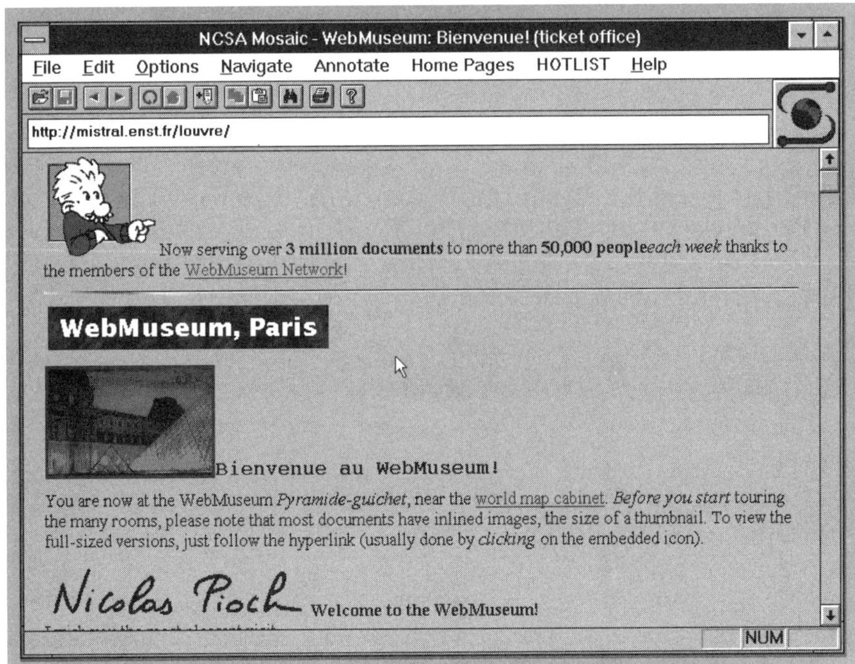

A WebMuseum Home Page as seen in a Windows Mosaic Browser

Objectives

Cruise the WebMuseum

Examine the works of three great artists

Find other on-line art museums, galleries, and exhibits

RESOURCE TABLE

CLIENT	GUI Browser
RESOURCE LOCATION	Locate information on the WebMuseum: Browser: URL: **http://mistral.enst.fr/**
SPECIAL ADVICE	Once you connect to your host, you will be asked to pick a server closer to home. Because this site is so popular, they have had to distribute access to different computers around the world. Don't worry, they all have the same information. Read the instructions on the Home Page. Use the down arrow keys to view more information. Select the hypertext pictures to view a larger image. For alternative locations, try the following: Browser: URL: **http://www.emf.net/louvre/** URL: **http://www.oir.ucf.edu/louvre/** URL: **http://sunsite.unc.edu/louvre/**

CyberLog 2

1. Use the information in the Resource Table to find and view the gallery of Famous Paintings at the WebMuseum. Find three artists that interest you. Take notes on each. Use the following chart to record your observations.

ARTIST NAME	BEST KNOWN WORKS OF ART	TIME PERIOD

CyberQuest 2

2. Select one of the artists from your list and research him or her more completely. Select any hypertext link that will tell you more about the artist.
3. While visiting the Louvre and the WebMuseum, take the Tour of Paris. Arrow down the Museum's Home Page to find the Tour of Paris.
4. How can you find other on-line museums, galleries, and art collections? Surf the Net and find other art collections.
5. Research famous composers on-line.

Astronomy

Hubble Space Telescope Update

Introduction

The Hubble Space Telescope (HST) has changed many of the basic theories of astronomy. Scientists from all over the world study the images sent back from the HST. Join the information team and keep up to date on what is happening in deep space.

Objectives

Connect to the Hubble Space Telescope information team

Explore the issues in current news releases

View the images from the Hubble Space Telescope

A Hubble Space Telescope Home Page as seen in a Macintosh Netscape Browser

RESOURCE TABLE

CLIENT	GUI Browser
RESOURCE LOCATION	Locate information on the Hubble Space Telescope: Browser: URL: **http://www.stsci.edu/EPA/Recent.html#SN1994I** NOTE: The EPA is uppercase. The R, S, and N for this URL are in uppercase. The last letter is a lowercase L.
SPECIAL ADVICE	If you need an alternative location, try the following: Browser: URL: **http://www.stsci.edu/EPA/Pictures.html** URL: **http://www.stsci.edu/public.html**

CYBERLOG 3

1. **Refer to the Resource Table to help you find information on the HST. Browse the images produced by Hubble. Record your five favorite images by writing a brief description of each.**

   Example: *X. Saturn Rings — Shows the rings of Saturn in two ways.*

A. __________ — ______________________________

B. __________ — ______________________________

C. __________ — ______________________________

D. __________ — ______________________________

E. __________ — ______________________________

2. **Locate and read Press Release PR95-04. There are a couple of ways to find the press release; for example, select Text of Press Releases under the More Information category, or select Press Release Text near the graphic of Quasar PKS2349.**

A. What is the date of the press release?

____

B. What is this press release about?

____

C. What is the name of the quasar being studied in this report?

____

D. What did astronomers expect to find with each quasar?

____

E. What led them to believe there is a problem with their theory about quasars?

____

3. **Locate and read Press Release PF95-07 about the Coma Cluster NGC 4881. Return to number 2 above to review how to locate the press releases.**

A. What is the date of the release?

____

B. What is the Coma Cluster?

____

C. How far away is NGC4881?

____

CyberQuest 3

4. **Read another press release of your choice and report on its contents. Create three questions of your own. Present their answers.**

5. **Explore URL: http://newproducts.jpl.nasa.gov/s19/s19.html**

Look for daily reports and news flashes on the Hubble Telescope. Report on what you find.

Business

Hooked on the Web

Introduction

The World Wide Web (WWW) Service Providers List is a group of organizations that provide basic Internet and WWW services. Getting you "hooked on the Web" is their business. As you might suspect, the Net is no longer a not-for-profit network. Many people, organizations, and businesses see the benefit of accessing the 30 million plus users of the Net. This activity explores how certain business groups are making money on the Net.

Objectives

Recognize that WWW service provider lists are accessible in many ways

Know what for-profit services are provided on the Net

Identify five different kinds of Net service providers, their locations, and the services they provide

RESOURCE TABLE

CLIENT	GUI Browser, Newsgroup, or E-mail
RESOURCE LOCATION	Locate service provider lists with one or more of the following tools: Browser: Enter **http://www.mhv.net/** Newsgroup: Enter **comp.infosystems.www.providers** or **alt.internet.services** E-mail: E-mail to **listproc@einet.net**
SPECIAL ADVICE	Use these alternative URLs to complete your Cyber Log if your above connection fails: **http://www.einet.net/** **http://www.lm.com/** **http://www.ip.net/** **http://www.wwa.com/** **http://www.garlic.com/** **http://branch.com/**

CYBERLOG 4

1. **Enter the URL found in the Resource Table. Read the document and log the name of five businesses, the on-line service they provide, and the URL or Location of their Home Page in the following table:**

NAME OF BUSINESS	SERVICE PROVIDED	URL OR LOCATION

CyberQuest 4

2. **Look up the five URLs / Locations you found in CyberLog 4. (If your connection fails, use the alternative addresses from the Special Advice section of the Resource Table.) Pick the one business you think will make the most money and create an advertisement listing its services and benefits to customers. Make sure your advertisement includes the following:**

- The kind of service provided
- Reasons why this business is successful
- Reasons why a customer (consumer) should use this service
- The current pricing
- Ways a customer can communicate with this business and buy the products or services listed

Design a full-page advertisement for a popular computer magazine.

Business

Computer Vendor Resources

Introduction

In today's technology-driven information society, change is the only constant. You can prepare for the changes to come by getting an idea of what the technology industry is working on now. Research the vast information provided by the companies that are leading the technology revolution.

Objectives

Explore the resources provided by major hardware and software vendors

Investigate future technology directions, products, and industry trends

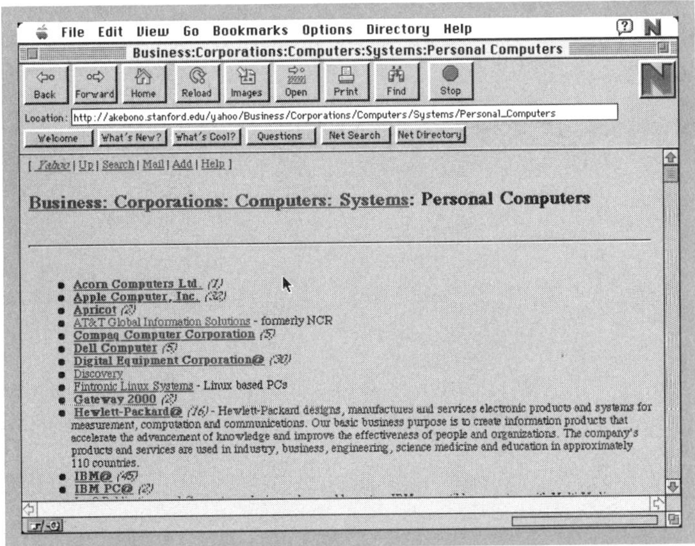

A Business Starting Points Home Page as seen in a Macintosh Netscape Browser

RESOURCE TABLE

CLIENT	GUI Browser
RESOURCE LOCATION	Locate information about computer software and hardware vendors: Browser: URL: **http://www.yahoo.com/Business/Corporations/Computers/Systems/Personal_Computers/** (This URL is for hardware vendors) URL: **http://www.yahoo.com/Business/Corporations/Computers/Software/** (This URL is for software vendors.) HINT: You may need to start at http://www.yahoo.com/, then select the categories Business, Corporations, Computers, etc.
SPECIAL ADVICE	For alternative locations, try the following: **http://www.microsoft.com** **http://www.compaq.com/** **http://www.novell.com/** **http://www.digital.com/** **http://www.hp.com/**

CYBERLOG 5

HARDWARE COMPANIES

1. **Using the first URL in the Resource Table, find five different computer hardware companies. Record the kinds of products they make and sell. This could include new computers, computer processor chips, printers, modems, or other hardware products. Some of these products may only be in the planning stages.**

	Company Name	Hardware Products This Company Makes and Sells
A.	____________	____________________
B.	____________	____________________

C. ____________ ____________________

D. ____________ ____________________

E. ____________ ____________________

2. **Which hardware product listed above do you think is the most promising? Why?**

____

____

SOFTWARE COMPANIES

3. **Using the second URL in the Resource Table, find five different computer software companies. Record the kinds of products they make and sell. This could include new word processors, spreadsheets, databases, games, financial programs, or other software products. Some of these may only be in the planning stages.**

	Company Name	Software Products This Company Makes and Sells
A.	____________	____________________
B.	____________	____________________
C.	____________	____________________
D.	____________	____________________
E.	____________	____________________

4. **Which software product listed above do you think is the most promising? Why?**

____

____

CyberQuest 5

5. **Of the five companies you listed in Cyber Log 5, which company would you like to work for? Prepare a list of reasons why you would like to work for that company. Prepare another list of ten different kinds of jobs your selected company may have available. Put a check mark by each job you would be interested in.**

Careers

Finding a Job

Introduction

Finding and keeping a job in the twenty-first century will be more challenging than ever before. The opportunities are there, but putting your finger on the right job in the field you are interested in will be continually more difficult. This activity helps you find invaluable vocational possibilities on the Net. After you connect with one or more of the locations provided in the Resource Table, complete the Cyber Log describing jobs you found interesting.

Objectives

Become familiar with on-line job-search opportunities

Go on-line to learn about a career that interests you

Identify five jobs that would interest you as a career

The Career Mosaic Home Page as seen in a Macintosh Netscape Browser

RESOURCE TABLE

CLIENT	GUI Browser or Gopher
RESOURCE LOCATION	Locate information on finding a job with the following: Browser: URL: **http://www.careermosaic.com/cm/home.html**
SPECIAL ADVICE	Finding a job is often more difficult than doing the job. Research is the key to finding employment in the future. Find out what your employer may expect in the way of skills and knowledge, and then plan your education accordingly. Some classes may not seem important now, but may be very important later when you are looking for work. For an alternative commercial job location service, try the following: Browser: URL: **http://www.careermag.com/careermag/**

CYBERLOG 6

1. **Job hunting can be a very challenging activity. This Cyber Log will help you get your feet wet hunting for jobs on-line. Refer to the Resource Table for help. Realize that the more you know about a potential job, the better chance you have for an interview. Therefore, fill out this table thoroughly.**

JOB TITLE	NAME OF EMPLOYER	EDUCATION REQUIRED	EXPERIENCE REQUIRED

CyberQuest 6

2. Pick your favorite job possibility from the list above and find out more about it. With your teacher's permission, call, mail, fax, send E-mail, or post a letter asking for more information about the job.

3. Prepare for a job interview with the employer you selected in number 2. Write down five questions you think they will ask you in the interview and prepare a response to each question.

4. Write five questions you have about the job you are interviewing for in number 3. What do you need to know about a job before you say, "Yes, I will take it"?

Economics

The Government's Economic Indicators

Introduction

Some of the most important economic statistics of the United States are easily available on the Net if you know where to look. Up-to-date statistics on unemployment, economic growth, housing starts, and interest rates can all be found with a little tunneling.

Objectives

Locate key government statistics on the Net

Find the answers to key economic questions on the Net

Condense a mountain of statistics into a presentable sound bite for radio

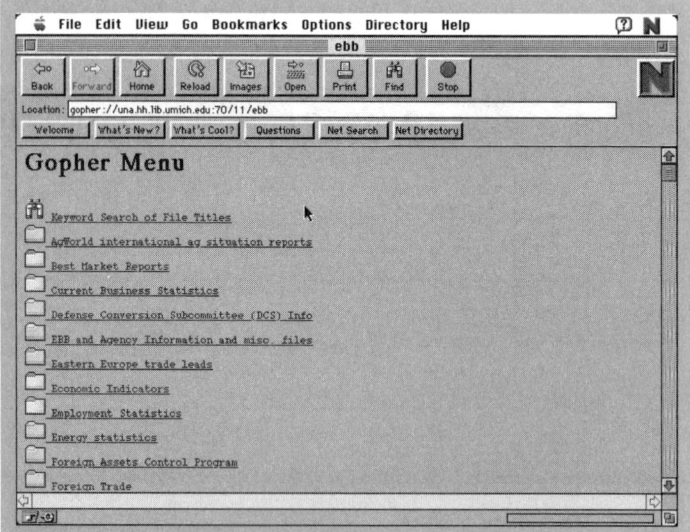

An Economic Indicators Gopher menu as seen in a Macintosh Netscape Browser

RESOURCE TABLE

CLIENT	GUI Browser or Gopher
RESOURCE LOCATION	Locate information on United States government statistics with the following tools: Browser: URL: **gopher://una.hh.lib.umich.edu:70/11/ebb** Select Economic Indicators and Best Market Reports. Gopher: Enter **gopher.gsfc.nasa.gov**, select Virtual Reference Shelf, then select Economic Bulletin Board and Exchange Rates. Try Economic Indicators and Best Market Reports.
SPECIAL ADVICE	Government statistics can be difficult to read and interpret. Keep searching the files until you find something in simple English that you can understand and record. Remember to arrow down. Sometimes the best information is found a few pages into the reports. If you don't like the topics, or if you have a hard time finding information, pick an economic topic of your own to complete the Cyber Log. If all else fails, or if the government reports start to drive you nuts, try this alternative economic URL from Yahoo: Browser: URL: **http://www.yahoo.com/economy/**

CYBERLOG 7

1. **You are a reporter from the local radio station. You have been asked to prepare a series of three short financial reports on the health of the economy. These "sound bite" reports will air on Monday: one on the morning news show, another on the afternoon news program, and the final one on the evening news program. Each report must be short, about 40-50 words, and not last more than 20 seconds. Pull your information from government statistics. Make sure you record where you found the statistics. See your Resource Table for possible sources.**

Sample Report: *The Government reported today that new home sales for the month of September were up 8.3%, which is a 2% increase over a year ago. New home construction was also up by 4% in September, according to a government report.*

RADIO KCBR ECONOMIC REPORTS FOR MONDAY

Monday Morning Report: *The Housing Industry*

Select Economic Indicators. Search the following files for tidbits of information:

Sources: ***Housing Starts, New Construction, Home Sales***

Write your radio spot here:

____
____
____
____

Monday Afternoon Report: *The Computer Industry*

Select Best Market Reports. Search the following files for tidbits of information:

Sources: ***Computer Software, Computers and Peripherals***

Write your radio spot here:

____
____
____
____

Monday Evening Report: *The Sports Industry*

Select Best Market Reports. Search the following files for tidbits of information:

Source: ***Sporting Goods and Recreational Equipment***

Write your radio spot here:

____
____
____
____

CyberQuest 7

2. **Now that you have some experience searching government records for tidbits of information, select a topic of your own to explore in more detail. There are government economic reports on thousands of issues. Believe it or not, there is a government report on popcorn sales to Middle Eastern countries. The report even lists how many kernels will pop in a bag of popcorn!**

Search the government statistics and files until you find something of interest. List the topic, and then make some general observations about it. Return to the same source one or two months later and see if anything has changed.

Topic: ____

Source: ____

General Observations:

____

____

____

____

Evaluation of Observations (one to two months later):

____

____

____

____

____

Education

Education Resources

Introduction

The Net is more than a cruising and surfing party. In fact, knowledge and learning are really what the Net is all about. In this activity, you will be given several sources of information on subjects you may encounter in school. You can find information on every subject from architecture to zoology.

A wise surfer once said, "A thousand mile journey begins with the first mouse click." So let's click that mouse NOW! The surf is up!

Objectives

Browse the contents of several subject lists

Complete a list of subject topics and URLs/locations

Find out how valuable these educational resources can be in your studies

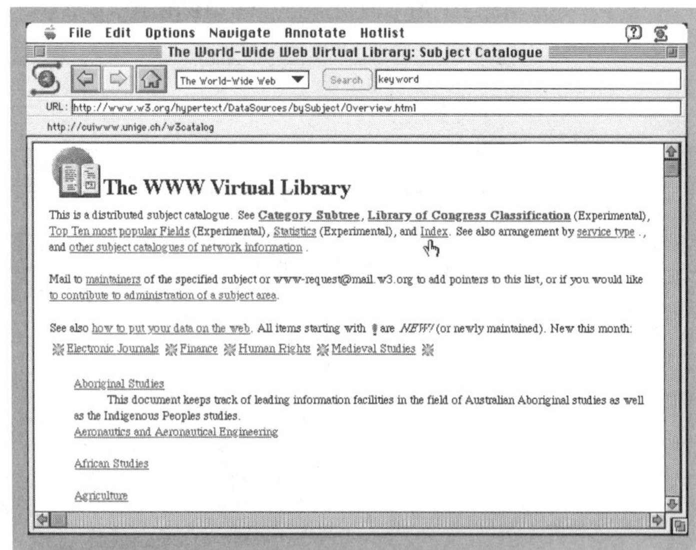

A WWW Virtual Library Home Page as seen in a Macintosh Mosaic Browser

RESOURCE TABLE

CLIENT	GUI Browser, Gopher, or FTP
RESOURCE LOCATION	Locate information on educational resources: Browser: URL: **http://www.w3.org/hypertext/DataSources/bySubject/Overview.html** URL: **http://www.yahoo.com/** URL: **http://www.cen.uiuc.edu/~jj9544/index.html** URL: **gopher://ds.internic.net/** Select Network Information Center, InterNIC Directory and Database Services (AT&T), select InterNIC Directory of Directories, then select Education. Gopher: Enter **ds.internic.net** Select Network Information Center, InterNIC Directory and Database Services (AT&T), select InterNIC Directory of Directories, then select Education. FTP: Enter **ds.internic.net/dirofdirs/education**
SPECIAL ADVICE	Use this URL in your Cyber Quest: Cyber Quest URL: **http://hillside.coled.umn.edu/others.html**

CYBERLOG 8

1. **To gain a better appreciation of the many educational subjects available on the Net, complete the following table using the URLs provided in the Resource Table. Search for the best Home Pages you can find on each subject. Then select two subjects of your own and record a good Home Page and URL location for each. Grade the quality of each Home Page: A, B, C, D, and F. Use + and - if you like.**

GRADE	SUBJECT	TITLE OF HOME PAGE	URL OR LOCATION ADDRESS
A+	*Art*	*The WebMuseum*	**http://mistral.enst.fr/**
	Business		
	Computers		
	Economics		
	English		
	Environment		
	Government		
	History		
	Humanities		
	Law		
	Science		
	Mathematics		

CyberQuest 8

2. **In teams of four, compare your subject lists. Discuss and demonstrate your Home Page choices. Prepare one list for your team of your very best choices.**

3. **Select one of your subject area Home Pages that you gave an A to, and prepare a short report on its contents and what interests you most.**

4. **Investigate other schools on the Net. The University of Minnesota maintains a list of Internet schools in their WWW Schools Registry. Use the URL in the Special Advice section of the Resource Table to visit the registry and find Internet schools in your state.**

Entertainment

Dave's Top Ten List

Introduction

Have you ever tried to repeat to a friend Dave Letterman's Top Ten List from the night before? Well, put your mind at ease. The Net posts Dave's Top Ten List in about a dozen different places. Some sites even post the lists from past shows. One Internet site boasts to having all of the Top Ten Lists since the show began!

Objectives

Search Top Ten Lists

Recognize parallels between Top Ten Lists and current events

Complete the Cyber Log questions dealing with Dave's Top Ten List

RESOURCE TABLE

CLIENT	GUI Browser
RESOURCE LOCATION	Locate Letterman's Top Ten List with the following tool: Browser: URL: **http://www.cbs.com/**
SPECIAL ADVICE	The true value of the Net is its ability to offer current data on issues and topics. If you need an alternative URL or Location, try the following: Browser: URL: **http://www.yahoo.com/Entertainment/Television/Shows/Talk_Shows/**, then select David Letterman, followed by Top Ten Lists.

CyberLog 9

1. **Complete the following table. If you would like to download and save the files feel free to do so. Make sure that you choose four Top Ten lists that are at least three months apart.**

LIST THE TOPIC OR THEME "TOP TEN REASONS..."	DATE AIRED	WHY IS THIS LIST FUNNY?

2. **Analyze the data recorded in the table above, then answer the following questions:**

A. Would any of these lists have been funny 100 years ago? If so, which ones?

B. Will any of the lists be funny 20 years from now? If so, which ones?

3. **Check the CBS Home Page in your Resource Table. Who are Dave's guests tonight?**

CyberQuest 9

4. **Do a search of people or topics covered. For example, find all of the Top Ten lists that have "Oprah" in them.**

URL: **http://www.cbs.com:80/lateshow/ttlist.html**

Then select the Top Ten List archive.

European Studies — Geography

Visit to European Web Sites

Introduction

Europe offers a state-of-the-art Internet system. In this activity, you will investigate and record unique information on the life, geography, and language of this continent. The Cyber Quest will allow your investigation to go even further, as you consider other European countries.

Objectives

Explore the information services and data available in European countries

Explore LEO, the German equivalent of the Net

Identify unique services provided by various countries' Home Pages

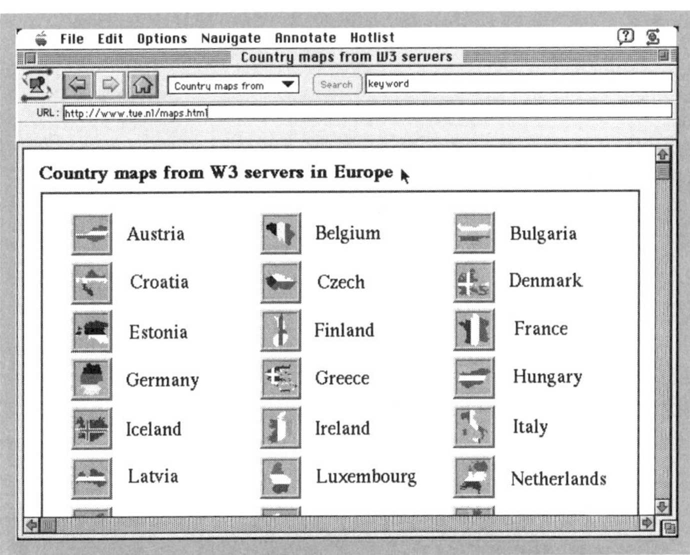

A list of W3 servers in Europe as seen in a Macintosh Mosaic Browser

RESOURCE TABLE

CLIENT	GUI Browser
RESOURCE LOCATION	Locate information on Europe's networks and on its geography, language, and culture: Browser: URL: **http://www.tue.nl/europe/**
SPECIAL ADVICE	If your connection fails, try this alternative. In fact, this option is so good, try it anyway. Browser: URL: **http://s700.uminho.pt/cult-europ.html**

CYBERLOG 10

1. **Use the first URL in the Resource Table to find and select three European countries of your choice. Take notes on each country. Later, from your notes prepare a report on the state of the Internet and the World Wide Web in these countries. For example, try to answer questions as to how many Internet or Web hosts and servers are available in these countries. Are the resources ahead or behind those found on the Internet in the United States? What kind of information can you find that can help you in your studies? in geography? in history? in foreign languages? in music or the arts? Can you get the local time and weather?**

EUROPEAN COUNTRY	NOTES ON INTERNET AND WEB RESOURCES AVAILABLE

2. **Use the second URL in the Resource Table to complete the following.**

A. What is LEO?

B. In what city is LEO located?

C. What are some of the resources and services provided by LEO?

3. **Take the tour of LEO's host city.**

CyberQuest 10

4. **Use the alternative URLs in the Special Advice section of the Resource Table to help you prepare a travel brochure for one of the countries in Europe. Gear your travel brochure to a high-tech electronic Internet traveler wanting to see in person sites that so far have only been available through a computer terminal.**

activity 11

General Resources

AskERIC

Introduction

In today's world, it is not as important to know the right answer as it is to know where to find the right answer. ERIC has been an excellent resource for finding answers for a long time. ERIC (Education Resource Information ClearingHouse) is one of the premiere services available to educational surfers. ERIC is a national information system that answers questions for students, teachers, and librarians.

Objectives

Learn about the ERIC database system

Find answers to educational questions

Learn more than one search method available to you on ERIC

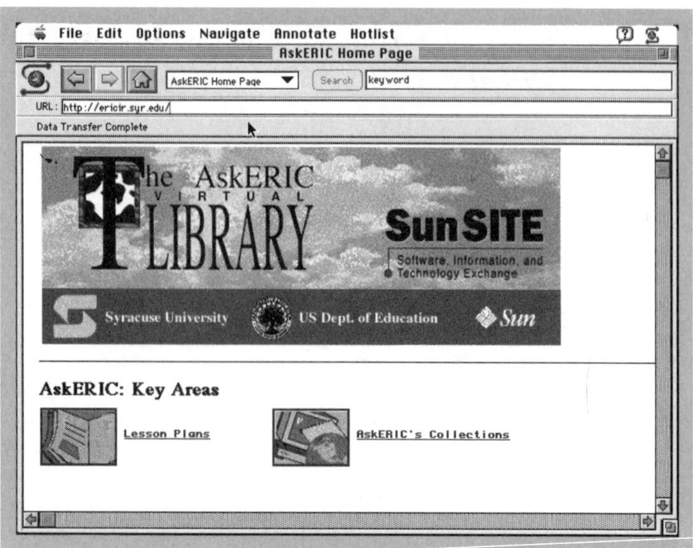

An AskERIC Home Page as seen in a Macintosh Mosaic Browser

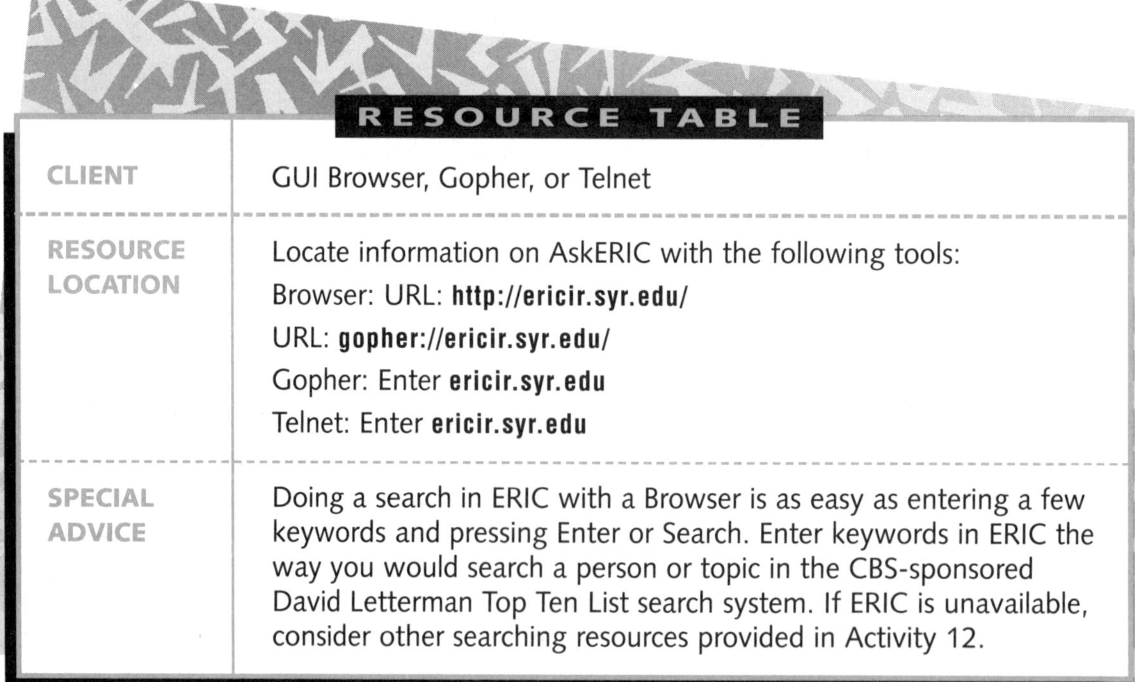

RESOURCE TABLE

CLIENT	GUI Browser, Gopher, or Telnet
RESOURCE LOCATION	Locate information on AskERIC with the following tools: Browser: URL: **http://ericir.syr.edu/** URL: **gopher://ericir.syr.edu/** Gopher: Enter **ericir.syr.edu** Telnet: Enter **ericir.syr.edu**
SPECIAL ADVICE	Doing a search in ERIC with a Browser is as easy as entering a few keywords and pressing Enter or Search. Enter keywords in ERIC the way you would search a person or topic in the CBS-sponsored David Letterman Top Ten List search system. If ERIC is unavailable, consider other searching resources provided in Activity 12.

CyberLog 11

1. **Log in to ERIC using one of the tools listed in the Resource Table.**

A. Where in the world is ERIC located?

B. What is the purpose of ERIC?

C. What are five services offered by ERIC?

2. **Use the Search AskERIC Frequently Asked Questions menu option. URL: gopher://ericir.syr.edu:70/11/FAQ/**

Search for the following terms by entering them in the search box and pressing Enter or Search. How many files or articles are returned to each? How long did it take to search these terms?

	HOW MANY ARTICLES WERE RETURNED	HOW LONG DID IT TAKE TO DO THE SEARCH?
COPYRIGHT SOFTWARE		
LEARNING		
SCHOOLS		

CyberQuest 11

3. **Select one of the articles from your word search and prepare a report on it.**

4. **Try searching other terms. Log the terms in the following table:**

TERMS SEARCHED	HOW MANY ARTICLES WERE RETURNED?	HOW LONG DID IT TAKE TO DO THE SEARCH?

General Resources

Searching with GUI Browser Clients

Introduction

In this activity, you will learn to use various search software clients adapted for your GUI Browser. Many of these searches work the same way as key-word searches. Search software makes it easier to find resources you want and need. There are many specialized search software clients available on the Net. Archie, Veronica, and WAIS are most often mentioned. The Web Crawler and ALIWEB are some others. Some work better or faster than others, but they all can be useful.

Objective

Search with the World Wide Web Worm, Lycos, Web Crawler Search, ALIWEB, Archie, WAIS, and Veronica

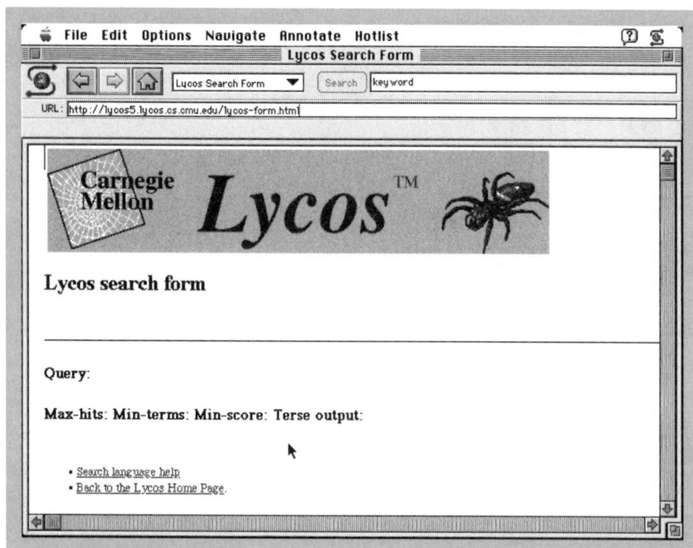

A Lycos search form as seen in a Macintosh Mosaic Browser

RESOURCE TABLE

CLIENT	GUI Browser or Gopher
RESOURCE LOCATION	Locate information on searching with the following tools: Browser: World Wide Web Worm Search: URL: **http://wwww.cs.colorado.edu/wwww** Lycos Search: URL: **http://lycos.cs.cmu.edu** Select a Lycos search form. WebCrawler Search: URL: **http://webcrawler.com** ALIWEB Search: URL: **http://web.nexor.co.uk/public/aliweb/search/doc/form.html** Archie Request Form: URL: **http://hoohoo.ncsa.uiuc.edu/archie.html** WAIS Search: URL: **gopher://joeboy.micro.umn.edu:70/77/books/.waisindex.index** Gopher Search with Veronica: URL: **gopher://mudhoney.micro.umn.edu:4326/7** Gopher: Enter **mudhoney.micro.umn.edu**
SPECIAL ADVICE	Go to the Internet Activities Home Page for an updated list of search engines. Browser: URL: **http://www.thomson.com/swpco/internet/wq50ab1.html**

CYBERLOG 12

1. **Search for keywords and titles with these various search options. You may wish to select one of your favorite artists from Activity 2. Search for the same information on each. Rank each in terms of ease of use, speed, and up-to-date information. (If you get no response, try another one and come back later.)**

   If you run out of ideas, search these words: environment, hubble, fractals, computer software, sports, art museums, and education.

	FAST? YES OR NO	EASY TO USE? YES OR NO	IS THE INFORMATION UP-TO-DATE YES OR NO
WORLD WIDE WEB WORM SEARCH			
WAIS SEARCH			
LYCOS SEARCH			
WEBCRAWLER SEARCH			
ALIWEB SEARCH			
ARCHIE SEARCH			
GOPHER SEARCH			

CyberQuest 12

2. **Pick the most efficient search client from the list above and research a topic for a report due in another class. Try several variations on your searches. For example, try rain forest, then rain forest Brazil or rain forest Belize. Summarize below how valuable the search client was in helping you complete your report.**

Geography — Geophysics

Volcanology

Introduction

Explore the massive impact of volcanoes by searching the resources on the Net. Take advantage of the Earth Observing System (EOS) team, the Jason Project, and the Alaska Volcano Observatory.

Objectives

Learn the terms related to volcanoes

Study infrared images of Mt. St. Helens and Pinatubo

Explore the images taken by volcanologists

Use distance scales to measure plume expansion

Use temperature scales and infrared satellite images to measure plume temperature

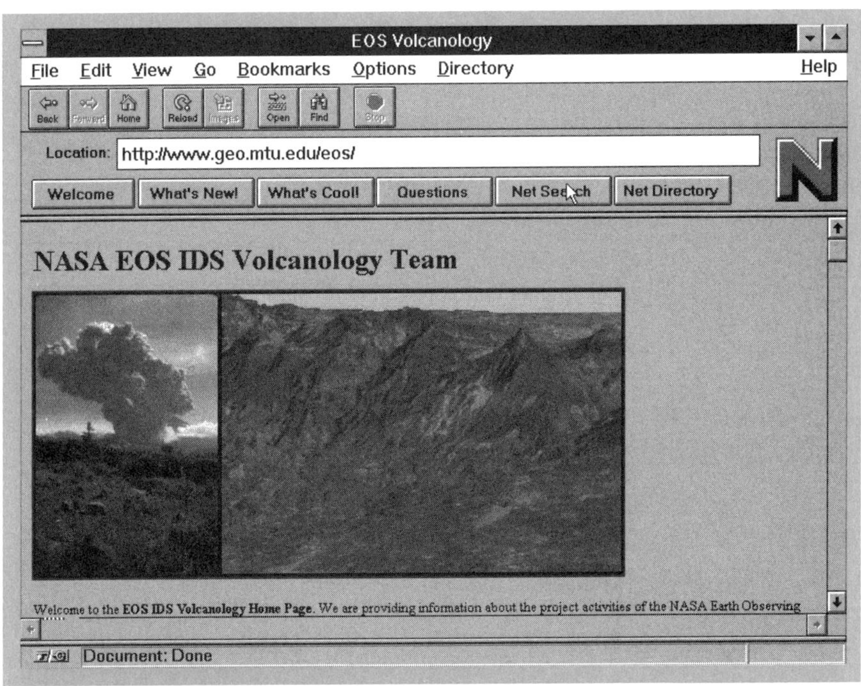

A NASA Volcanology Home Page as seen in a Windows Netscape Browser

RESOURCE TABLE

CLIENT	GUI Browser
RESOURCE LOCATION	Browser: URL: **http://www.geo.mtu.edu/eos/**
SPECIAL ADVICE	For some alternative locations, try the following: Browser: URL: **http://www.avo.alaska.edu/** URL: **http://volcano.und.nodak.edu/** URL: **http://seawifs.gsfc.nasa.gov/JASON.html** URL: **http://info.er.usgs.gov/**

CYBERLOG 13

1. **From the Home Page of the EOS, http://www.geo.mtu.edu/eos, select the topic Volcanoes Studied by the Team. Select Mt. St. Helens. Read the introductory notes and define the following terms:**

A. Plenian eruption______________________________

B. Co-ignimbrite ______________________________

C. Column ______________________________

D. Plume ______________________________

2. **From the "Map Showing the Outline of Eruption Cloud Area," calculate how long it took the plume to reach Wyoming.**

   Eruption time: 8:50

   Wyo Boarder time: ______

   Lapsed time: __________

3. **From the "Visible GEOS-3 Images," explain the meaning of:**

   the light-toned regions ____________________

   the dark-toned regions ____________________

4. **From the "Thermal Infrared GOES-3 Images" at 0850 Pacific time, there is a -65°C temperature reading in the column. Is this accurate? ______ Explain what happened to produce this reading.**

   ____

5. **Return to the "Volcanoes Studied" and select the "Pinatubo" volcano.**

After viewing the four time periods (from 1331-1631) and reading the information, is the eruption expanding equally in all directions? ______

Explain. ____

____

____

CyberQuest 13

The "AVHRR Thermal Infrared Images" record the temperatures in the plume. Using the scale in the bottom right corner of the image, fill in the table. Record all temperatures.

White	_____	to	_____	Yellow	_____	to	_____
Blue	_____	to	_____	Orange	_____	to	_____
Lt. Blue	_____	to	_____	Red	_____	to	_____
Green	_____	to	_____	Black	_____	to	_____
Pink	_____	to	_____				

Government and Civics

U.S. House of Representatives

Introduction

Government is most effective when citizens know how it works and who is in charge. Both the Democrats and Republicans have had their chances at controlling the House of Representatives and the Senate throughout the years. With all the changes, knowing your new congressional leaders, their positions, and their responsibilities can be very valuable.

Objectives

Study the leaders of Congress

Identify your representatives and senators

Learn how to contact your representatives and senators on-line

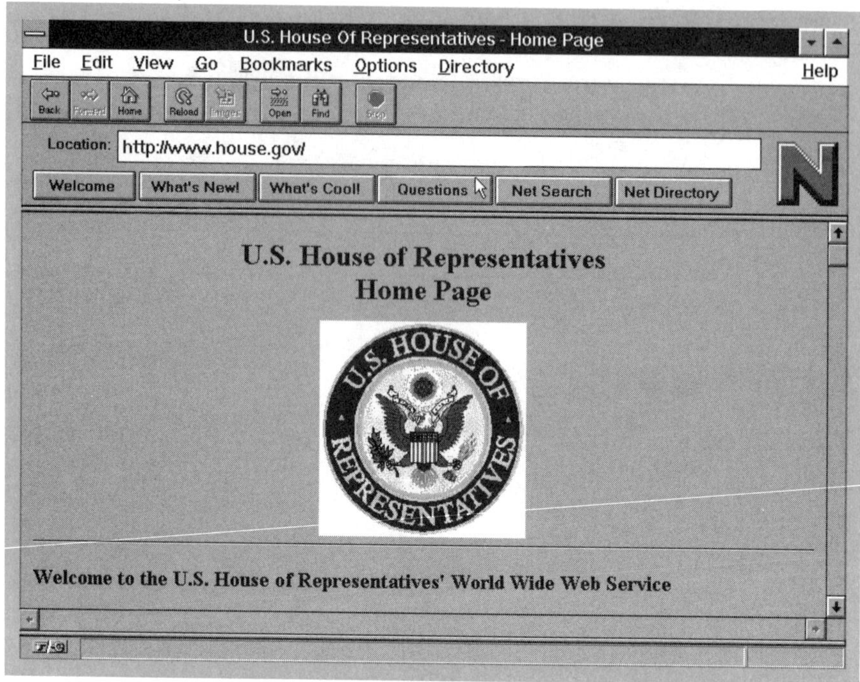

The House of Representatives Home Page as seen in a Windows Netscape Browser

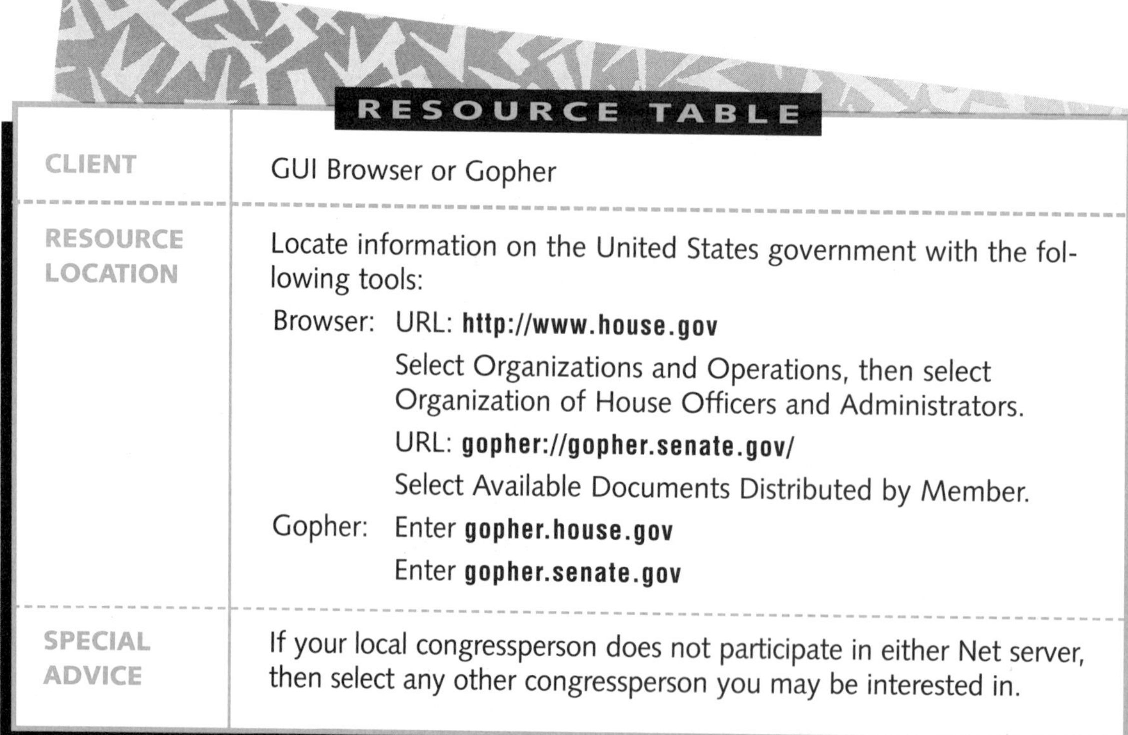

RESOURCE TABLE

CLIENT	GUI Browser or Gopher
RESOURCE LOCATION	Locate information on the United States government with the following tools: Browser: URL: **http://www.house.gov** Select Organizations and Operations, then select Organization of House Officers and Administrators. URL: **gopher://gopher.senate.gov/** Select Available Documents Distributed by Member. Gopher: Enter **gopher.house.gov** Enter **gopher.senate.gov**
SPECIAL ADVICE	If your local congressperson does not participate in either Net server, then select any other congressperson you may be interested in.

CYBERLOG 14

Complete the following questions to the best of your ability:

1. **Access this chart by following the URL provided in the Resource Table. Label each box below with the appropriate information.**

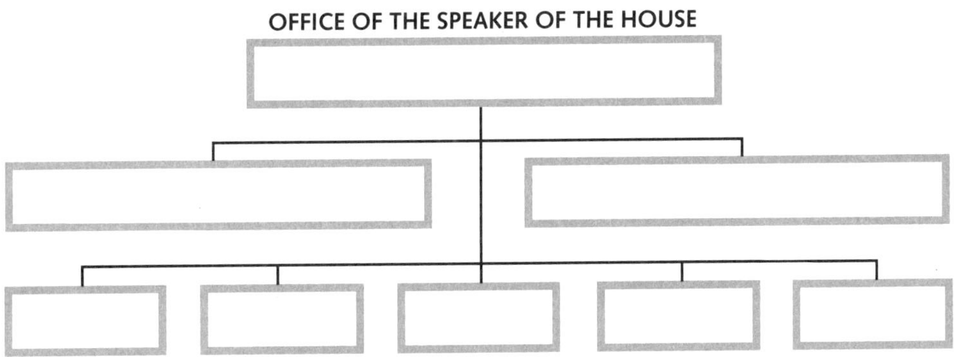

2. **Surf to the U.S. House of Representatives Member Directory. Locate your representative in the House of Representatives and record the following information:**

   District: ________________ Washington Office: ________________

   E-mail Address: __________ Service Start Date: ________________

   One Committee: _________ One Legislation Sponsored: ___________

3. **Go to the Senate Gopher Server and examine the available documents distributed by members. Determine the percentage of senators that actually use this server to provide those they represent with up-to-date information. (Assume there are 100 senators that could use this system.) (Example: 55 out of 100 = 55%) _____%**

CYBERQUEST 14

4. **Create a letter you could E-mail to a senator or representative, asking his or her position on funding for the Net. Submit the letter to your teacher to review.**

History

The Mayflower Compact and the Monroe Doctrine

Introduction

The Internet makes available the original texts of many of our national historical documents. Explore the original text of the *Mayflower Compact*. Then read President Monroe's address that began the policy known as the *Monroe Doctrine*.

Objectives

Read the *Mayflower Compact*

Identify the major values of these early settlers

Identify changes in language usage

Read the text of President Monroe's address

Identify several events that were happening at the time of this address

Explore the impact of this address on later presidents

ftp://ftp.spies.com/Gov/US-History/mayflow.cp
File Edit View Go Bookmarks Options Directory Help
Back Forward Home Reload Images Open Find Stop
Location: ftp://ftp.spies.com/Gov/US-History/mayflow.cp
Welcome What's New! What's Cool! Questions Net Search Net Directory
THE MAYFLOWER COMPACT:
"In the name of God, Amen. We, whose names are underwritten, the Loyal Subjects of our dread Sovereign Lord, King James, by the Grace of God, of England, France and Ireland, King, Defender of the Faith, e&.
Having undertaken for the Glory of God, and Advancement of the Christian Faith, and the Honour of our King and Country, a voyage to plant the first colony in the northern parts of Virginia; do by these presents, solemnly and mutually in the Presence of God and one of another, covenant and combine ourselves together into a civil Body Politick, for our better Ordering and Preservation, and Furtherance of the Ends aforesaid; And by Virtue hereof to enact, constitute, and frame, such just and equal Laws, Ordinances, Acts, Constitutions and Offices, from time to time, as shall be thought most meet and convenient for the General good of the Colony; unto which we promise all due

Text of the *Mayflower Compact* as seen in a Windows Netscape Browser

RESOURCE TABLE

CLIENT	GUI Browser
RESOURCE LOCATION	Locate the documents on the *Mayflower Compact* and the *Monroe Doctrine* with the following tools: Browser: URL: **ftp://ftp.spies.com/** Select directories */Gov* then */US-History*. Look for the files *mayflow.cp* and *monroe.doc*. FTP: Enter **ftp.spies.com** Then search the directories as shown above.
SPECIAL ADVICE	With FTP, log in as anonymous. Use your E-mail address as the password.

CYBERLOG 15

Answer the following questions to the best of your ability. Use the address in the Resource Table to search for the Mayflower Compact and the Monroe Doctrine.

1. **Who wrote the *Mayflower Compact*?**

2. **When was the *Mayflower Compact* created?**

3. **List five important values expressed in the *Mayflower Compact*.**

A. ______________________________

B. ______________________________

C. ______________________________

D. ______________________________

E. ______________________________

4. **What was the date of Monroe's address?**

5. **Who was the president addressing?**

6. **In your own words, what is the *Monroe Doctrine*?**

____

____

CyberQuest 15

7. **Had the Native Americans created the *Monroe Doctrine* before the arrival of the Pilgrims, how would that have affected colonization in the Americas? Complete a report on this topic with a word processor or handwritten on a separate paper.**

History

Introduction

The Web can preserve the history of peoples, places, and events. One of the most tragic events in the history of civilization was the Holocaust. Those who lived through that terrible period of history are remembered on Web sites around the world.

Objectives

Use the Net to become more personally aware of the Holocaust tragedy

Learn about the Holocaust from the eyewitness accounts provided on the Net

Examine various memorials to the Holocaust tragedy around the world

RESOURCE TABLE

CLIENT	GUI Browser
RESOURCE LOCATION	Locate information on the Holocaust on the WWW. Browser: URL: **http://www.ushmm.org/** Browser: URL: **www.channels.nl/annefran.html**
SPECIAL ADVICE	You can find many more sites by searching the word HOLOCAUST in a search engine.

CyberLog 16

1. **Visit each of the sites listed in the Resource Table. If for any reason these sites are down, key the word *Holocaust* in a search engine to find alternative sites. Answer the following questions.**

A. Who developed and ran the camps discussed in the Holocaust pages?

B. What different peoples and nationalities were victims of the Nazi holocaust?

C. Pick one of the camps, such as Auschwitz. Prepare a short report of 50-100 words on the camp and what happened there.

2. **Prepare a short report on Anne Frank. (Use the URL: http://www.channels.nl/annefran.html or search for Anne Frank in a search engine as explained in Activity 12.) Answer some of the following questions in your report.**

A. Where did she live?

B. Where did she hide from the Nazis?

C. What eventually became of her?

D. How did we find out about her life?

E. In which country is the Web site **http://www.channels.nl/annefran.html** located?

Journalism

On-Line Newspapers and Publications

Introduction

There is a movement away from printed magazines and newspapers. On-line newspapers and magazines are considered a wave of the future. In this activity, you will access a listing of commercial on-line publication projects. This list includes address information, contact information, and a description of each service. In the Cyber Quest, you will see what is happening on the college scene with college on-line newspapers.

Objectives

Recognize the impact of on-line communication media

Identify different kinds of news media available on-line

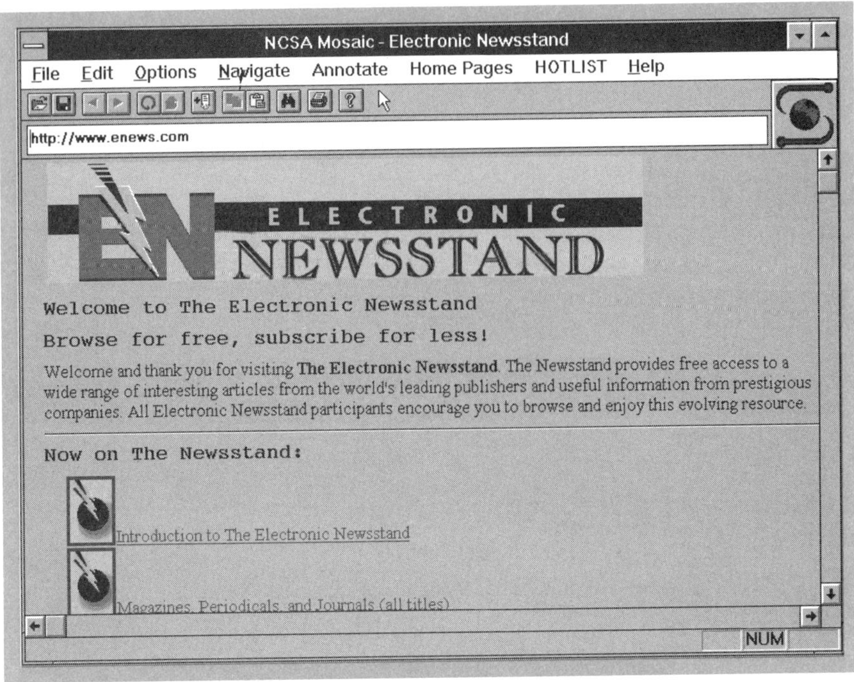

The Electronic Newsstand Home Page as seen in a Windows Mosaic Browser

RESOURCE TABLE

CLIENT	GUI Browser or E-mail
RESOURCE LOCATION	Locate information on journalism with the following tools: Browser: URL: **http://www.enews.com/** To receive this file by E-mail, send your message to **majordomo@marketplace.com.** In the body of the message, enter *get online-news online-newspapers.list*. The file will be delivered to you as an E-mail message.
SPECIAL ADVICE	Many colleges also provide on-line newspapers. Check Browser: URL: **http://www.yahoo.com/News** and then search for University New.

CyberLog 17

1. From the Electronic Newsstand Home Page, select Magazines, Periodicals and Journal (All Titles), then open the Best of the Newsstand and browse through the articles. Fill in the table below as you view the documents.

ARTICLE NAME	SOURCE OF THE ARTICLE	OVERVIEW OF ARTICLE

CyberQuest 17

2. Check out some of the university campus newspapers. Use the alternative URL provided in the Special Advice section of the Resource Table and pick several of the colleges of your choice. List the college, the name of the paper, and the URL or location of the newspaper.

COLLEGE	NAME OF SCHOOL PAPER	URL OR LOCATION

Language Arts

Purdue University On-Line Writing Lab

Introduction

Writing can be a challenging task. The Net provides a whole new world of assistance to help you with your writing. Search the Purdue University On-line Writing Lab (OWL) for help, writing tools, and advice on your writing. The Purdue Writing Lab has more than 100 different documents with a wide-ranging collection of pointers. You can even E-mail the lab with specific questions about the writing process.

Objectives

Contact the Purdue Writing Lab with either your Browser, Gopher, FTP, or E-mail client

Discover new ways to improve your writing

Identify five significant writing resources at this on-line location

Prepare and submit a grammar question that will help you with your next essay or paper

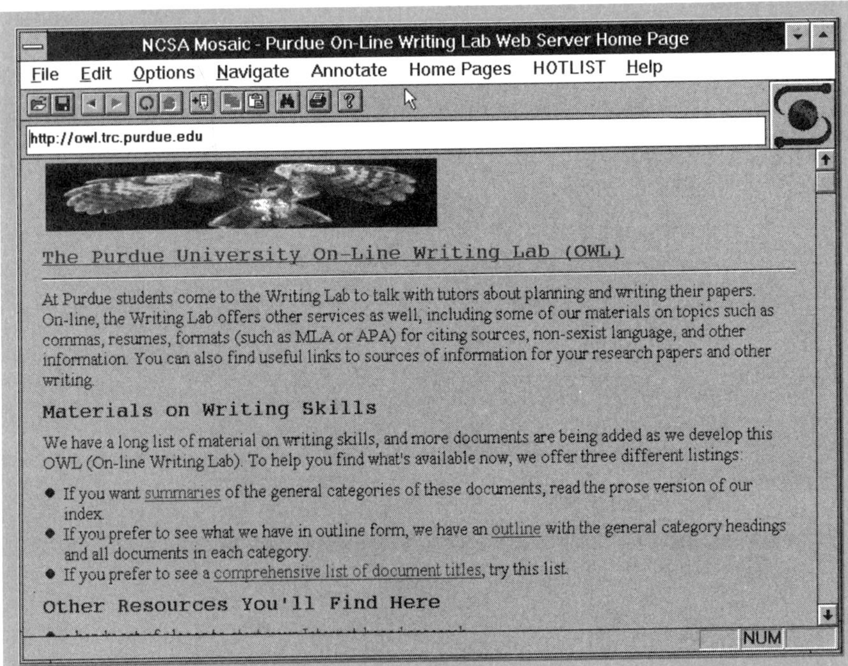

The Purdue Writing Lab Home Page as seen in a Windows Mosaic Browser

RESOURCE TABLE

CLIENT	GUI Browser, Gopher, FTP, or E-mail
RESOURCE LOCATION	Locate the Purdue Writing Lab with the following tools: Browser: URL: **http://owl.english.purdue.edu/** **gopher://owl.english.purdue.edu/** E-mail your request to **owl@sage.cc.purdue.edu.** The subject should be Owl-request and the body contains your question. Allow 48 hours for the return of your E-mail.
SPECIAL ADVICE	Observe Netiquette while doing this activity. Do not submit repetitive requests. Do not send silly requests. Don't waste the time of this resource! Keep your questions short and to the point.

CYBERLOG 18

1. **Cruise this site for five writing resources. Record the name of the resource, and explain why the resource is valuable to you.**

NAME OF RESOURCE	WHY IS THIS RESOURCE VALUABLE TO YOU?

2. Complete the questionnaire found at hyperlink "Fill out our OWL user survey."

CyberQuest 18

3. OWL allows you to ask questions of the students and professors that work at the Purdue Writing Lab. Identify three weaknesses in your writing. Create a carefully worded letter asking for help with your writing. You can address issues like punctuation, capitalization, paragraphing, and sentence structure. Submit your letter to your teacher. Your teacher will select one letter or combine the ideas from several letters. Don't send one letter per student because this excellent resource could be overwhelmed.

____

____

____

____

____

____

____

Latin American Studies — Geography

Hola!

Introduction

Learn Spanish direct from Latin America. Explore the geography of many countries with the virtual reality of the Net. Latin America is considered a set of developing countries. However, Latin America's Internet capability may surprise you. With the Net just a few keystrokes away, valuable and up-to-date information can be surfed, which helps you be more aware of these countries and their Web capabilities.

Objectives

Read the local news from all over Latin America

Explore the geography of Latin America

Explore the resources and programs of the Latin American universities

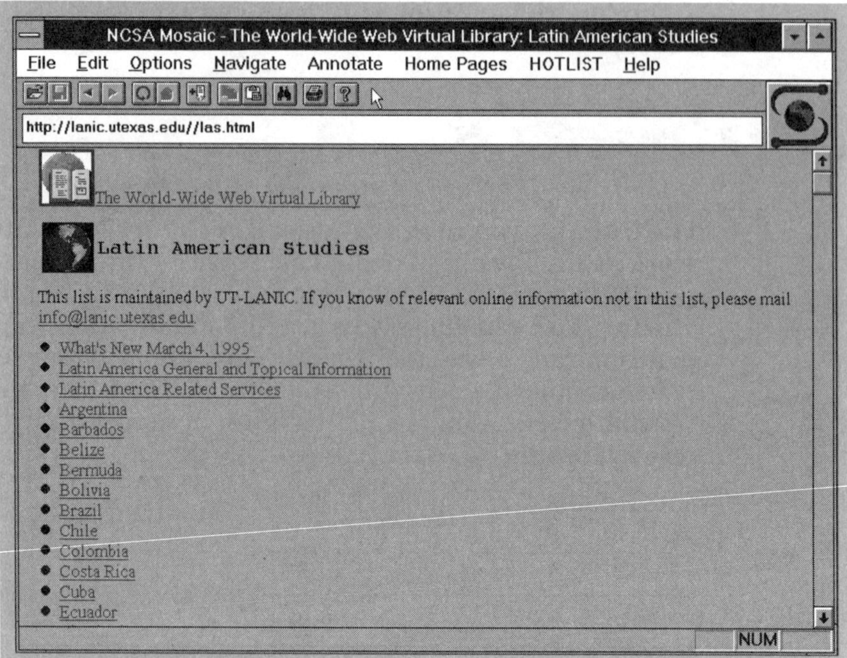

A Latin American Starting Points Home Page as seen in a Windows Mosaic Browser

RESOURCE TABLE

CLIENT	GUI Browser
RESOURCE LOCATION	Locate information on Latin American countries with the following tools: Browser: URL: **http://lanic.utexas.edu/las.html** URL: **http://sunsite.dcc.uchile.cl/chile/chile.html** URL: **http://www.univalle.edu.co/Colombia.html** URL: **http://www.mty.itesm.mx/MexWeb/Mapa1/**
SPECIAL ADVICE	Browser: URL: **http://www.w3.org/pub/DataSources/WWW/Servers.html**

CyberLog 19

1. **Select five Latin American countries. Read and record three facts or pieces of new information you learn about these countries.**

Country: Information and Facts:

____

____

____

Country: Information and Facts:

____

____

____

Country: Information and Facts:

____

____

____

Country: Information and Facts:

____

____

____

Country: Information and Facts:

____

____

____

2. **Latin America has many fine universities. Identify ten universities in at least three different countries, and list a notable resource or program from each.**

	Country	University	Describe the resource
1.	______	______	______________________
2.	______	______	______________________
3.	______	______	______________________
4.	______	______	______________________

5. ______ ______ ____________________________________

6. ______ ______ ____________________________________

7. ______ ______ ____________________________________

8. ______ ______ ____________________________________

9. ______ ______ ____________________________________

10. ______ ______ ____________________________________

CyberQuest 19

3. Some countries have provided maps on the Internet.

Select four countries and access their maps. Identify four cities and four legends from each map (i.e., roads, lakes, rivers, mountains, locations, scale of map, etc.).

Country:______________	Legends:
City 1:______________	1.______________________________
City 2:______________	2.______________________________
City 3:______________	3.______________________________
City 4:______________	4.______________________________

Country:______________	Legends:
City 1:______________	1.______________________________
City 2:______________	2.______________________________
City 3:______________	3.______________________________
City 4:______________	4.______________________________

Country:________________

City 1:________________

City 2:________________

City 3:________________

City 4:________________

Legends:

1.______________________________

2.______________________________

3.______________________________

4.______________________________

Country:________________

City 1:________________

City 2:________________

City 3:________________

City 4:________________

Legends:

1.______________________________

2.______________________________

3.______________________________

4.______________________________

Law

Take It to the Supreme Court

Introduction

Have you ever wanted to be a Supreme Court Justice? In this activity, you will learn the way the Supreme Court thinks. You can learn how they arrive at decisions on famous legal cases. You will visit Project Hermes and obtain files on Supreme Court opinions. Learn as much as you can about the opinions of a specific judge.

Objectives

Become better acquainted with major Supreme Court decisions

Understand why a particular justice made a particular decision

Learn to analyze, evaluate, and make your own conclusions

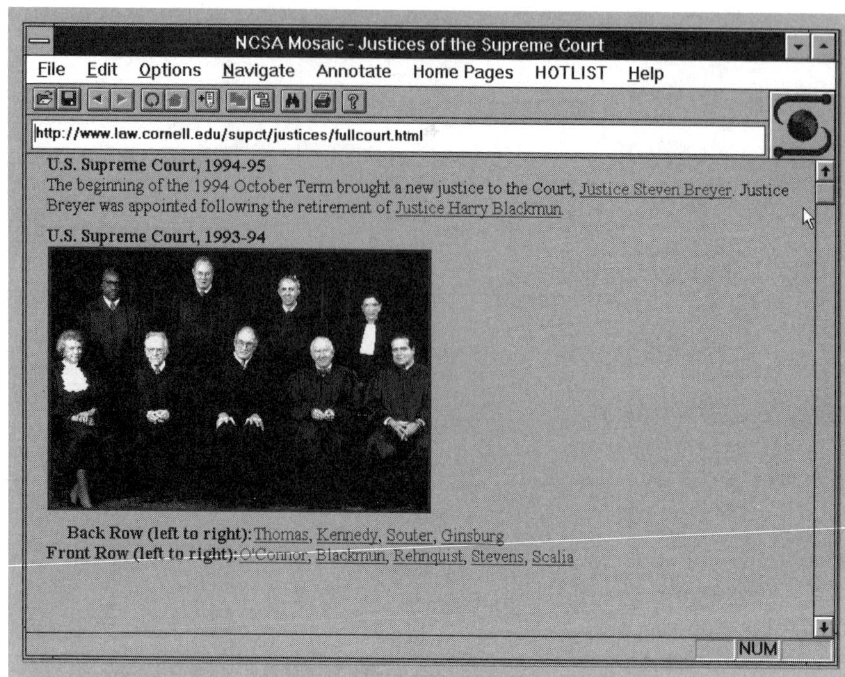

The Cornell Supreme Court Home Page as seen in a Windows Mosaic Browser

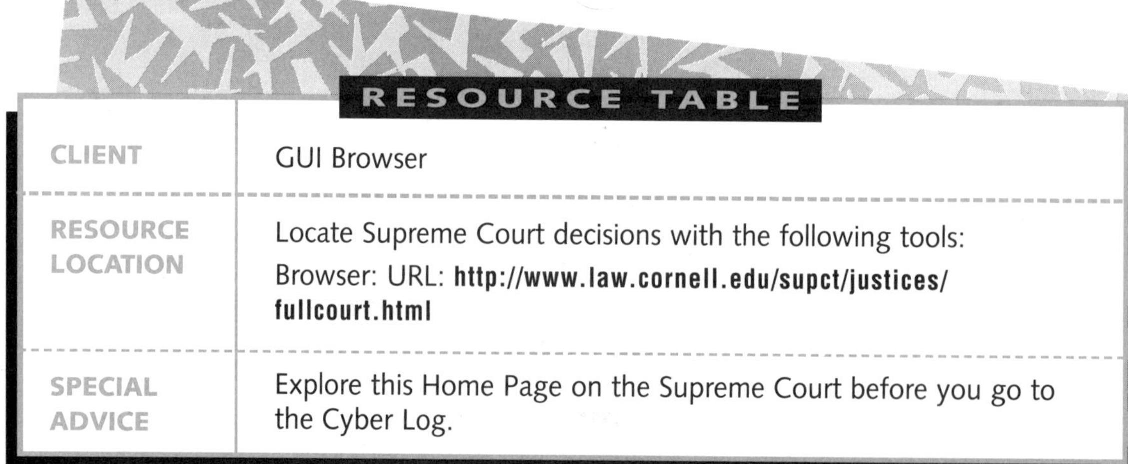

RESOURCE TABLE

CLIENT	GUI Browser
RESOURCE LOCATION	Locate Supreme Court decisions with the following tools: Browser: URL: **http://www.law.cornell.edu/supct/justices/fullcourt.html**
SPECIAL ADVICE	Explore this Home Page on the Supreme Court before you go to the Cyber Log.

CyberLog 20

1. **Connect to the resource as listed in the Resource Table for this activity. Use the full URL (. . . fullcourt.html). Choose a justice by clicking on him or her in the picture. Read the biography and record the following information:**

A. What is the name of the justice you have selected?

B. How old is this justice?

C. What specific assignments did this justice have during his or her career?

D. What president appointed this person as an Associate Justice?

CyberQuest 20

2. **Read through a case of one justice. It is a hypertext link from the biography page labeled Recent Decisions. Answer the following questions:**

A. What was the name of the justice?

B. What is the name of the case you have selected?

C. Describe what the case was about.

D. What points were presented in the decision by the Court?

E. What was the ruling of the Court on this case?

Marketing

InterNIC-PC Catalog

Introduction

In this activity, you will examine several computer products, then record the best three prices you can find for each product listed. Also list anything special that ought to be considered regarding each product. The Cyber Quest in this activity will give you a chance to anticipate your own school's next major computer product purchase. In addition, you will also get price quotes for your configuration one to two months later to see how the prices changed.

Objectives

Learn comparative shopping on the Net quickly, easily, and electronically

Develop critical marketing-oriented synthesis and evaluation skills

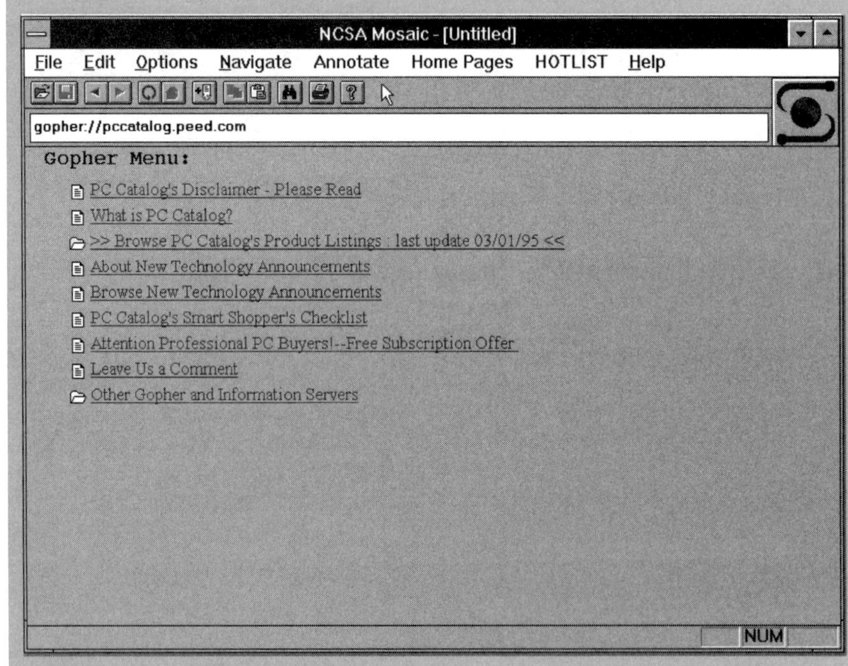

A Gopher menu as seen in a Windows Mosaic Browser

RESOURCE TABLE

CLIENT	GUI Browser or Gopher
RESOURCE LOCATION	Locate marketing data on computer products with the following tools: Browser: URL: **http://www.yahoo.com/Business_and_Economy/Companies/Computers** URL: **http://www.peed.com/** URL: **http://www.pc-today.com/manufacturers.html**
SPECIAL ADVICE	You can do a lot of shopping on the Net. You can find nearly any computer of piece of computer equipment on the Net. If you get stuck, use a search engine (Activity 12) or look for additional resources on the Internet Activities Home Page at: Browser: URL: **http://www.thomson.com/swpco/internet/wq50ab1.html**

CYBERLOG 21

1. **Review the PC Catalog on-line. Complete the table below for the various products listed. For the Cyber Quest activity, return to this chart in two months and see how much prices have changed.**

PRODUCT AND PRODUCT FEATURES	MAIL ORDER VENDOR OR COMPANY NAME	PRICE PER UNIT / PRICE TWO MONTHS LATER
Computer: (List the features like CPU/mhz, RAM, floppy drives, hard disk capacity, etc.)		

PRODUCT AND PRODUCT FEATURES	MAIL ORDER VENDOR OR COMPANY NAME	PRICE PER UNIT / PRICE TWO MONTHS LATER
Monitor: (Dot pitch, screen size, resolution, graphics card, etc.)		
Modem: (Baud rate, Internal/ external, etc.)		
CD-ROM: (MPC compliant, capacity, buffer size, access and data transfer rate, etc.)		
Laser Printer: (Memory, pages per minute, dpi, toner cartridge life, etc.)		

PRODUCT AND PRODUCT FEATURES	MAIL ORDER VENDOR OR COMPANY NAME	PRICE PER UNIT / PRICE TWO MONTHS LATER
Software Applications: (List choices, word processing, spreadsheets, database, games, etc.)		

CyberQuest 21

2. **Return to this chart in two months and see how much prices have changed. Record your new prices. Then briefly answer this question: What could have caused these prices to go up and down?**

Mathematics

Bring Home the Goods with AMS

Introduction

The American Mathematical Society (AMS) is one of the richest mathematical resources on the Net. Many math-related opportunities are presented on this Home Page. The Home Page is appropriately labeled e-MATH (which stands for electronic math). This Home Page is the Internet's version of a mathematician's survival kit on the Net.

Objectives

Discover all the options available to the math-minded on the AMS Home Page

Complete the Cyber Log with specific direction from your teacher

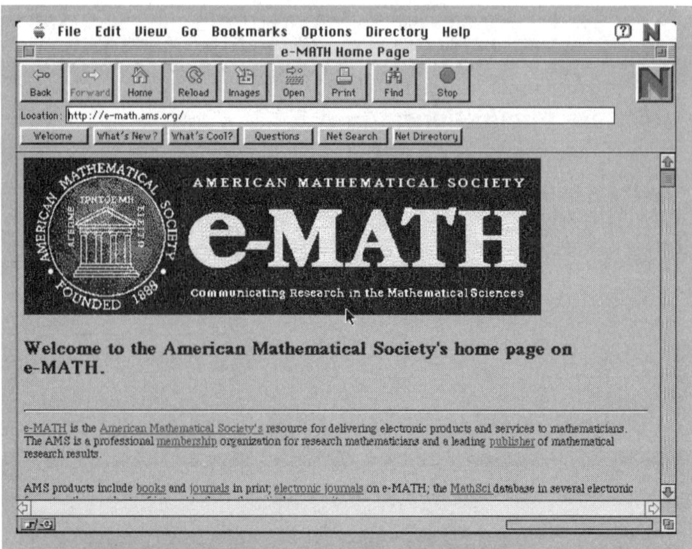

The e-Math Home Page as seen in a Macintosh Netscape Browser

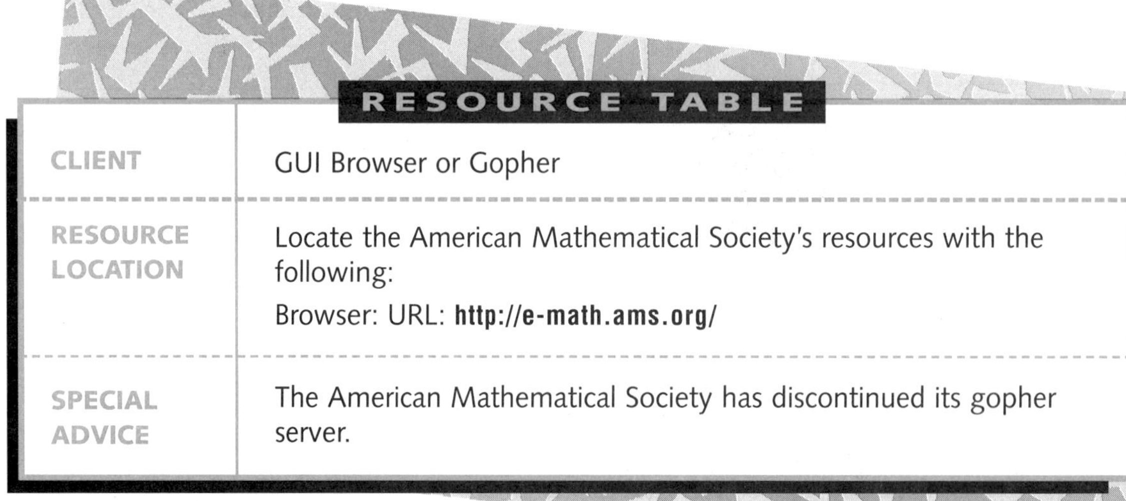

RESOURCE TABLE

CLIENT	GUI Browser or Gopher
RESOURCE LOCATION	Locate the American Mathematical Society's resources with the following: Browser: URL: **http://e-math.ams.org/**
SPECIAL ADVICE	The American Mathematical Society has discontinued its gopher server.

CYBERLOG 22

1. **Investigate five math-related hypertext-linked areas valuable to you. Record the URL for each link and describe the potential use.**

URL/LOCATION	HYPERTEXT LINK TITLES	HOW COULD YOU USE THIS INFORMATION?

CYBERQUEST 22

2. **Investigate more thoroughly one of the hypertext links you recorded in the Cyber Log. Summarize how this link is uniquely valuable in helping you gain a better appreciation and understanding for the current mathematics topic you are learning. *(Remember, this link needs to offer a unique capability. In other words, you could not get this assistance and exposure any other way.)***

Mathematics

Fractals, Expanding the Universe

Introduction

Fractals describe complex images. Computer technologies have increased the potential of this field of mathematics. There are challenges for the beginner and questions that will challenge the most advanced student in the fractal universe.

Objectives

Access current information on fractal development

Learn the eight major fractal divisions

View the images created by fractal equations

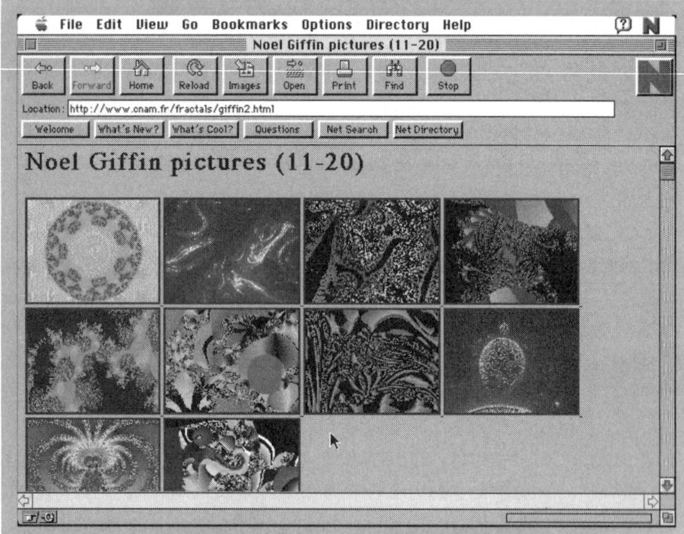

A Fractals Home Page as seen in a Macintosh Netscape Browser

RESOURCE TABLE

CLIENT	GUI Browser
RESOURCE LOCATION	Locate resources on fractals: Browser: URL: **http://www.cnam.fr/fractals.html**
SPECIAL ADVICE	For an alternative location on fractals, try this: Browser: URL: **http://spanky.triumf.ca/**

CyberLog 23

Complete the following questions as thoroughly as possible:

1. **Find the definitions to the terms below in the section Fractal FAQs**
   fractal: ______________________
   strange attractor: ______________________
   Mandelbrot set: ______________________
   Julia set: ______________________
   Lyapunov fractals: ______________________
   chaos: ______________________

2. **Scroll down the Home Page to the bullets. View at least one of each type listed. WARNING: The animations require an mpeg viewer to be installed. You may not be able to view the animation selections.**

DIVISION	IMAGE VIEWED	YOUR OBSERVATION
Example: *ifs*	*fern2.gif*	*Looks like a fern leaf. Notice that each segment of the fern leaf is a repetition of the whole.*
Mandelbrot		
Noel Giffin		
Miscellaneous		
Flame		
Lyapunov		
Mandelbrot 3D		
Paolo Cozzi		

CyberQuest 23

3. **Summarize the impressions you have of a fractal image. Are there any that remind you of some real-life scene or some other familiar object? Pick a fractal from the Cyber Log and describe in some detail what it looks like. Try to draw similar patterns with a draw or paint program.**

Meteorology

Visiting NCAR

Introduction

Current information! That is what the Internet is all about. In no other subject is current information so vital as in the study of weather or meteorology. In this activity, you will take a look at current weather information for the continental United States. The images you are about to see are updated every hour. They include visible and infrared photos, complete surface weather maps, and weather warnings.

Objectives

Locate current weather information

Record weather conditions across the continental United States

The NCAR Meterology Home Page as seen in a Macintosh Netscape Browser

RESOURCE TABLE

CLIENT	GUI Browser
RESOURCE LOCATION	Locate information on meteorology with the following URLs: Browser: URL: **http://www.ncar.edu/**, scroll down to Weather-Information, select Current Satellite images. For additional information use these sites: URL: **http://www.ucar.edu/** URL: **http://www.ssec/wisc.edu/data/index.html** For current weather related information from schools, try this site: URL: **http://www.aws.com/globalwx.html**
SPECIAL ADVICE	In this activity, you will work with infrared, visual, and surface weather maps and data. You may also want to try this site: **http://www.atmos.uiuc.edu**

CYBERLOG 24

1. **Answer the following questions with the help of the URLs in the Resource Table. Make sure you scroll up and down the entire screen to find your answer.**

A. What does NCAR stand for? ______________________________

B. Summarize NCAR's mission statement. ______________________

____

____

____

____

2. **Fill in the table from the current images and information. You will need to estimate the location of each city on the six U.S. weather maps found at the URL / Location indicated in the Resource Table.**

CITY, STATE	CLOUD COVER (Sunny, partly cloudy, overcast)	PRECIPI-TATION (rain, snow, clear, scattered showers)	TEMPERA-TURE (record the degrees from the map)	DEW POINT (record the degrees from the map)	WIND VELOCITY (record the velocity from the map)
New York, NY					
Atlanta, GA					
Dallas, TX					
Salt Lake City, UT					
Los Angeles, CA					
Your Town					
Time					
Date					

CyberQuest 24

3. **Search the same weather information you see above for cities in Canada. What is the average temperature difference between three Canadian cities and the cities listed in the Cyber Log?**

4. **Check out the weather in Africa and in Asia. Explore the following URL from Antarctica. Can you find the current weather at the South Pole?**

URL: **http://quest.arc.nasa.gov/livefrom/livefrom.html**

Music

Popular Lyrics

Introduction

Do you need the lyrics to your favorite songs? You can look up the lyrics to thousands of today's popular songs on the Net. In this activity, you will search for four of your favorite songs and record the lyrics of each. You will also be asked to record some information about each song in the Cyber Log and answer some questions about the songs you have selected in the Cyber Quest.

Objectives

Observe specific information about four songs of your choice

Answer the questions regarding your choices

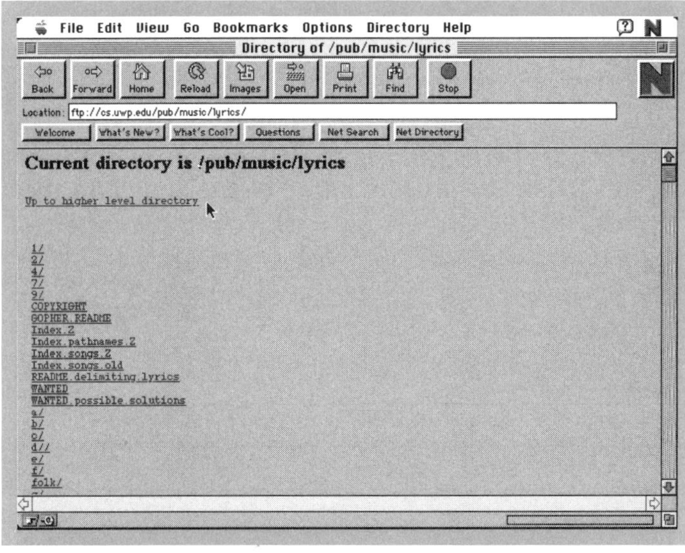

An FTP directory as seen in a Macintosh Netscape Browser

RESOURCE TABLE

CLIENT	GUI Browser or FTP
RESOURCE LOCATION	Locate musical information with the following tools: Browser: URL: **ftp://cs.uwp.edu/pub/music/lyrics/** then select the alphabetic letter subdirectory that represents an artist or song you are interested in. FTP: Enter **ftp.uwp.edu/pub/music/lyrics/** then select the alphabetic letter subdirectory that represents an artist or song you are interested in.
SPECIAL ADVICE	Lyrics provides the words to thousands of popular songs. **Read the copyright statement!** Search for your favorite artist by using a search engine. See Activity 12.

CyberLog 25

1. **Read the copyright statement at the beginning of the screen. Select four songs, each from a different artist. Record the name of the song and the artist, then record the lyrics.**

   Song Title:

   Artist Name:

   Lyrics:

   ____

   ____

   ____

   ____

   Song Title:

   Artist Name:

   Lyrics:

   ____

   ____

   ____

   ____

Song Title:
Artist Name:
Lyrics:

Song Title:
Artist Name:
Lyrics:

CyberQuest 25

2. **Compare the lyrics of two artists. What is similar or different about their lyrics? What do they sing about? How do their styles differ?**

Photography

Ansel Adams

Introduction

This activity gives you the opportunity to study the techniques of a true master photographer. Even though the Net started off as a text-based, electronic superhighway, today it can bring you up close and personal with many visual experiences.

Objectives

Study the photos of Ansel Adams

Review his work

Study other photography-related activities

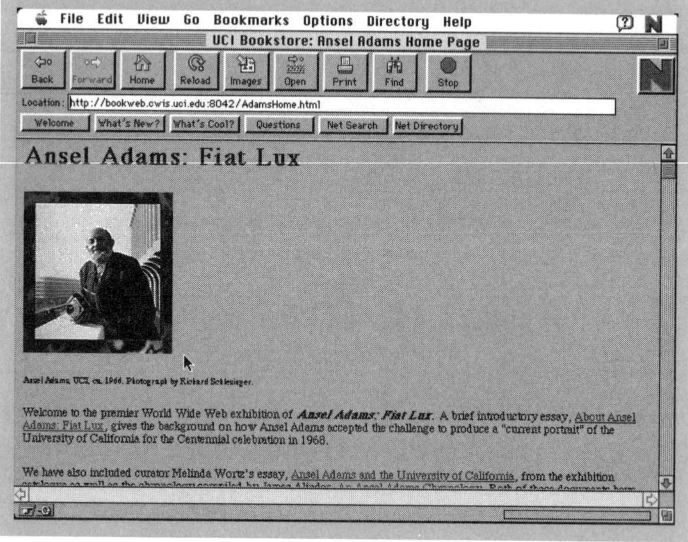

The Ansel Adams Home Page as seen in a Macintosh Netscape Browser

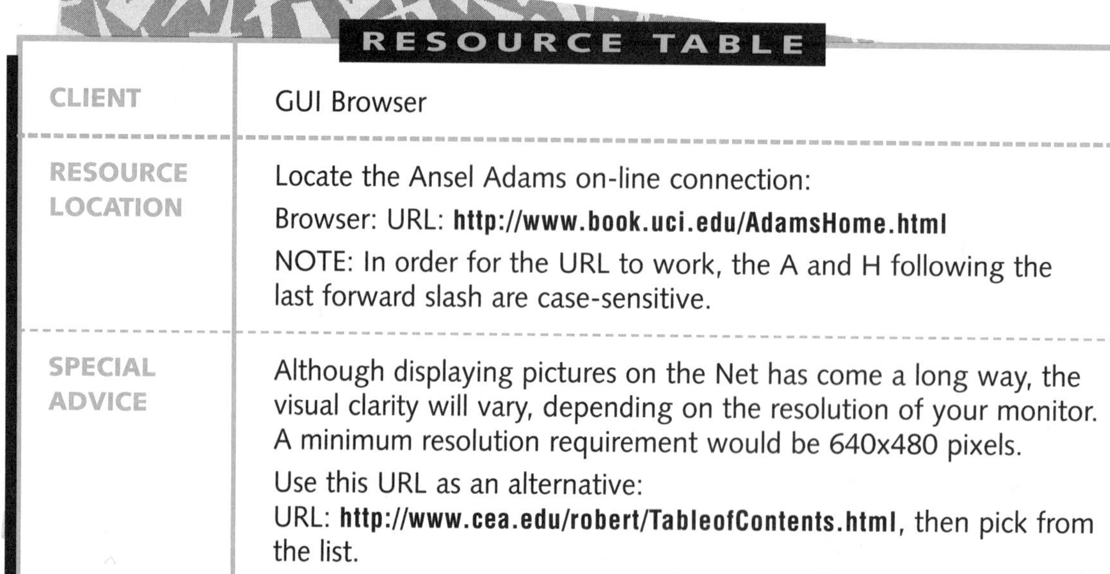

RESOURCE TABLE

CLIENT	GUI Browser
RESOURCE LOCATION	Locate the Ansel Adams on-line connection: Browser: URL: **http://www.book.uci.edu/AdamsHome.html** NOTE: In order for the URL to work, the A and H following the last forward slash are case-sensitive.
SPECIAL ADVICE	Although displaying pictures on the Net has come a long way, the visual clarity will vary, depending on the resolution of your monitor. A minimum resolution requirement would be 640x480 pixels. Use this URL as an alternative: URL: **http://www.cea.edu/robert/TableofContents.html**, then pick from the list.

CyberLog 26

1. At the bottom of the Home Page is the Exhibit Organization. Select the Tour The Fiat Lux Exhibition. Select the Natural Reserve System. Review five photographs by Ansel Adams.

DATE	TITLE	DESCRIPTION

2. Is there a recurring theme in his work? If so, what is it?

____

____

From the Home Page hypertext link, An Ansel Adams Chronology, answer the following:

3. When and where was the first public demonstration of the daguerreotype?

____

4. Ansel worked at the ____________________ National Park.

5. What organization was he president of? ____________________

6. Where were the headquarters of this organization? ________________

CyberQuest 26

7. For a change of pace, try a USENET Newsgroup on photography.

   USENET: **rec.photo.darkroom**

   URL: **http://www.yahoo.com/Art/Photography/**, then select the USENET, followed by a Newsgroup called **rec.photo.darkroom**.

   This Newsgroup provides information on setting up your own photo lab and darkroom. List the essential elements of a well-equipped lab and darkroom.

Science

Virtual Frog Dissection

Introduction

Explore the anatomy of a frog without the messy cleanup and smelly stuff they use in the biology lab. This environmentally correct frog dissection program is a must for all future biologists.

Objectives

Learn the major organs of a frog

Study the skeletal structure of a frog

Select various dissection options

RESOURCE TABLE

CLIENT	GUI Browser
RESOURCE LOCATION	Locate historical information on the virtual frog dissection: Browser: URL: **http://george.lbl.gov/ITG/Whole.Frog/frog/frog.anatomy.html** NOTE: ITG and W and F following ITG must be capitalized. Try this URL to complete the Cyber Quest: URL: **http://george.lbl.gov/ITG.hm.pg.docs/dissect/info.html** Select the hypertext link START. NOTE: ITG is in capital letters.
SPECIAL ADVICE	This is a development project of the NREN multi-gigabit network being called the electronic superhighway.

CyberLog 27

1. **For each of the following views, list the parts of the frog shown on your screen.**

Skeletal View

___

___

Digestive View

___

___

Nervous System View

___

___

Organs View

___

___

CyberQuest 27

2. **Read the instructions provided with the virtual frog dissection. Fill out your requests and options on-line. View the frog without skin. Then show each organ by itself. Describe the various organs of the frog in the following table. Try to draw them as well.**

ORGAN NAME	DESCRIPTION AND SKETCH OF EACH ORGAN

3. When you feel you know enough about frog innards, try the game provided in the Virtual Frog Builder hypertext link. Record your impression on how much you believe this game tested your knowledge of frog dissection.

____

____

____

____

Science

NASA SpaceLink

Introduction

The National Aeronautic and Space Administration (NASA) was one of the primary developers of the Internet. Join the NASA space exploration teams with their on-line resources.

Objectives

Connect to NASA's SpaceLink education resources

Research information about current and past projects

Record highlights of the Hubble Space Telescope

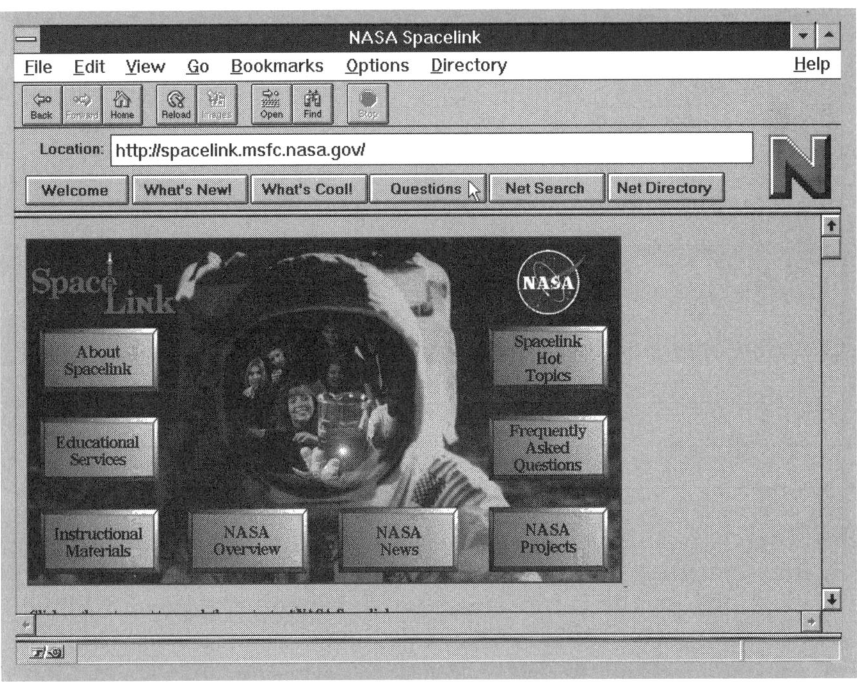

The NASA SpaceLink Home Page as seen in a Windows Netscape Browser

RESOURCE TABLE

CLIENT	GUI Browser, Gopher, or Telnet
RESOURCE LOCATION	Locate NASA SpaceLink information with the following tools: Browser: URL: **http://spacelink.msfc.nasa.gov**, and then URL: **http://quest.arc.nasa.gov**
SPECIAL ADVICE	For an alternative location to NASA information, try the following: Browser: URL: **http://hypatia.gsfc.nasa.gov/NASA_homepage.html** URL: **http://spacelink.msfc.nasa.gov/html/resources.html** Gopher: URL: **gopher://spacelink.msfc.nasa.gov** Telnet: URL: **telnet://spacelink.msfc.nasa.gov**

CYBERLOG 28

Answer the questions below each topic.

1. **Select Education Services. Identify three of NASA's educational services.**

A. ______________________________

B. ______________________________

C. ______________________________

2. **Select Hot Topics. NASA is hosting current projects with education. In late 1994, they featured Antarctica Live with television broadcasts and interactive sessions on the Internet between the South Pole and participating schools. List two of their current projects.**

A. ______________________________

B. ______________________________

3. **Select NASA News. From the section Years in Review, choose 1994. List three highlights from the Hubble Space Telescope.**

A. ______________________________

B. ______________________________

C. ______________________________

CyberQuest 28

4. **Research the education resources available through NASA. Identify three that you would like to participate in.**

URL	TITLE	DESCRIPTION

5. **Try the alternative URLs in the Special Advice section of your Resource Table. Summarize where each one takes you and what each URL does.**

____

____

____

____

____

Sports

Schedules Ahoy, Matey

Introduction

You can sail the seven seas and back again, but as long as you are surfing the Net, you will always know where, when, and what professional football, baseball, basketball, or hockey team is playing your favorite team. If you are a real sports enthusiast, then this activity will keep you in touch with every game of every team of every major professional sport you can name.

Objectives

Understand the significant challenge behind scheduling professional sports

Surf the sports calendar

RESOURCE TABLE

CLIENT	GUI Browser
RESOURCE LOCATION	Locate sport schedules with the following tools: Browser: URL: **http://ESPNET.SportsZone.com/mlb** baseball URL: **http://ESPNET.SportsZone.com/nfl** football URL: **http://ESPNET.SportsZone.com/nba** basketball URL: **http://ESPNET.SportsZone.com/nhl** hockey
SPECIAL ADVICE	These locations are excellent examples of how the Net can be used to maintain current information.

CYBERLOG 29

1. **Examine all four major sports schedules and then fill in the table appropriately.**

SPORT AND TEAM	NUMBER OF TEAMS	EARLIEST START DATE	LATEST ENDING DATE	NUMBER OF CITIES	ALL CITIES THAT COMPETE WITH THIS TEAM IN GIVEN SPORT
Football					
Basketball					
Baseball					
Hockey					

CyberQuest 29

After examining the four major sports teams and their schedules, respond to the following questions:

2. **Which sports' schedules overlap each other? How many months do they overlap?**

 ____

 ____

3. **Which cities have more than one professional team in the same sport?**

 ____

4. **Name five cities that have more than one sport.**

 ____

 ____

5. **Do you believe there are too many or too few professional teams? Why?**

 ____

Sports

A Picture Is Worth a Thousand Words

Introduction

The entire sports field has been vastly improved through pictures. When athletes see what they are doing from the perspective of the camera, it helps them improve their performance. Pictures also help to popularize their sports and create superstars of many athletes. This activity provides you a resource location on the Net where you can download sports GIF picture files of all types.

Objectives

Retrieve graphical (GIF) pictures over the Net

See some real large sumo wrestlers

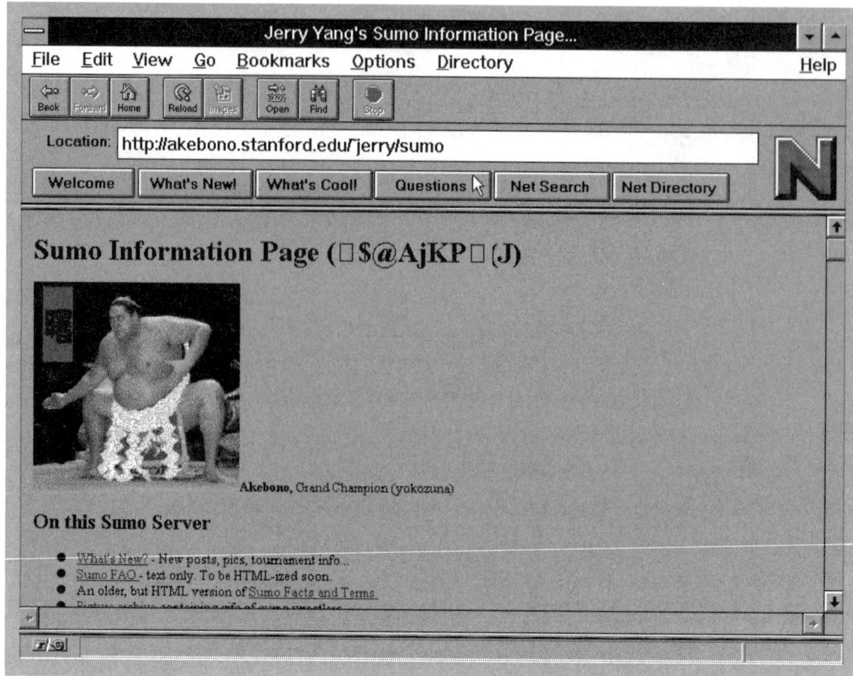

Sumo wrestlers on a Home Page as seen in a Windows Netscape Browser

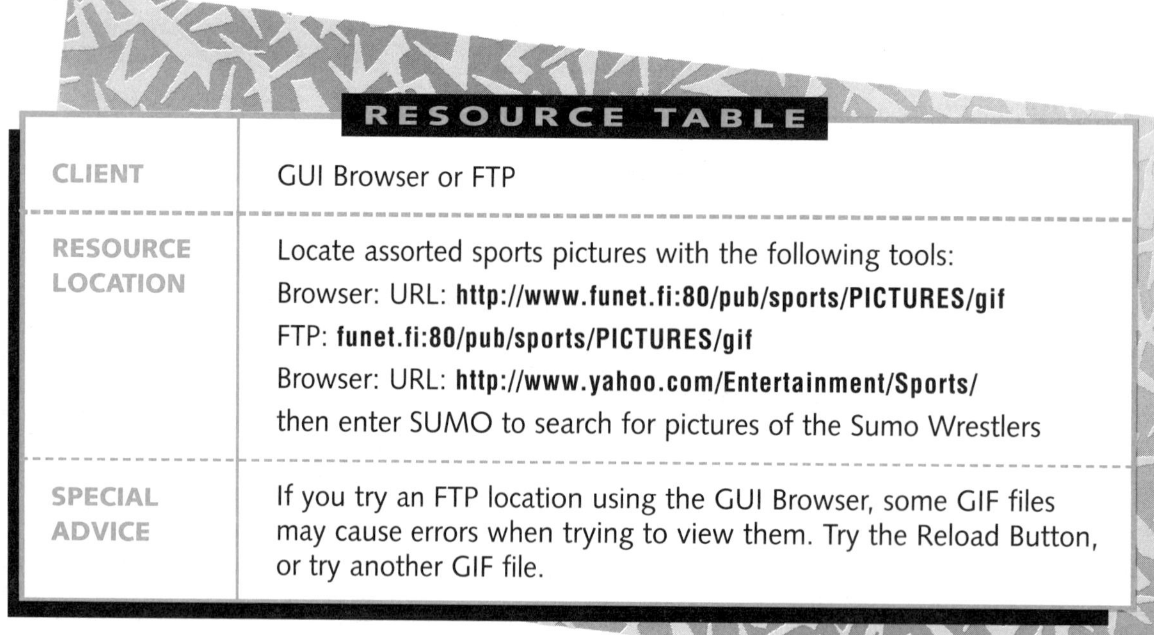

RESOURCE TABLE

CLIENT	GUI Browser or FTP
RESOURCE LOCATION	Locate assorted sports pictures with the following tools: Browser: URL: **http://www.funet.fi:80/pub/sports/PICTURES/gif** FTP: **funet.fi:80/pub/sports/PICTURES/gif** Browser: URL: **http://www.yahoo.com/Entertainment/Sports/** then enter SUMO to search for pictures of the Sumo Wrestlers
SPECIAL ADVICE	If you try an FTP location using the GUI Browser, some GIF files may cause errors when trying to view them. Try the Reload Button, or try another GIF file.

CyberLog 30

1. **Access the location indicated in the Resource Table. With your GUI Browser, select and view four different sports GIF files, then complete the table below. If you only have an FTP client, then you will need to download four different sports GIF pictures for your viewing pleasure. Enter the information about each GIF file in the table below or in a word processor. *If all you have is an FTP client, make sure your teacher provides you with a GIF file viewer and instructions on how to view the graphic files you've selected.***

PICTURE DESCRIPTION	FILE NAME	APPROXIMATE SIZE (1/8, 1/4, 1/3, 1/2, 2/3, 3/4, FULL SCREEN)

CyberQuest 30

Answer the following questions about the sumo GIF files found in the Resource Table:

2. **What was the largest size (1/8, 1/4, 1/3, 1/2, 2/3, 3/4, Full Screen) of any GIF file you downloaded? What is the file size of this GIF file? Describe the clarity of the picture and the impression it leaves with you.**

   ____

   ____

3. **What was the smallest size (1/8, 1/4, 1/3, 1/2, 2/3, 3/4, Full Screen) of any GIF file you downloaded? What is the file size of this GIF file? Describe the clarity of the picture and the impression it leaves with you.**

   ____

   ____

Technology and Computers

Surfing the Technology Wave

Introduction

The technology wave is always bringing another new idea to shore. If you're not always on your toes, you can get in over your head. This activity will help you be more alert to the changing technology scene, especially in computer science. What better place to keep up with computers and technology than on the Net? This activity will help you continue to surf the technology wave.

Objectives

Launch your Newsgroup, FTP, or Telnet program

Recognize multiple resource locations for learning computer science technology

Record in your Cyber Log multiple sites of interest by general surfing

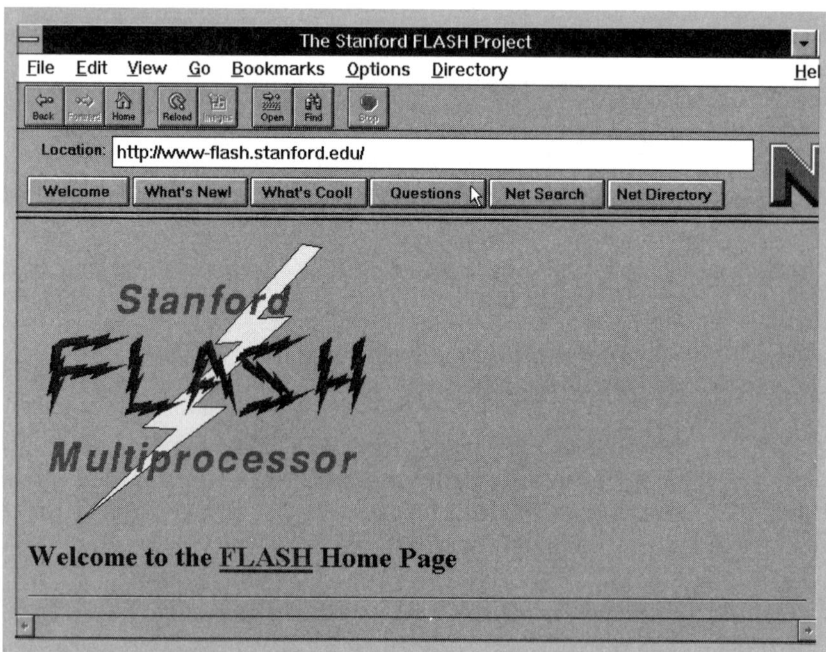

The Stanford FLASH Home Page as seen in a Windows Netscape Browser

RESOURCE TABLE

CLIENT	GUI Browser
RESOURCE LOCATION	Locate assorted computer science topics with the following tools: Browser: URL: **http://www.yahoo.com/Science/Computer_Science/** NOTE: the S and the C and S in Science/Computer_Science are capital letters.
SPECIAL ADVICE	This location is so rich with possible areas of interest, you may want to focus on your own personal or school needs before you branch out too far and wide.

CYBERLOG 31

1. **Surf the Net for areas of specific interest on computers and other technologies and complete the table below. The URLs / Locations provided in the Resource Table mainly talk about computer science. If you find other sources of information, include them in your table.**

COMPUTER SCIENCE AREA OF INTEREST	ACCESS METHOD AND ADDRESS	BRIEF DESCRIPTION

CyberQuest 31

2. **Submit a one-page report on an area of computer science that you found interesting. The report should deal with a concept or subject you did not previously know about. The possibilities are endless. Just catch a good wave to surf and ride it all the way to shore. Summarize below what your report will cover.**

____

____

____

____

____

activity 32

Travel and Tourism

Vacations

Introduction

The United States State Department provides free information for travelers visiting foreign countries. You can also access weather information for many of your vacation destinations. In this activity, you will select several countries and find out what the travel status is. Later, take a virtual trip to the countries you selected.

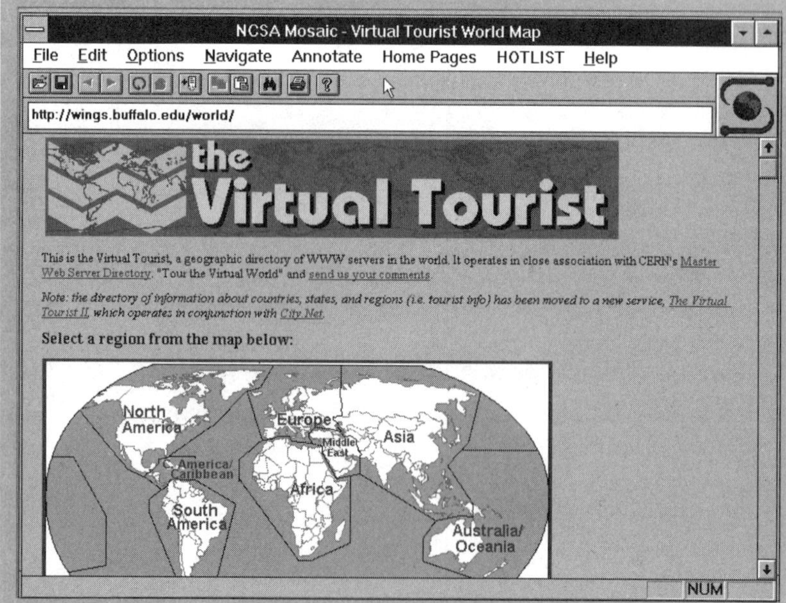

The Virtual Tourist Home Page as seen in a Windows Mosaic Browser

Objectives

Access information regarding travel in several foreign countries

Take a virtual trip to the countries you selected

RESOURCE TABLE

CLIENT	GUI Browser or Gopher
RESOURCE LOCATION	Access travel information from the government and other sources: Use this URL for question number 4, specifically: Browser: URL: **www.vtourist.com/webmap** For the Cyber Quest Virtual Vacation, select The Virtual Tourist II. Click on the maps to find the country you wish to visit. URL: **gopher://info.umd.edu/** Follow the same Gopher path listed below to find the Travel Advisories. Gopher: **info.umd.edu** Then select Educational Resources, select Academic Resources by Topic, then select United States and World Politics, Culture and History, then select Travel Information, then select Travel Warnings & Consular Information Sheets.
SPECIAL ADVICE	You may have to hunt around a bit for the Travel Advisories. Once you find them, record the path if it is different than those shown above. The Virtual Tourist may not give you any additional information, but at least you will know where the country is on the map!

CyberLog 32

1. List some countries that are currently on the Travel Warning list and state briefly the reason for the warning.

COUNTRY	REASON FOR TRAVEL ADVISORY

2. Select one of the countries and summarize the information provided by the State Department. Prepare a report of 150 to 300 words on this country.

3. What are the top three reasons given for a country being listed as unsafe?

4. Use the first URL in the Resource Table for the Virtual Tourist II. On the maps provided at this resource, locate each of the countries you listed in number 1. On a separate piece of paper, draw a rough sketch outline from the on-line map.

CyberQuest 32

5. Would you be willing to travel to a country that currently has a Travel Warning? Indicate why or why not.

6. Visit the U.S. State Department Gopher again. Using the Information Sheets found at this Gopher, examine the three countries. Complete the following table:

COUNTRY	U.S. EMBASSY LOCATION	HEALTH CONDITIONS

GLOSSARY

a

Address The number sequence that identifies a unique user or computer on a network. Every computer and user on the Internet must have a different address for the system to know where to send E-mail and other computer data. (See Names.)

Articles Information, ideas, and comments posted on USENET and E-mail lists.

b

Backbone The Internet backbone was created by the National Science Foundation. The backbone links major computer centers together with a high-speed telecommunication connection. Subnetworks attach to the backbone.

Bits Per Second A measurement of speed for network telecommunications systems. A bit is the smallest piece of information communicated by computers. The number of bits that pass through a modem determines the speed of a modem.

Bookmark A means of collecting favorite Home Pages and addresses in Netscape and in other Gopher and Internet Clients for future reference.

bps See Bits Per Second.

Browsers Browsers are the newest and most significant new software tools on the Internet. Browsers, like Netscape and Mosaic, are user-friendly viewers, and are required to navigate the World Wide Web and to manipulate hypertext documents. Well-designed Browsers have the other major Internet software tools built right into their software.

c

Category Collection of related Newsgroups.

Client The term given to any computer that is connected to the Internet and has the software it needs to share information over the Internet.

Client Software Software that allows your computer to talk, communicate, and share information with Internet host computers and Internet servers.

com Indicates a commercial domain.

Connections The software and hardware links between computers are called connections. The speed and compatibility of your computer's connection to your Internet host computer will determine the efficiency with which you can access Internet resources. (See SLIP and PPP)

Cybernetics The science that compares the functions of the brain with the functions of a computer.

Cyberspace A term given to the electronic, computerized world of the Internet. Often called virtual reality. When you are on the Internet or the

World Wide Web, you are in Cyberspace.

d

Directory A storage location, like a file folder, where related data and files are stored.

Distributed Network The Internet is a distributed network, meaning that there is not one central authority or group guiding its growth, use, and development. If one part of the Internet goes down, as in a natural disaster like an earthquake, Internet communications can be transferred to other lines of communication, and the downed portion of the network can be bypassed until repairs are made.

Domain Name System A system of computers and software that allows Internet names like **karl@dixon.edu** to be converted into a number like **158.90.62.25** and back again.

Domains A division or section of the Internet. For example, the military is one domain, education is another. Service providers like America Online and Prodigy have their own domains. Domains can be divided geographically, by country, region, or state, or by other similarities, such as business, commerce, government agencies, or private organizations.

Download To copy files, data, information, and software from a remote host computer to your computer or to another computer.

DNS See Domain Name System.

Dumb Terminal A dumb terminal is attached to a mainframe or minicomputer. The terminal does not do any of the computer processing. Dumb terminals allow input from the user and display the processing taking place on a host computer.

Dynamic Constantly changing.

e

edu Indicates an educational domain.

E-Mail E-mail is short for electronic mail. Electronic mail is the most widely used feature of the Internet. Mail is written in an E-mail program and transmitted over networks to other users with compatible E-mail software.

Emulate To imitate. (See Dumb Terminal.)

Etiquette Rules of conduct and behavior. (See Netiquette.)

f

FAQ's Frequently Asked Questions. Hosts will post answers to their most frequently asked questions.

Flamers Newsgroup or E-mail users who send flames or written rebukes.

Flames Rebukes sent by agitated Internet users to people who violate rules of Internet Netiquette, or who spam the Internet.

FTP File Transfer Protocol. FTP software transfers files, information, and data from one computer to another.

g

Gateways Tools that allow commercial E-mail software to communicate with each other.

Gopher A system of menus that allow users with Gopher Client software to access information on computers called Gopher Servers.

Gopher Client Software that allows users access to Gopher Servers.

Gopher Servers Software that allows Gopher Clients access to Gopher files, directories, and menus.

Gopherspace The Internet pathways available from a Gopher Client.

gov Indicates a governmental domain.

Groups USENET Newsgroups.

GUI Graphical User Interface. GUI, pronounced *gooie*, replaces commands with pictures, or icons, in software usually associated with Windows or Macintosh computers.

h

Hits A hit is recorded anytime someone connects to a remote computer, site, or Home Page.

Home Page A Home Page is like an index that contains related information on a single topic in a hypertext WWW environment.

Host Any computer providing network services and resources to other computers is called a host. Host computers are also called servers. Servers are the key computers in networks.

Hotlist A catalog or list of Home Pages in Mosaic.

HTML (See HyperText Markup Language.)

HTTP (See HyperText Transfer Protocol.)

Hypermedia Computer data that creates hypertext links between more than one kind of media. Types of media include video, pictures, graphics, animation, and text. (See Multimedia.)

Hypertext A system of information retrieval, where selected keywords are linked to text and other information in the same document or in another document. Clicking on a hypertext word will execute a command to find the text you have selected. Hypertext links are not limited to the local computer network. Hypertext links can take you to information located on another computer in another part of the world.

HyperText Markup Language A set of commands that describe a file to a GUI Browser.

HyperText Transfer Protocol Protocols are instructions that tell computers how to handle and send hypertext documents and data from one computer to another.

i

Icon A picture or graphic that represents something. For example, an icon of a printer may represent the Print command. (See GUI.)

Incompatability When software from a client computer does not communicate with the software on an Internet host, there is an incompatibility. Incompatibilities exist with different versions of software, when internal software settings do not correspond, or for a variety of other reasons. Hardware may also be incompatible, limiting Internet access.

Internet The name given to the current telecommunications system between networks of computers. The Internet is often called a "network of networks." The Internet will grow into the electronic superhighway of the future. The Internet is often called the Net because it is the largest computer network in the world.

IP Internet Protocol, an address label for Internet packages called packets. IP makes sure the packets arrive at the correct destination.

l

Links Hypertext Words that jump automatically to another selection of text.

Lurkers Newsgroup or E-mail users who read groups but don't post their own articles.

m

Menu A menu is a list of choices.

mil Indicates a military domain.

Modem A simple communications tool that converts computer signals into signals that can travel over telephone lines.

Moderated Screened by a person or group for anything going into a Newsgroup for distribution to its readers. Moderators cut out unnecessary postings and articles that do not fit the topic of the group.

Multimedia Systems that use more than one medium. A multimedia computer can utilize various types of media including video, sound, pictures, graphics, animation, and text.

n

Names A unique or different name is required for Internet users. In common speech, the words *name* and *address* are often used interchangeably. Technically speaking, a name involves the use of words (**eugene@dixon.edu**), and an address is a number like **158.95.6.2**.

net Indicates a network provider domain.

Net Short for Network.

Netiquette Internet rules of behavior and conduct.

Network Two or more computers linked together to share information and data.

Network Administrators The most important person on a network is the Network Administrator. These people manage all the hardware and software issues on a network and keep things running. They manage the security of the network and grant network rights to users. Network Administrators are often overworked and underpaid, but they usually have some really cool computers.

Newbies New members of discussion groups.

Newsgroup Participants who follow threads of a particular topic with the help of a USENET newsreader.

Newsreader Software tool required to read and participate in USENET Newsgroups.

o

On-line Using computer connections to networks.

org Indicates an organizational domain.

p

Packets The bundles of data that can be transmitted over the Internet.

Password A special word used to secure computer systems. Passwords are usually created by authorized users under the directions of a Network Administrator. Hosts use passwords to distinguish users that are allowed on a computer network from those that are trying to gain illegal or unauthorized entry.

Platforms There are many different and sometimes incompatible computer hardware and software systems, called platforms.

Post To send articles to Newsgroups or to electronic bulletin board systems.

PPP Point to Point Protocol. One of the types of connections that allow Internet communications over a modem. PPP allows your computer to act like you have a direct connection to the Internet. (See SLIP.)

r

Resources Anything you can find on the Internet is a resource, including software, files, data, information, services, and people.

s

Saints People who provide help to new members of discussion groups.

Server Any computer providing network services and resources to other computers. Server computers are also called hosts. Servers are the key computers in networks.

Service Providers Companies that provide Internet connections.

SLIP Serial Line Internet Protocol. One of the types of connections that allow Internet communications over a modem. SLIP allows your computer to act like you have a direct connection to the Internet. (See PPP.)

Spam Unwanted Internet garbage, particularly advertising on the public Internet.

Subject Line The title of a Newsgroup posting or article.

Subscribers Participants in a Newsgroup or E-mail discussion list.

Superhighway Another name for Cyberspace. Also, the name given to the Internet of the future.

Surf Exploring the Internet. When you surf, you are looking for interesting information.

t

TCP Transmission Control Protocol. TCP keeps track of every item in a packet or package that is transmitted over the Internet. If an item arrives broken or incomplete, TCP asks the host computer to send the packet over again.

Telnet Telnet provides the ability to log in to remote servers or host computers and to use its resources as if you were a computer terminal on that particular host computer.

Telnet Session Anytime you log in to a Telnet computer, you start a Telnet session. When you log out of Telnet, you end the session.

Text-Based Internet systems that rely on words rather than on graphics and pictures.

Thread A series of messages on the same theme or topic.

Title The particular name of a Newsgroup within its category.

Transfer Rate The speed at which data is exchanged between computers.

u

Uniform Resource Locator An address or reference code that makes it possible for a GUI Browser like Mosaic or Netscape to locate hypertext and hypermedia documents on any WWW host server in the world.

Unique Different, individualized.

Unmoderated Not screened for anything going into a Newsgroup for distribution to its readers. Therefore, group members must be more aware of what is and is not appropriate for the group.

URL See Uniform Resource Locator.

USENET A huge collection of computers that allow you to post, distribute, or publish Newsgroup articles. USENET is one of the most widely used Internet services.

User-Friendly Easy-to-use software. User-friendly software is intuitive; in other words, people are able to guess by the name, icon, or location of a command what a particular software command will do.

w

Wizards Newsgroup experts.

WWW The World Wide Web, or W3. WWW is a system of computers that can share information by means of hypertext links.

List of URLs/Locations

The following is a list of URLs/Locations featured in *Internet Activities*. The list has sections for FTP, Gopher, Newsgroup, and Web sites. For each site, the address is listed in the left column and the subject area of the site is listed in the right column. At the end of the list are blank spaces for you to enter your own favorite new sites discovered as you surf the Net.

URL/Location	Subject Area
FTP	
ftp://ftp.lib.virginia.edu/pub/alpha/vat/archeology	Leon Battista Alberti and Flavio Biondo
ftp://sunsite.unc.edu	Bees
Gopher	
gopher://gopher.micro.umn.edu/	
gopher://gopher.micro.umn.edu:70/1	Mother of All Gophers at the University of Minnesota
gopher://marvel.loc.gov/	Library of Congress MARVEL Gopher
gopher://space.mit.edu:79/Ønasanews	MIT
gopher://gopher.tc.umn.edu:70/11/Libraries/Electronic%20Books	Zen and the Art of the Internet
gopher://gopher.micro.umn.edu	Veronica
gopher://marvel.loc.gov/	Library of Congress
Newsgroup	
news.misc	
news.admin.misc	
misc.answers	
alt.best.of.internet	
rec.arts.tv	
alt.usenet.alt.usenet.offline-reader	

URL/Location	Subject Area
WEB Sites	
http://www.ncsa.uiuc.edu/demoweb/demo.html	NCSA Demo Page
http://newproducts.jpl.nasa.gov/s19/s19.html	Jet Propulsion Lab
http://newproducts.jpl.nasa.gov/s19/caltech.html	Cal Tech Home Page
http://web.mit.edu/	MIT Home Page
http://nearnet.gnn.com/gnn/usl/ora/index.html	O'Reilley and Associates, Inc.
http://www.w3.org/hypertext/www/TheProject.html	CERN in Switzerland
http://www.eit.com:80/web/netservices.html	Locate Internet Resources
http.//nearnet.gnn.com/gnn/helpdesk/tools/ index.html	Locate Tools
http://www.eit.com/help/search.html	A Guide To Cyberspace
http://www.yahoo.com/Computers/Internet.	Yahoo Computer Category
http://www.digital.com/gnn/wic/index.html	The Whole Internet Catalog
http://www.cs.indiana.edu/docproject/ zen/zen-1.0_toc.html	Zen and the Art of the Internet
http://www.w3.org/hypertext/datasources/news/ news.html#125	
http://Info.cern.ch/hypertext/www/newsgroups/html	Newsgroup Reader
http://www.pop.psu.edu/~barr/ alt-creation-guide.html	Mosaic or WWW
http://sunsite.unc.edu/expo/deadsea.scrolls.exhibit/ intro.html	Dead Sea Scrolls
http://mistral.enst.fr/	WebMuseum
http://www.stsci.edu/EPA/Recent.html#SN1994I	Hubble Space Telescope
http://www.yahoo.com/Business/Corporations/ Computers/Systems/Personal_Computers/	Computer Hardware Vendors
http://www.yahoo.com/Business/Corporations/ Computers/Software/	Computer Software Vendors
http://www.careermosaic.com/cm/home.html	Information on Finding a Job
http://www.w3.org/hypertext/DataSources/ bySubject/Overview.html	Information on educational resources
http://www.cbs.com/	Letterman's Top Ten List
http://www.tue.nl/europe	Europe's Geography,Language, and Culture
htpp://www.leo.org/leo_e.html	

URL/Location	Subject Area
http://ericir.syr.edu/	Information on AskERIC
http://wwww.cs.colorado.edu/wwww	World Wide Worm Search
http://lycos.cs.cmu.edu	Lycos Search
http://www.webcrawler.com	WebCrawler Search
http://web.nexor.co.uk/public/aliweb/search/doc/form.html	ALIWEB Search
http://hoohoo.ncsa.uiuc.edu/archie.html	Archie Request Form
http://www.geo.mtu.edu/eos/	GUI Browser
http://www.house.gov	U.S. House of Representatives
http://www.enews.com/	Information on Journalism
http://www.yahoo.com/News	College Newspapers
http://owl.english.purdue.edu/	Purdue Writing lab
http://lanic.utexas.edu/las.html	Information on Latin American Countries
http://www.law.cornell.edu/supct/justices/fullcourt.html	Supreme Court Decisions
http://e-math.ams.org/	American Mathematical Society
http://www.cnam.fr/fractals.html	Fractals
http://www.book.uci.edu./AdamsHome.html	Ansel Adams
http://george.lbl.gov/ITG/Whole.Frog/frog/frog.anatomy.html	Virtual Frog Dissection
http://spacelink.msfc.nasa.gov	
http://quest.arc.nasa.gov	NASA SpaceLink
http://ESPNET.SportsZone.com/mlb	
http://ESPNET.SportsZone.com/nfi	
http://ESPNET.SportsZone.com/nba	
http://ESPNET.SportsZone.com/nhl	Sports Schedules
http://www.funet.fi:80/pub/sports/PICTURES/gif	Sports Pictures
http://www.yahoo.com/Science/Computer_Science/	Assorted Computer Science Topics

Your Favorite New Sites

URL/Location **Subject Area**

Index

V

W

Z

Free On-Line Hours

Turn This Page to Start Your Adventures...